Cyber Risk is a Myth

In boardrooms and C-suites across the globe, a dangerous disconnect persists. Security teams speak in technical jargon about vulnerabilities and patches while executives think in terms of revenue, reputation, and operational continuity. This communication gap isn't just inconvenient; it's potentially financially devastating.

The business world has created an artificial distinction between "cybersecurity risks" and "business risks" that causes substantial confusion and poor decision-making. Whether your manufacturing plant on the Gulf Coast goes offline because of ransomware or a hurricane, the business impact remains the same: lost production, missed deliveries, and financial damage. The root cause matters far less than the business outcome.

Cyber Risk is a Myth: A Business Approach to Integrated Risk Management removes this artificial separation. Drawing on court cases, stock market data, and hard evidence, this book establishes a revolutionary premise: when properly understood and communicated, security risks ARE business risks. They require the same frameworks, language, and decision processes as any other business risk.

This book provides a practical methodology for translating technical security concerns into business language, integrating security into enterprise risk frameworks, building compelling business cases for security investments, and developing metrics that resonate with executives. The result? Better-informed decisions, appropriate resource allocation, and security that truly enables business success.

Additional resources to accompany the book are available at kaynemcgladrey.com/myth/.

Cyber Risk is a Myth

A Business Approach to Integrated Risk Management

Kayne McGladrey

CRC Press
Taylor & Francis Group
Boca Raton London New York

CRC Press is an imprint of the
Taylor & Francis Group, an **informa** business

Designed cover image: Shutterstock ID: 1982527613

First edition published 2027
by CRC Press
2385 NW Executive Center Drive, Suite 320, Boca Raton FL 33431

and by CRC Press
4 Park Square, Milton Park, Abingdon, Oxon, OX14 4RN

CRC Press is an imprint of Taylor & Francis Group, LLC

ISBN: 978-1-041-24904-7 (hbk)
ISBN: 978-1-041-24905-4 (pbk)
ISBN: 978-1-003-74414-6 (ebk)

DOI: 10.1201/9781003744146

Typeset in Sabon
by KnowledgeWorks Global Ltd.

Mike Riffon, for reminding me to celebrate both the little and the big wins.

Decro Wong, who took a risk on hiring me.

Dean Thompson, one of the best mentors I've had over my career.

Jack Nichelson, Cheri Hotman, Jim Lola, and Gabriella Williams, who all believed in this book.

Contents

About the Author

Kayne McGladrey is a CISSP-certified cybersecurity executive, author, and senior IEEE member with nearly three decades of experience in cybersecurity. He began his career as a systems administrator before moving into advisory roles where he helped Fortune 500 and Global 1000 companies translate technical risks into business decisions. McGladrey created the vendor-agnostic GRC Maturity Model, a four-stage framework that guides organizations in assessing and advancing their GRC capabilities.

He has spoken at RSA, Black Hat, Gartner IT Security and Risk, ISACA GRC, and other major conferences, emphasizing the need to treat risk management as a core business function rather than a static checklist.

McGladrey's thought leadership appears in *CSO Online*, *Dark Reading*, *Forbes*, the *Financial Times*, and *The Wall Street Journal*, where he discusses AI-driven threats, regulatory trends such as the EU AI Act, and the business value of cybersecurity. He mentors emerging security professionals, contributes to IEEE policy discussions, and continues to shape enterprise security strategy through writing, podcasting, and consulting.

Introduction

Impostor syndrome is relatively common in the field of cybersecurity, and it's still pronounced for me at times, even after over 20 years of working in the field. I'd dropped out of college after the first semester of my theatre program, giving up on my childhood dream of being on stage because I realized the improbability of it. I knew I didn't want to go back to working in fast food, and I had an interest in computers and security. With those few skills, I interviewed for my first consulting job and joined a startup as employee #4 with a salary of less than half the market rate.

In the decades since, I've run worldwide professional services, been a CISO at an aerospace and defense firm, provided executive advisory services for CISOs and boards across three continents, been named a Senior Member of the Institute of Electrical and Electronics Engineers for my contributions to cybersecurity, written for publications as diverse as *Reader's Digest* through *CISO Magazine*, hosted and been a guest on many podcasts, won awards for thought leadership in risk management, cybersecurity, and AI governance, and been a part of many stressful and difficult conversations about cybersecurity risks.

My origin story seems utterly improbable given today's emphasis on an endless number of certifications, educational requirements, and years of experience to join the profession.

In 2023, I started thinking about writing a book about cybersecurity risk management and outlining some chapters on my mobile while I was waiting in airports and other odd moments. However, while working at a GRC startup, I came to realize that there was no useful, hands-on guide for improving GRC maturity, which led to my first book, *The GRC Maturity Model*, published by Hyperproof. While I was writing that book, I continued to think about the book I'd meant to write, a book challenging my industry's assumptions about risk management.

In 2024 and through 2025, I started workshopping a presentation about risk management. Based on the consistently positive audience feedback, I decided to write the book you're currently reading. The book and the talk are based on a very simple premise: I feel like I've been in an extended Alcoholics Anonymous meeting for nearly thirty years. We keep doing the same thing and expecting different results.

I do not believe we have a technology problem; at the core, I believe that we have a communications problem. Cybersecurity professionals are not generally taught business skills. MBA students are not taught many cybersecurity skills. And when the two groups get together in meetings, we typically talk past one another with a lack of common ground or understanding. I've seen this at small startups, multinational companies, and in numerous languages. Similarly, most business books don't cover cybersecurity adequately, and a lot of the best technology risk management books are either dense or overly academic.

This book is an attempt to close that communications gap.

I'm certain that I made mistakes while writing this book. After all, I started writing in markdown in Notepad++, as I don't like dealing with the red squiggle or blue squiggle of modern word processors. A podcast about how a judge had publicly castigated an attorney over a malformed court case citation, where they'd cited an actual case but incorrectly formatted the number, which led me to move the entire content into Word so that I could use the 'references' feature. And because I'm a CISO, not an author, I didn't think to check for a template that was formatted for a book.

Bellingham, WA, is home for me and is located north of Seattle, where gold miners stopped before leaving to seek their fortunes in Alaska. Those gold miners spent most of their money on pickaxes and shovels, and I'm reminded of that story often as I look at what it takes to publish a book – you can spend quite a lot on a newer shovel or a better pickaxe, but the best tools do not guarantee you'll strike gold. This is also like cybersecurity, where the best tools will not guarantee that your organization will not have a data breach. Some of these tools are incredibly expensive for a niche function, like adding an index to a book, which feels very similar to pricing for niche functionality in cybersecurity. This first edition was intentionally created using the familiar tools I had at hand, and improved by the delightful and patient editorial team at Taylor & Francis.

This book is meant for the people I spend the most time with – executives, CISOs, attorneys, senior leaders, and senior cybersecurity experts. I hope this book confirms much of what you've wanted to say.

Finally, I don't know how people read business books in 2026, particularly given the convenience of AI at providing summaries with varying degrees of accuracy. As such, I've added executive summaries and tool listings to every chapter. Readers might not read every page; this is expected. Please use the executive summaries at the start of every chapter to determine which content best meets your needs.

What's in this book?

- Words. Quite a lot of them.
- Stories. Although nearly all these stories are from my career or from close friends, I can't divulge the specific details of these stories. Industries, locations, and identifying details have been substantially changed.

- Case studies. These are the direct opposite of stories, based exclusively on court case documents and news stories from legitimate sources.
- Worksheets, exercises, workshop ideas, and templates. I spent years in the executive advisory space and have created and collaborated on items like this; however, because of prior confidentiality agreements, I had to create these exclusively for this book as I don't have copies of older documents used with Clients. These are available as separate downloads from kaynemcgladrey.com/myth/.

Chapter 1

The myth of "cyber risk"

Chapter in One Sentence: The concept of "cyber risk" as distinct from business risk is a costly myth that fragments accountability, misaligns resources, and ultimately leaves organizations more vulnerable to the threats they seek to mitigate.

1.1 EXECUTIVE SUMMARY

This chapter challenges the artificial separation between "cyber risk" and "business risk," arguing that this division creates harmful disconnects throughout organizations. When a ransomware attack halts production, is it a "cyber" problem or a business continuity issue? The truth is that these are not separate domains but the same fundamental business risks manifesting through technology.

This artificial division emerged historically as computing evolved into a specialized technical discipline with its own terminology, certifications, and professional identity. Organizational structures reinforced this separation, with security teams typically reporting through IT rather than risk management channels. The "cyber" prefix itself became a marker of specialized knowledge, creating both a professional identity for security practitioners and a barrier to entry for business stakeholders.

The costs of this separation are substantial. Communication barriers develop as security teams discuss threats in technical terms that fail to resonate with business leaders. Accountability becomes fragmented, with critical risks falling into gaps between technical and business domains. Resources are misallocated as security investments disconnect from business priorities. Organizations may achieve compliance while failing to address their actual risk exposure.

Evidence increasingly shows that organizations integrating cybersecurity into broader business risk frameworks achieve better outcomes – experiencing fewer breaches, responding more effectively when incidents occur, and allocating resources more efficiently. The Equifax breach vividly demonstrated how technical vulnerabilities directly translate to business catastrophes, with

DOI: 10.1201/9781003744146-1

a single unpatched software vulnerability resulting in over $700 million in settlement costs and lasting reputational damage.

Integration doesn't diminish technical expertise but enhances its effectiveness by connecting it to business objectives. By viewing security risks through a business lens, organizations can prioritize based on business impact rather than technical severity alone. This requires developing shared language, metrics, and processes that bridge traditional silos and create joint accountability for managing what are shared organizational risks.

1.2 KEY TAKEAWAYS

- The separation between "cyber risk" and "business risk" is artificial and creates harmful disconnects in how organizations allocate resources and make decisions
- Technical security language often obscures business relevance, creating barriers to effective communication and risk management
- Organizations with integrated risk approaches experience fewer breaches, more effective incident response, and better alignment of security investments with business objectives
- Integration enhances security effectiveness by ensuring limited resources address the risks with the greatest business impact
- Begin integration by developing a common risk language that connects technical vulnerabilities directly to business outcomes

1.3 APPLICATION QUESTIONS

1. How does your organization's security language and reporting translate technical vulnerabilities into business impacts that executives can understand and prioritize?
2. Where in your organization does accountability become fragmented between security and business teams, potentially creating vulnerability gaps?
3. What practical steps could you take to better integrate security considerations into business decision-making processes at your organization?

1.4 TOOLS REFERENCED IN THIS CHAPTER

All tools available at kaynemcgladrey.com/myth/

- Exercise: "Decoding Security-Speak"
- Cybersecurity Translation Cheat Sheet
- Security Investment Prioritization Matrix
- Risk Integration Maturity Assessment
- Exercise: "Risk Translation"

- Executive Security Communication Template
- Security-Business Integration Workshop

1.5 INTRODUCTION

Is "cyber risk" truly distinct from business risk? Or is this separation an artificial construct that creates more problems than it solves?

When a ransomware attack halts production at a manufacturing facility, is that a "cyber" problem or a business continuity issue? When customer data is exposed through a web application vulnerability, is that a "technical security" failure or a threat to brand reputation and customer trust? When an employee falls for a phishing email that leads to a wire transfer fraud, is that a "cybersecurity incident" or a financial loss?

This artificial division between "cyber risk" and "business risk" permeates modern organizations, creating harmful disconnects between technical security functions and broader business operations. Security teams focus on vulnerabilities, threats, and controls, while business leaders concentrate on revenue, costs, and strategic objectives. The two groups often speak different languages, operate with different priorities, and struggle to find common ground in addressing what are, fundamentally, shared organizational risks.

This chapter aims to show why this separation is both artificial and counterproductive. It will show how treating cybersecurity risks as a special category, distinct from other business risks, creates significant problems in how organizations allocate resources, make decisions, and protect their most valuable assets. This foundational misconception affects every aspect of how organizations approach security, often leading to suboptimal outcomes despite substantial investments.

The impacts of this artificial division are far-reaching. Resources are frequently misallocated, with security investments disconnected from business priorities. Decision-making becomes fragmented, with security and business leaders operating from different playbooks. Organizational effectiveness suffers as unaligned objectives create friction rather than synergy. Most importantly, this separation often leaves organizations vulnerable precisely where business and technical domains intersect.

Throughout this chapter, we will explore several key questions: How did cybersecurity and business risk become separated in the first place? What role does specialized language play in maintaining this divide? What are the tangible costs of keeping these risk domains siloed? What evidence exists that integrated approaches yield better outcomes? And finally, what principles can guide organizations toward a more unified approach to risk?

The stakes here are considerable. Integrating cyber risks within the broader business context isn't just a semantic preference but a strategic necessity. Organizations that continue to treat cyber risk as a distinct category find themselves with fragmented defenses, misaligned priorities, and

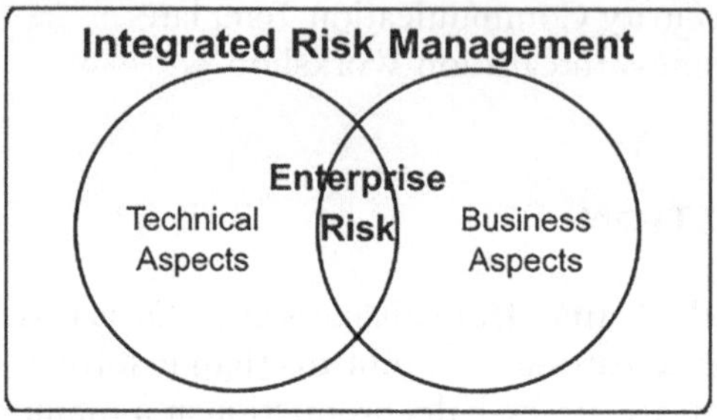

Figure 1.1 Integrated risk management

persistent vulnerability gaps. Conversely, those that recognize the artificial nature of this separation and take steps to integrate cyber risk within their broader enterprise risk frameworks often achieve better protection at lower cost, with fewer surprises and more stakeholder confidence as illustrated in Figure 1.1.

By the end of this chapter, readers should understand why the concept of "cyber risk" as a separate category is problematic, how it came to be, what costs it imposes, and how a more integrated approach can deliver superior outcomes. This understanding will serve as the foundation for subsequent chapters that explore specific methods for assessing, communicating, and managing technology-related risks as integral components of enterprise risk.

CISO Tip: When discussing security risks with your board, start with business impact rather than technical details. Frame each risk in terms of how it affects business goals they already care about.

CFO Tip: Ask your security team to quantify risks in financial terms – even rough estimates provide better context than technical severity scores alone.

1.6 THE HISTORICAL SEPARATION OF CYBERSECURITY AND BUSINESS RISK

The artificial division between cybersecurity and business risk appears to have deep historical roots that stretch back to computing's earliest days. Understanding how this separation developed helps explain why many organizations continue to struggle with fragmented risk management approaches. This section examines the technical origins of cybersecurity as a specialized discipline and traces how organizational structures and regulatory frameworks may have reinforced the separation between security concerns and broader business objectives.

1.6.1 The birth of cybersecurity as a technical discipline

STORY

In 1999, a regional bank established one of the first dedicated information security departments that I worked with. Housed in the basement of their operations building, the two-person team focused exclusively on securing the bank's computing infrastructure. Their workspace – intentionally isolated for "security reasons" – sat three floors away from the executive suite where business decisions were made.

The security team diligently built firewalls, implemented access controls, and established the bank's first security policies. Their tools were specialized and their language technical. They generated weekly reports filled with metrics on blocked connection attempts, virus detections, and system vulnerabilities. These reports, proudly delivered to senior management, were often set aside or rapidly skimmed during meetings focused on loan portfolios, market expansion, and customer acquisition.

When the bank suffered its first significant security incident – unauthorized access to customer records – the disconnect became painfully apparent. While the security team had identified the relevant vulnerability months earlier, the significance of this risk never translated into terms that resonated with business leaders. Their technical warning about inadequate authentication controls, potentially allowing lateral movement through internal systems had failed to communicate what was at stake: customer trust, regulatory compliance, and financial liability.

This physical and linguistic separation created a pattern that would persist for decades across industries: security teams addressing "cyber risks" while business leaders managed "business risks," neither fully understanding how completely intertwined these concerns had become.

The roots of today's cybersecurity/business risk divide can be traced to the earliest days of computing. As organizations began adopting information technology in the 1960s and 1970s, security considerations focused almost exclusively on physical access to mainframe computers and protecting sensitive data from unauthorized viewing or modification. These concerns were primarily technical in nature, addressed by technical specialists using technical solutions.

The earliest computer security professionals were often former system administrators or programmers who developed specialized knowledge of system vulnerabilities, access control mechanisms, and data protection techniques. Their focus was primarily on protecting the systems themselves rather than explicitly linking those protections to business value. This technical orientation made sense in an era when computing was still a specialized function, largely separate from core business operations.

As computing evolved through the 1980s and 1990s, so too did cybersecurity as a discipline. The growing use of personal computers, local area networks, and eventually the internet created new security challenges that required increasingly specialized knowledge. During this period, cybersecurity began to solidify as a distinct career path, complete with its own educational programs, certifications, and professional communities.

This early specialization created the foundation for today's separation between cybersecurity and business risk. As security practitioners developed deeper technical expertise, they tended to communicate primarily with other technical specialists, using increasingly specialized language that became less accessible to business stakeholders. Meanwhile, business leaders often viewed technology as a supporting function rather than a core business driver, further reinforcing the separation.

By the early 2000s, cybersecurity had become an established technical discipline with its own methodologies, frameworks, and body of knowledge. The Certified Information Systems Security Professional (CISSP) certification, launched in 1994, had grown to become an industry "gold standard." Academic programs in information security were expanding, and a distinct professional identity had formed around cybersecurity expertise.

This historical development, while creating valuable technical depth, also contributed significantly to today's separation of cyber and business risks. Security was established as a specialized technical function, often reporting through IT rather than risk management channels, with its own terminology, priorities, and perspective that sometimes diverged from broader business concerns.

This historical separation led to the siloed governance structures we'll examine in Chapter 7, where we explore how organizations can mature toward more integrated governance models.

1.6.2 The emergence of "cyber risk" as a distinct category

As cybersecurity threats grew more sophisticated and their business impacts more significant, the concept of "cyber risk" began to appear as a distinct category within organizational risk frameworks. This categorization was reinforced by several factors that, while practical in the short term, ultimately deepened the divide between cybersecurity and business risk.

Regulatory frameworks played a significant role in establishing cyber risk as a separate category. The Health Insurance Portability and Accountability Act (HIPAA) in 1996, the Gramm-Leach-Bliley Act in 1999, and later regulations like the General Data Protection Regulation (GDPR) created specific compliance requirements around information security and privacy. These regulations often treated information security as a distinct domain requiring specialized oversight, further cementing the separation between cyber and other business risks.

Organizational structures likewise reinforced this separation. As cyber threats became more prominent, many organizations formed specialized security departments, often headed by newly created Chief Information Security Officer (CISO) roles. While providing focused attention on security concerns, these specialized departments sometimes operated in relative isolation from broader risk management functions. Reporting structures varied, but many CISOs reported to Chief Information Officers (CIOs) rather than to Chief Risk Officers (CROs), Chief Legal Officers (CLOs), or other senior executives, creating an additional layer of separation between security and business risk management.

Investment patterns also contributed to the division. As high-profile breaches made headlines, boards and executives increased cybersecurity budgets, often treating these investments as a specialized expense category rather than integrating them into broader risk management spending. This pattern of separate funding streams further reinforced the notion that cyber risk was fundamentally different from other business risks.

Perhaps most significantly, the "cyber" prefix itself became a marker of specialized knowledge, creating both a professional identity for security practitioners and a barrier to entry for business stakeholders. Terms like "cyber threat," "cyber-attack," and "cyber risk" signaled that these concepts belonged to a specialized domain requiring specialized expertise, making it easier for business leaders to delegate these concerns entirely to technical specialists.

1.6.3 Unintended consequences of separation

The historical separation of cybersecurity from business risk has led to several unintended but significant consequences that continue to undermine organizational security and performance.

Perhaps the most fundamental consequence is the communication barrier that has developed between technical security professionals and business leaders. Security teams often discuss vulnerabilities, threats, and controls in highly technical terms that fail to resonate with business stakeholders. Meanwhile, business leaders speak of market share, customer experience, and revenue growth in terms that may seem disconnected from security concerns. This communication gap makes it difficult to achieve a shared understanding of risks and appropriate responses.

This communication barrier frequently results in a lack of shared priorities and objectives. Security teams may prioritize addressing technical vulnerabilities based on severity scores, while business leaders focus on initiatives that drive revenue or operational efficiency. Without a common framework for evaluating priorities, organizations struggle to allocate resources effectively, often leading to misalignment between security investments and business objectives.

Separation also creates difficulties in allocating resources based on business impact. When cyber risks are evaluated using technical criteria rather than business impact metrics, investment decisions may not reflect the actual risk to the organization. A technically severe vulnerability in a low-value system might receive more attention than a moderate vulnerability in a business-critical application, leading to suboptimal resource allocation.

According to Deloitte's Audit Committee Practices Report (Deloitte, 2025), a majority of audit committees, 62%, have primary oversight of cybersecurity risks, and half of respondents rank cybersecurity as the number-one area of focus for the audit committee over the next 12 months. Enterprise risk management (ERM) is a significant priority for organizations, with 52% of respondents indicating that the audit committee has primary oversight of ERM. This dual focus on both cybersecurity and ERM by audit committees underscores the convergence of cyber and broader business risks. This integration at the governance level challenges the separation of cyber risk and supports the effectiveness of holistic risk oversight.

This research shows a growing recognition at the board level that cybersecurity risks cannot be effectively managed in isolation from broader enterprise risks. The high percentage of audit committees overseeing both areas suggests an increasing understanding that integrated risk management is more effective than siloed approaches.

Despite this growing awareness at the governance level, many organizations continue to operate with separated risk frameworks at the operational level. This disconnect between governance expectations and operational reality creates additional challenges as boards seek integrated risk information, while organizational structures continue to produce siloed risk assessments.

Understanding how this separation developed historically provides important context, but the real question organizations struggle with is the effects of this separation. The following section examines how the language barriers created by specialization actively impede effective risk management.

CISO Tip: Map your security organization's history against your company's digital transformation journey to identify where disconnects began.

CFO Tip: Review your organization's budget structure – if security investments are isolated from business unit budgets, you may be reinforcing the separation of security and business risk.

Language barriers created by specialized terminology often reinforce the historical separation, creating ongoing challenges for effective risk communication.

1.7 THE LANGUAGE PROBLEM: HOW TERMINOLOGY CREATES ARTIFICIAL DIVIDES

Language shapes organizational thinking in ways that often go unrecognized. The terminology used to describe risks can either bridge understanding or create barriers between stakeholders. This section explores how specialized cybersecurity language may contribute to the artificial separation between technical and business concerns and examines strategies for developing shared risk vocabulary that connects security issues directly to business outcomes.

1.7.1 The power of labels in shaping organizational thinking

The language we use to describe risks fundamentally shapes how we think about and respond to them. In organizational settings, labels serve not just as descriptors but as powerful framing devices that influence perception, priority, and ownership of various concerns.

The term "cyber risk" itself creates a cognitive frame that places certain risks in a specialized category, distinct from ordinary business risks. This framing influences how organizations structure their response to these risks, often leading to specialized handling rather than integration with broader risk management processes. The mere act of labeling certain risks as "cyber" can signal that they require specialized expertise, potentially discouraging business leaders from engaging deeply with these issues.

This cognitive framing extends beyond just the "cyber" prefix. Consider how differently stakeholders might perceive these alternative descriptions of the same underlying risk:

- "A DDoS attack vulnerability in our web infrastructure" (technical framing)
- "A risk of website unavailability affecting customer transactions" (business framing)
- "A potential interruption to our $2M daily online revenue stream" (financial framing)

While describing the same fundamental issue, each framing invites different levels of engagement from different stakeholders and suggests different prioritization approaches.

The "cyber" prefix has become particularly problematic as an exclusionary marker. It signals specialized knowledge and can create the impression that only technical experts should be concerned with these issues. When a risk is labeled as a "cyber risk," business executives may feel less qualified to question assessments or proposed solutions, potentially leading to reduced scrutiny of security investments or strategies.

This exclusionary effect operates in both directions. Security professionals may view business risks as outside their domain of concern, focusing narrowly on technical vulnerabilities rather than their business implications. Business leaders, meanwhile, may delegate "cyber" issues entirely to technical teams, missing opportunities to integrate these considerations into strategic planning. The result is a form of mutual exclusion that leaves critical risks inadequately addressed at the intersection of business and technology.

Research in cognitive psychology suggests that such labeling affects not just communication, but actual information processing. When information is categorized as belonging to a specialized domain, individuals typically apply domain-specific mental models rather than more general reasoning. In the context of organizational risk, this means that risks labeled as "cyber" are likely to be processed differently than those labeled as "financial" or "operational," even when the underlying business impacts are similar.

1.7.2 The role of technical jargon in creating barriers

Beyond the broad labeling of risk categories, specific technical terminology creates additional barriers to integrated risk management. Security professionals routinely use specialized jargon that, while precise and efficient for technical communication, often obscures business relevance and impedes cross-functional understanding.

Common examples of security terminology that create barriers include:

- Vulnerability severity ratings (CVSS scores) that don't translate to business impact
- Technical threat descriptions that fail to articulate potential business consequences
- Control frameworks (e.g., NIST, ISO, CIS-CSC) that don't clearly map to business objectives
- Security metrics that measure technical outcomes rather than business risk reduction

When security teams communicate using such terminology without translation, business stakeholders may struggle to connect technical details to business priorities. A "critical" vulnerability according to a CVSS score might not represent a critical business risk if it affects a low-value system or if compensating controls reduce the likelihood of exploitation. Yet, without clear translation between technical and business risk frameworks, such distinctions may be lost.

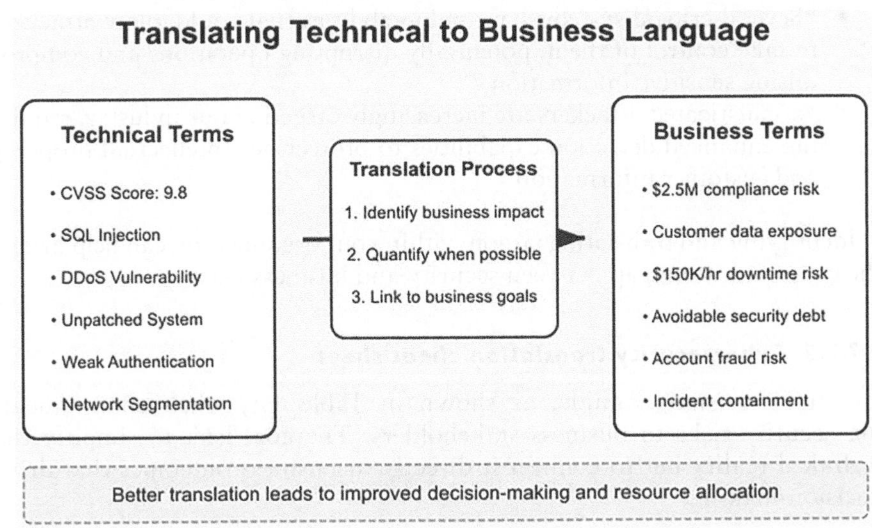

Figure 1.2 Translating technical to business language

This translation problem cuts to the heart of the cyber risk integration challenge. Security practitioners need technical precision to address specific vulnerabilities, while business leaders need business-relevant information to make sound risk decisions. Without effective translation between these domains, organizations struggle to develop a shared understanding of risk that supports both technical accuracy and business relevance. This terminology gap creates what we'll explore in Chapter 2 as a fundamental translation problem, where technical security language fails to drive executive action despite clearly identified risks as shown in Figure 1.2.

1.7.2.1 Exercise: "Decoding security-speak"

Consider the following security statements:

- "We need to implement a web application firewall to address OWASP Top 10 vulnerabilities."
- "Our environment contains several systems with RCE vulnerabilities requiring immediate patching."
- "The latest threat intelligence indicates increased APT activity targeting our sector."

How might these be translated into business-relevant statements? For example:

- "We need to implement additional web protection to prevent unauthorized access to customer data that could lead to regulatory penalties and reputational damage."

- "Several critical systems have vulnerabilities that could allow attackers to take control of them, potentially disrupting operations and compromising sensitive information."
- "Sophisticated attackers are increasingly targeting our industry, requiring enhanced detection capabilities to protect our intellectual property and customer information."

Identifying and translating jargon within your organization can help bridge the communication gap between security and business teams.

1.7.2.2 Cybersecurity translation cheat sheet

Use this translation guide, as shown in Table 1.1, when communicating security risks to business stakeholders. The goal isn't to simplify the technical reality but to connect it directly to business outcomes that drive decision-making.

Table 1.1 Cybersecurity translation cheat sheet

Technical language	*Business translation*	*Business impact*
"Critical vulnerability with CVSS score of 9.8"	"High-priority security weakness that requires immediate attention"	Potential for unauthorized access to financial systems with $X exposure
"DDoS mitigation capabilities"	"Protection against website/service disruption attacks"	Each hour of downtime costs $XX,XXX in lost revenue and customer trust
"Zero-day exploit"	"Previously unknown security flaw actively being used by attackers"	Immediate risk to business operations requiring rapid response
"Endpoint detection and response"	"Technology that identifies and contains security incidents on employee devices"	Reduces breach containment time from days to hours, limiting average incident cost by XX%
"Identity and access management weakness"	"Issues with who can access what information and systems"	Risk of unauthorized access to sensitive data with regulatory penalties of $X per record
"Insufficient encryption practices"	"Customer/financial data not properly protected"	Potential regulatory fines of up to X% of annual revenue and litigation costs averaging $X million
"Security awareness training gaps"	"Employees not adequately prepared to recognize threats"	60% of breaches involve human error, averaging $X.X million in costs per incident
"Lack of network segmentation"	"Systems not properly separated to prevent spread of attacks"	Increases breach costs by XX% due to broader organizational impact

1.7.3 Reframing the language of risk

Adopting business-centric risk language represents a powerful opportunity to overcome the artificial division between cyber and business risk. When security concerns are framed in terms of their business implications rather than their technical characteristics, they become more accessible to business stakeholders and easier to integrate into broader risk management frameworks.

The benefits of business-centric risk language include:

- Clearer prioritization based on business impact rather than technical severity
- Better alignment between security investments and business objectives
- More effective communication between security and business teams
- Improved ability to integrate technology risks into enterprise risk frameworks
- Enhanced executive engagement in security risk decisions

Effective examples of translating technical risks into business terms include:

- Instead of "we have 237 critical vulnerabilities," say "we have identified 15 systems with security gaps that could affect customer data, potentially resulting in regulatory penalties of up to $2 million, legal costs averaging $850,000 per system, and customer churn projected to reduce annual revenue by $3.2 million."
- Rather than "we need enhanced endpoint detection and response," say "our current ability to detect and contain security incidents affecting employee systems takes 72 hours, creating a $150,000 exposure per incident. With improved detection tools, we can reduce containment time to 4 hours, cutting per-incident costs by 60% and realizing an estimated annual savings of $1.8 million based on our historical incident rate."
- Instead of "our application lacks proper authentication controls," say "the current login system for our customer portal creates an unacceptable risk of unauthorized access to account information, which could breach our customer trust commitments and violate regulatory requirements. Based on industry benchmarks, a breach of this system would cost approximately $245 per compromised record, totaling $4.9 million with our current user base, while the solution requires a one-time investment of $275,000 and $60,000 in annual maintenance."

According to the 2024 ACC Chief Legal Officers Survey (Association of Corporate Counsel, 2024)

- "Thirty-four percent of CLOs say that data breaches are the biggest data-related threat that they are focused on mitigating in 2024… yet just 9 percent are 'very confident' in their organization's ability to mitigate emerging data risks."

- "The top 3 issues that keep CLOs up at night are regulations and enforcement (53 percent), privacy and data security (41 percent), and cybersecurity threats (37 percent)."
- "Forty percent of CLOs rank operational efficiency as their law department's top strategic initiative for the coming year..."

The clustering of data risk, regulatory, privacy, and cybersecurity concerns – alongside operational efficiency – illustrates that cyber risk cannot be managed in a vacuum. The low confidence in mitigation further highlights the limitations of siloed approaches and the need for integrated, cross-functional strategies.

This research highlights how legal officers are increasingly concerned with cybersecurity issues, yet few feel confident in their organization's ability to mitigate these risks. This suggests that the traditional approach of treating cybersecurity as a separate technical domain is failing to produce adequate confidence among key stakeholders. The research also demonstrates how cybersecurity concerns are intimately connected with regulatory compliance, privacy considerations, and operational efficiency – all fundamental business concerns that transcend purely technical categorizations.

Integrated language supports integrated thinking. When organizations adopt a common risk language that bridges technical and business considerations, they enable more holistic risk assessment and more effective risk management. This language shift doesn't require technical teams to abandon precision, but rather to supplement technical details with business context that helps stakeholders understand why technical issues matter to the organization's success.

Language barriers represent just one facet of the cyber-business risk divide. When these communication problems persist, they create measurable organizational costs that extend far beyond simple misunderstandings. The next section examines the tangible business impact of maintaining siloed risk approaches.

CISO Tip: Create a "translation guide" specific to your organization that connects technical terms to your company's strategic objectives.

CFO Tip: Request security briefings that express metrics in financial terms – ROI, cost avoidance, and risk reduction as a percentage of asset value.

1.8 THE COSTLY REALITY OF RISK SILOS

The separation between cyber and business risk appears to create measurable organizational costs that extend far beyond simple communication challenges. This section examines the tangible impacts of fragmented risk management, from accountability gaps to resource misallocation as seen in Figure 1.3. Real-world examples, including the Equifax breach, show how technical vulnerabilities can translate directly into business catastrophes when organizations maintain artificial divisions between security and business concerns.

1.8.1 Fragmented accountability and its consequences

When organizations separate cyber risk from business risk, accountability becomes fragmented, often leading to significant vulnerability gaps. This fragmentation manifests in several ways, each carrying substantial costs.

The most common accountability problem is the "not my responsibility" syndrome. When risks sit at the intersection of business processes and technical systems, ownership often becomes unclear. Technical teams may view certain risks as business process issues, while business units may consider them technology problems. This ambiguity can leave important risks inadequately addressed, as each group assumes the other is handling the concern.

Consider a common scenario involving third-party vendors with access to sensitive data. The procurement team may view security assessment of these vendors as IT's responsibility, while IT sees vendor management as a business function. Meanwhile, legal believes both teams are addressing the risk, and

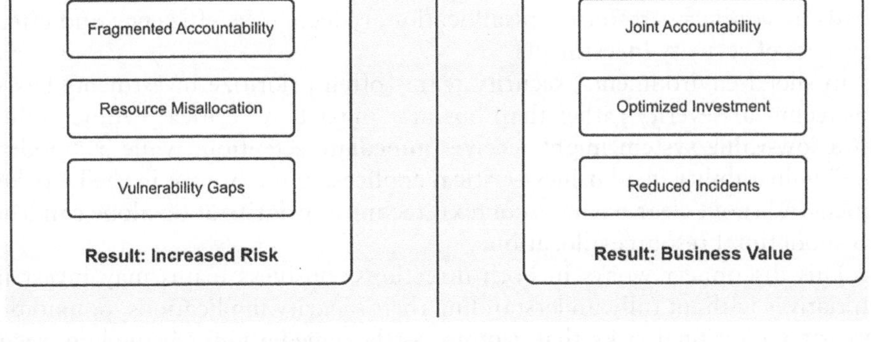

Figure 1.3 The cost of separation vs. integration

compliance assumes existing processes are sufficient. Because of this, critical vulnerabilities may persist despite each group believing protections are in place.

This fragmentation becomes particularly problematic during security incidents. Unclear ownership of risk often translates to unclear ownership of incident response. When a data breach occurs, questions about who should lead the response, what actions should be taken, and how communications should be handled can delay effective action, potentially increasing the impact of the incident.

The costs of this miscommunication can be substantial. Organizations with fragmented accountability typically experience:

- Longer time to detect security incidents as responsibilities for monitoring fall between organizational cracks
- Slower incident response because of confusion about roles and authorities
- Incomplete risk remediation as partial solutions are implemented without coordination
- Duplicative or conflicting controls as different groups implement solutions independently
- Blind spots where risks aren't adequately addressed by any group

These consequences stem directly from the artificial separation between technology risks and business risks. When organizations treat cybersecurity as a specialized domain distinct from business risk management, fragmentation becomes almost inevitable, creating gaps that adversaries can readily exploit.

1.8.2 Resource misallocation and inefficient protection

Beyond accountability issues, the separation of cyber risk from business risk leads to significant resource misallocation, reducing the efficiency and effectiveness of security investments.

In siloed environments, security teams often prioritize investments based on technical severity rather than business impact. A "critical" vulnerability in a low-value system might receive immediate attention, while a "moderate" vulnerability in a business-critical application might wait in the IT ticket queue. Without clear business context, technical prioritization alone can lead to suboptimal resource allocation.

This disconnect works in both directions. Business teams may invest in initiatives without fully understanding their security implications, potentially creating additional risks that require costly remediation. Meanwhile, security teams may implement controls that impede business processes, creating friction that leads to workarounds or exceptions that ultimately reduce security effectiveness.

Examples of resource misallocation in siloed environments include:

- Over-investment in protecting low-value assets while under-investing in high-value ones
- Implementation of security controls that create business friction without commensurate risk reduction
- Duplicative technology investments across different business units addressing similar risks
- Expensive technical solutions for risks that could be more efficiently addressed through process changes
- Failure to consider total cost of ownership for security solutions, including operational impacts

These inefficiencies represent a hidden cost of treating cyber risk as separate from business risk. Organizations often focus on the direct costs of security technologies and staff while overlooking the indirect costs of misaligned investments, business disruption, and suboptimal risk reduction.

More fundamentally, separation creates challenges in effectively comparing security investments with other business investments. When cyber risks are evaluated using different frameworks and metrics than other business risks, organizations struggle to make consistent decisions about where to allocate limited resources for maximum risk reduction.

🔗 *Downloadable Resource: Security Investment Prioritization Matrix*

1.8.3 Case study: Equifax – when technical vulnerabilities become business catastrophes

1.8.3.1 Context

Equifax, one of three major consumer credit reporting agencies in the United States, holds sensitive personal and financial information on more than 200 million U.S. consumers. As a steward of these data, the company's business model depends entirely on its ability to securely maintain and manage access to vast quantities of personally identifiable information (PII), including Social Security numbers, birthdates, addresses, driver's license numbers, and credit card information.

In 2017, Equifax found itself at the center of one of the most significant data breaches in history – an event that would transform the company, lead to unprecedented regulatory consequences, and provide a clear and compelling case of how technical vulnerabilities translate directly to business risks as illustrated in Figure 1.4.

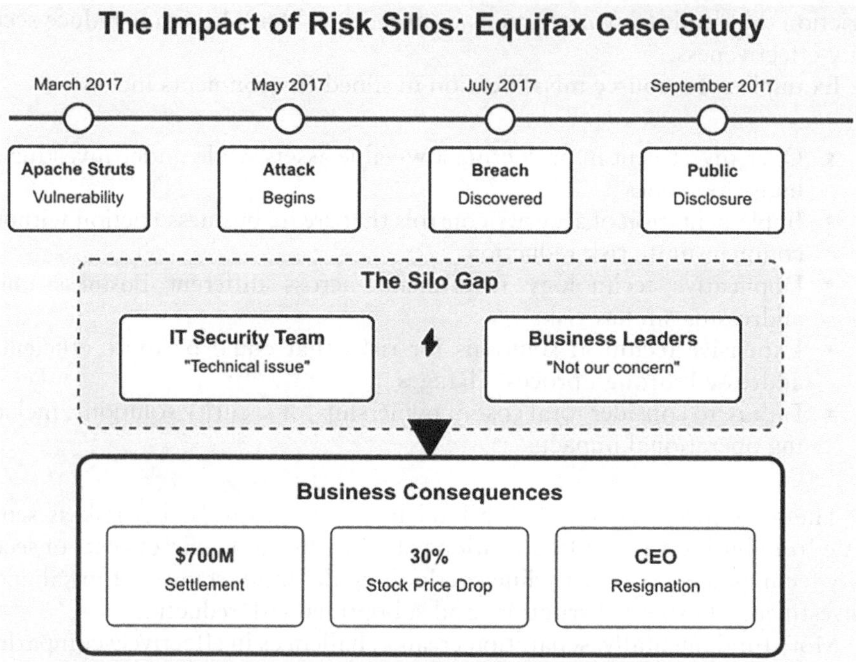

Figure 1.4 Equifax case study

1.8.3.2 Challenge

On September 7, 2017, Equifax announced that unauthorized parties had accessed the personal information of approximately 147 million U.S. consumers – nearly half the U.S. population. The breach exposed critical personal data including names, Social Security numbers, birth dates, addresses, and in some instances, driver's license numbers and credit card information.

The root cause? A critical vulnerability in Apache Struts, an open-source web application framework used by Equifax. The U.S. Computer Emergency Readiness Team (US-CERT) had alerted Equifax to this vulnerability on March 8, 2017, and a patch was available. However, despite Equifax's security team disseminating the alert internally and ordering patches within 48 hours, the company failed to apply the patch to its vulnerable Automated Consumer Interview System (ACIS) Dispute Portal.

This single technical failure exposed fundamental flaws in Equifax's security practices:

1. The patch management policy didn't require employees to acknowledge receipt of critical patch directives or confirm that patches were applied

2. The company relied on an automated vulnerability scanner that wasn't configured to search all potentially vulnerable systems
3. The databases weren't properly segmented, allowing attackers who breached one system to access many others
4. Administrative credentials were stored in plain text in an unsecured file share
5. Over 145 million Social Security numbers and other sensitive information were stored in plain text

For over four months, the vulnerability remained unaddressed, allowing attackers to access and extract data between May 13 and July 30, 2017, before Equifax finally discovered the breach.

1.8.3.3 Approach

Equifax's response to the breach demonstrated the company's struggle to transition from treating this as merely a technical incident to recognizing it as a full-scale business crisis:

Initially, the company established a dedicated website (equifaxsecurity2017.com) and offered free credit monitoring services to affected consumers through TrustedID Premier. However, these efforts were marred by technical problems, confusing information, and terms of service that initially appeared to require consumers to waive their right to sue.

As the scale of the business impact became clear, Equifax's approach changed:

1. CEO Richard Smith resigned in late September 2017, replaced by interim CEO Paulino do Rego Barros Jr.
2. The company fired its Chief Information Officer after he was charged by the Securities and Exchange Commission for insider trading (selling company shares between discovering the breach and public disclosure)
3. Equifax signed consent agreements with banking regulators from eight U.S. states
4. The company hired a new Chief Information Security Officer (CISO) in July 2018 to integrate more robust security practices
5. Equifax implemented comprehensive information security program improvements mandated by regulatory settlements

1.8.3.4 Outcome

The consequences for Equifax were severe and far-reaching, affecting every aspect of the business:

Financial Impact: In July 2019, Equifax agreed to a settlement (Federal Trade Commission v. Equifax, Inc., 2019) with the Federal Trade Commission,

Consumer Financial Protection Bureau (CFPB), and 50 U.S. states and territories totaling between $575 million and $700 million. This included:

- $300 million for a consumer fund to provide credit monitoring and compensation
- Up to $125 million additional if the initial $300 million proved insufficient
- $175 million to 48 states, the District of Columbia, and Puerto Rico
- $100 million in civil penalties to the CFPB

Regulatory Consequences: The settlement required Equifax to implement a comprehensive information security program including:

- Designating employees responsible for the program
- Conducting annual security risk assessments
- Implementing safeguards like patch management, network segmentation, and encryption
- Obtaining third-party assessments of its security program every two years

Leadership Changes: CEO Richard Smith and CIO Jun Ying both departed the company, along with other executives.

Stock Price Impact: Equifax's stock price dropped approximately 30% in the days following the breach announcement and took nearly a year to recover.

Long-term Business Requirements: The settlement mandated Equifax to:

- Provide all U.S. consumers with six free credit reports each year for seven years
- Offer affected consumers free credit monitoring services for up to 10 years
- Provide free identity restoration services to all affected consumers for seven years

1.8.3.5 Lessons

The Equifax breach vividly demonstrates this chapter's core argument: cybersecurity risks are business risks with technical components, not a separate category of concern. Several critical lessons emerge:

1. **Technical vulnerabilities create direct business consequences.** What began as a simple failure to patch a software vulnerability culminated in hundreds of millions in settlement costs, executive departures, and long-term regulatory oversight. The Apache Struts vulnerability wasn't just an IT problem – it was a business risk that materialized with catastrophic consequences.
2. **Artificial separation between technical and business risks creates dangerous blind spots.** Equifax's security team issued an order to patch systems, but the order wasn't delivered to the individual responsible. This communication breakdown reflects how technical tasks like patching

are often isolated from business risk management frameworks – creating a dangerous gap where critical risks go unaddressed.

3. **Governance failures amplify technical vulnerabilities.** Beyond the unpatched vulnerability, Equifax demonstrated systemic governance failures: unsegmented networks, plain-text storage of sensitive data, insufficient monitoring, and inadequate detection capabilities. These weren't merely technical shortcomings but fundamental business governance failures.
4. **Stock value directly reflects security practices.** The immediate 30% drop in Equifax's stock price demonstrates how quickly the market penalizes inadequate security practices once they become visible. This direct connection between security practices and shareholder value underscores why security belongs in business risk discussions.
5. **Security investments must align with business value at risk.** With 147 million consumer records at stake, Equifax's security investments were clearly insufficient given the business value at risk. A proper business risk assessment would have identified that the ACIS Dispute Portal accessed critical data assets requiring proportional protection.

The Equifax case demonstrates why organizations must stop thinking about "cyber risk" as something distinct from business risk. When a technical vulnerability can trigger over $700 million in settlement costs, executive departures, and years of regulatory scrutiny, it's clear that these risks belong squarely in enterprise risk management frameworks, not siloed in technical departments.

For executives and boards, the message is clear: technical vulnerabilities directly impact business outcomes. Treating security as just a technical function rather than a core business risk management activity creates the exact conditions for an Equifax-style disaster.

In a more integrated risk environment, this vulnerability would have been evaluated based on its potential business impact – considering the sensitivity of the data potentially exposed and the regulatory, financial, and reputational consequences of a breach. Such an evaluation would likely have resulted in faster patching, additional compensating controls, or other risk mitigation measures that might have prevented the breach or reduced its impact.

The Equifax breach demonstrates how technical vulnerabilities directly translate into business catastrophe. We'll see similar patterns in Chapter 2's analysis of the Capital One breach, where failures in risk communication led to significant business damage.

1.8.4 The compliance trap

Regulatory frameworks, while intended to improve security, often inadvertently reinforce the separation between cyber and business risk. Many compliance requirements focus on specific technical controls or processes without explicitly connecting them to business objectives, potentially leading organizations to pursue compliance as an end rather than as part of a broader risk management strategy.

This "compliance trap" occurs when organizations focus on meeting regulatory requirements rather than addressing their actual risk exposure. For example, a healthcare organization might implement all required HIPAA security controls while failing to address business-specific risks that fall outside the regulation's explicit requirements. The result is a false sense of security, as compliance doesn't equal adequate risk management.

Checkbox compliance approaches are particularly dangerous. When organizations treat compliance as a series of boxes to check rather than as part of a comprehensive risk management program, they may implement controls without ensuring their effectiveness or relevance to the organization's specific risk profile. This mechanical approach can consume significant resources while providing limited actual risk reduction.

When compliance becomes disconnected from risk reality, organizations face several challenges:

- Resources allocated to compliance activities may not address the most significant business risks
- Controls implemented for compliance may not be operationally effective in the specific environment
- The focus on documentation may overshadow actual security effectiveness
- Organizations may fail to address new risk factors or influences that aren't yet covered by regulatory frameworks
- Security becomes reactive to regulatory changes rather than proactive to modern threats

According to the World Economic Forum's Global Cybersecurity Outlook 2025 (World Economic Forum, 2025), key challenges include supply chain vulnerabilities, a growing skills gap, and fragmented regulatory landscapes, with the report calling for enhanced collaboration across sectors and a security-first mindset to bolster overall cyber resilience. The identification of supply chain and regulatory risks as core cyber challenges, and the explicit call for cross-sector collaboration, highlight the inadequacy of treating cyber risk as a standalone issue. Integrated, collaborative approaches are necessary to address the complex, interconnected nature of modern risk.

This research highlights the growing complexity of the cybersecurity risk landscape, particularly regarding supply chain vulnerabilities and fragmented regulations. These challenges cannot be addressed through traditional siloed approaches but require collaboration across organizational boundaries – both within organizations and between them. The mention of a "security-first mindset" suggests the need to embed security considerations into business processes rather than treating them as separate technical concerns.

The compliance trap represents one of the most persistent challenges in integrating cyber and business risk. Regulatory frameworks, while valuable, often reinforce the notion that cybersecurity is a specialized domain requiring specialized handling. Organizations seeking to overcome the artificial division between cyber and business risk must find ways to fulfill compliance obligations while maintaining a broader, more integrated approach to risk management.

This compliance trap creates what we'll discuss in Chapter 5 as the "compliance-only mindset," where organizations invest only enough to satisfy regulatory requirements rather than addressing their actual risk exposure.

The evidence from cases like Equifax demonstrates clear organizational costs of separation. However, a growing body of research and organizational experience points toward better outcomes when organizations adopt integrated approaches. Let's examine what this evidence reveals about the benefits of integration.

CISO Tip: Document instances where security recommendations were ignored due to communication gaps, then calculate the actual costs when incidents occurred.

CFO Tip: Compare the complete costs of security incidents (including business disruption, reputation damage, and recovery efforts) against proposed preventative investments.

1.9 EVIDENCE FOR INTEGRATION: BETTER BUSINESS OUTCOMES

Growing evidence suggests that organizations adopting integrated risk approaches may achieve superior business outcomes compared to those maintaining traditional silos. This section presents research findings and organizational trends that show integration benefits, while addressing common objections that stakeholders often raise when considering unified risk management approaches.

1.9.1 Evidence of integration success

Beyond theoretical arguments for integrating cyber risk into broader business risk management, there is growing evidence that such integration delivers measurable benefits. While comprehensive industry data comparing siloed versus integrated approaches remains limited, we can infer potential benefits associated with the de-duplication of risk assessment and management efforts. Comprehensive and empirical data comparing siloed versus integrated risk approaches in similar industry cohorts represents a significant research gap in our industry. Organizations implementing integration should establish baseline measurements to track efficiency gains.

According to PwC's 2024 Global Digital Trust Insights (PwC, 2024),

> These top 5% – our stewards of digital trust – are reaping benefits that others are missing. They're experiencing fewer breaches, and the attacks that do hit them aren't as costly. Managing risk is easier because they've streamlined their security solutions. And they've positioned themselves for greater productivity and faster growth, outpacing the competition as they plunge into new technologies with confidence that they are well protected.

This finding provides direct evidence that organizations with integrated, enterprise-wide risk management – not siloed cyber risk programs – achieve superior business outcomes, including reduced breaches and higher productivity.

This research is particularly significant because it connects security outcomes directly to business performance. The "stewards of digital trust" identified in the study don't just have better security metrics; they demonstrate higher productivity and stronger business results. This suggests that properly integrated risk management doesn't just reduce negative outcomes, but actively contributes to business success.

Additional research supports these findings. Studies have consistently found that organizations with integrated risk approaches experience:

- Faster detection and response to security incidents
- Lower overall cost of security incidents when they occur
- More efficient allocation of security resources
- Better alignment between security investments and business objectives
- Higher confidence in security effectiveness among executives and board members

The fiscal impact of this improved performance can be substantial. Organizations with integrated risk approaches typically report lower per-record costs in data breaches, shorter breach resolution times, and reduced total cost of risk management when considering both direct and indirect costs.

Perhaps most compelling is evidence regarding risk visibility. Organizations with integrated approaches consistently report fewer "surprise" incidents – events that were not previously identified as significant risks. This suggests that integration improves risk identification and assessment, helping organizations expect and prepare for potential incidents rather than simply reacting to them. In Chapter 4, we'll explore specific enterprise risk management frameworks that provide structured approaches for achieving this integration, helping organizations to manage security risks alongside other business risks.

1.9.2 Organizational trends toward integration

Recognizing the benefits of integration, many organizations are moving toward more unified risk approaches. This movement reflects both growing awareness of the limitations of siloed risk management and increasing pressure from stakeholders for more comprehensive risk oversight.

According to Hyperproof's 2025 IT Risk and Compliance Benchmark Report (Hyperproof, 2025), "91% of respondents have a centralized team to manage GRC. This is the highest number reported in the six years of the survey, up from 88% in the previous year." Most organizations now recognize the importance of taking a unified approach to risk and compliance management, indicating a strong trend toward integration in the market. This statistic directly demonstrates the industry-wide move away from treating cyber risk in isolation. The centralization of GRC functions shows that organizations recognize the interconnectedness of cyber, compliance, and operational risks, and that integrated approaches are now the norm for effective risk management.

This trend toward centralization represents a significant shift from earlier organizational models that treated various risk domains as separate concerns. The high percentage of organizations adopting centralized GRC functions suggests that integration is becoming the standard approach rather than an exceptional practice.

Several organizational models are emerging to support integration:

- Unified risk management teams that bring together specialists from different risk domains
- Integrated risk committees that coordinate risk activities across traditional silos
- Cross-functional risk assessment processes that evaluate risks from multiple perspectives
- Common risk frameworks that apply consistent evaluation criteria across risk types
- Shared risk reporting mechanisms that provide comprehensive visibility to stakeholders

Executive perspectives on integration benefits also reveal growing support for unified approaches. In surveys and interviews, executives consistently cite improved decision-making, more efficient resource allocation, and better strategic alignment as key benefits of integrated risk management. Many also note improved board engagement, as integrated risk information provides a more comprehensive view of organizational risk posture.

As these organizational changes continue, they are likely to accelerate the shift toward integrated risk management. As more organizations demonstrate the benefits of integration, others will follow, hopefully reducing the artificial separation between cyber and business risk.

Chapter 4 explores specific ERM frameworks that enable this integration, providing structured approaches for connecting security risks to enterprise risk management.

1.9.2.1 Risk integration maturity assessment

- **PURPOSE:** Helps organizations evaluate how effectively they've integrated cybersecurity risk with broader business risk management, identifying specific improvement opportunities.

- **WHEN TO USE:** During strategic planning, prior to major security initiatives, or as part of annual security program assessments.

Rate each dimension from 1 (Siloed) to 5 (Fully Integrated), following the criteria in Table 1.2.

Table 1.2 Risk integration maturity assessment

Integration dimension	*Siloed (1)*	*Developing (3)*	*Integrated (5)*	*Your score*
Governance structure	Security and risk functions report through separate channels with minimal coordination	Some cross-functional coordination exists but with separate decision processes	Unified governance structure with security fully integrated into enterprise risk management	
Risk assessment method	Separate methodologies for cyber and business risks	Common methodology but separate execution	Single, unified risk assessment process incorporating both technical and business factors	
Risk language	Heavy technical jargon in security; financial terms in business risk	Some translation between domains but inconsistent	Consistent enterprise-wide risk terminology with both technical precision and business clarity	
Budget allocation	Security budget separate from business unit budgets	Some input from business units on security spending	Security investments allocated based on business risk and owned jointly	
Incident response	Technical team handles incidents with minimal business involvement	Business stakeholders involved after technical assessment	Joint business and technical teams with pre-defined business impact thresholds	
Risk appetite definition	Separate risk appetites for security vs. business	Coordinated but separate risk appetite statements	Unified risk appetite framework applied consistently across domains	
Metrics and reporting	Technical metrics for security; financial metrics for business risk	Some cross-domain reporting but separate primary metrics	Integrated metrics linking security activities directly to business outcomes	
Ownership and accountability	Security owns "cyber" risk; business units own "business" risk	Shared responsibility but unclear boundaries	Clear joint accountability with defined roles for both technical and business stakeholders	

Scoring Guide:

- 8–16: Highly Siloed – Significant barriers between security and business risk
- 17–24: Beginning Integration – Early efforts to connect domains but substantial gaps remain
- 25–32: Advancing Integration – Good foundation but opportunities for deeper coordination
- 33–40: Mature Integration – Highly effective risk integration with minor refinement opportunities

IMPLEMENTATION TIPS:

- Have both security and business leaders complete the assessment independently, then compare results
- Focus improvement efforts on dimensions with the largest gaps between current and desired states

Use assessment results to build a roadmap for risk integration initiatives

1.9.3 Addressing common objections to integration

Despite growing evidence supporting integration, some stakeholders continue to resist unified risk approaches. Understanding and addressing these objections is essential for organizations seeking to overcome the artificial division between cyber and business risk.

One common concern is that integration might dilute technical expertise, potentially reducing the effectiveness of specialized security functions. This concern often stems from misunderstanding what integration involves. Effective integration doesn't eliminate specialization, but rather connects specialized expertise more directly to business objectives. Technical security professionals still maintain deep domain knowledge, but they apply that knowledge with greater awareness of business context and in closer coordination with other risk functions.

Integration can enhance technical depth by ensuring that security specialists understand the business context in which they operate. This context helps them target their expertise more effectively, focusing on the vulnerabilities and controls that matter most to the organization rather than pursuing technical perfection in areas of limited business significance.

Technical security expertise requires deep, specialized knowledge that shouldn't be diluted. Network protocol analysis, vulnerability research, and incident forensics demand focused expertise that generalists cannot easily replicate. The goal isn't to eliminate specialization but to connect it more effectively to the business context.

However, security and business teams often operate with fundamentally different time horizons – security thinks in terms of potential future threats while the business focuses on quarterly results. Professional identities built around specialized knowledge can create resistance to integration efforts. Performance metrics that reward functional rather than cross-functional success reinforce siloed behaviors.

Another objection relates to regulatory compliance. Some practitioners worry that integrated approaches might compromise compliance with specific security regulations. However, integrated risk management can often enhance compliance by connecting regulatory requirements to broader business objectives. This connection helps organizations implement compliance controls more effectively and adapt them more readily to changing regulatory expectations.

Some examples of organizations that have successfully preserved technical depth while improving business alignment include:

- Financial institutions that maintain specialized security teams but integrate their assessments into enterprise risk frameworks
- Healthcare organizations that align security controls with patient safety and privacy objectives
- Manufacturing companies that connect cybersecurity with operational technology safety and reliability
- Technology companies that integrate security into product development processes

Resistance to change represents perhaps the most significant obstacle to integration. Established organizational structures, professional identities, and measurement systems all reinforce the separation between cyber and business risk. Overcoming this inertia requires deliberate effort, clear leadership support, and practical transition strategies that acknowledge the challenges of organizational change.

Strategies for overcoming resistance include:

- Starting with shared language and metrics to build collective understanding
- Creating cross-functional teams to address specific high-priority risks
- Implementing joint risk assessment processes that bring together different perspectives
- Gradually aligning reporting structures and incentives with integrated objectives
- Celebrating early wins that demonstrate the benefits of integration

By acknowledging and addressing these objections directly, organizations can navigate the transition to more integrated risk approaches while preserving the specialized expertise needed to address complex technical risks.

With evidence supporting integration benefits and methods for addressing common objections, the question becomes practical: how can organizations begin moving toward more unified risk management? The closing section of chapter one provides suggested steps for starting this transformation.

CISO Tip: Present security initiatives with clear KPIs that demonstrate business value, not just technical effectiveness.

CFO Tip: Consider security investments as "business resilience spending" rather than technical overhead to better align with enterprise risk management.

1.10 A UNIFIED RISK MODEL: BRINGING CYBER AND BUSINESS TOGETHER

Moving from fragmented to integrated risk management requires both conceptual understanding and practical implementation strategies. This section outlines foundational principles for viewing cybersecurity through a business lens and provides actionable steps that organizations can take to begin bridging the artificial divide between technical and business risk concerns.

1.10.1 Principles of integrated risk management

Moving from the current fragmented approach to a more integrated risk model requires certain foundational principles. These principles don't eliminate the need for specialized knowledge, but place that knowledge within a broader business context.

Core principles for viewing cyber risks through a business lens include:

1. Business impact as the primary measure of risk significance. Rather than evaluating risks based solely on technical severity, integrated approaches assess risks based on their potential impact on business objectives, considering factors like financial loss, operational disruption, regulatory penalties, and reputational damage.
2. Common risk criteria across all risk domains. Integrated approaches use consistent criteria to evaluate distinct types of risks, enabling meaningful comparison and prioritization across traditional silos.
3. Shared ownership between technical and business stakeholders. Integrated risk management recognizes that effective risk mitigation requires both technical expertise and business process changes, making risk management a shared responsibility.
4. Transparent translation between technical and business perspectives. While maintaining necessary technical detail, integrated approaches ensure technical risks are consistently translated into business terms that non-technical stakeholders can understand and act upon.

Business impact analysis plays a crucial role in risk prioritization. By systematically evaluating how specific risks might affect business operations, financial performance, regulatory compliance, and customer relationships, organizations can develop a more nuanced understanding of risk significance that goes beyond technical severity ratings.

Creating a common risk language across the organization supports integration by ensuring that different stakeholders can communicate effectively about shared risks. This doesn't mean eliminating technical terminology but supplementing it with a business context that helps non-technical stakeholders understand why technical issues matter to the organization's success.

1.10.1.1 Exercise: "Risk translation"

Practice converting these technical risks into business terms:

- Technical: "Our web application has SQL injection vulnerabilities in several input fields."
- Business: "Our customer portal has weaknesses that could allow attackers to access our customer database, potentially exposing personal and financial information that would trigger regulatory reporting requirements and damage customer trust."
- Technical: "We lack adequate network segmentation between operational technology and IT networks."
- Business: "Our manufacturing systems are connected to our corporate network in ways that could allow a security incident to spread from office systems to production facilities, potentially causing production outages costing $500,000 per day."
- Technical: "Our current intrusion detection system has limited visibility into encrypted traffic."
- Business: "Our ability to detect potential data theft is limited, creating a risk that sensitive information could be exfiltrated without detection, potentially leading to competitive disadvantage and intellectual property loss."

This translation exercise helps bridge the gap between technical and business perspectives, ensuring that security concerns are understood in terms of their business implications.

Downloadable Resource: Executive Security Communication Template

1.10.2 Practical first steps toward integration

While full integration of cyber risk into business risk management may require significant organizational changes, organizations can begin with practical steps that deliver immediate benefits while building momentum for broader transformation.

Organizational structure considerations include:

- Creating cross-functional risk committees that bring together security, IT, legal, compliance, and business representatives
- Establishing dotted-line reporting relationships between security teams and business units to strengthen alignment
- Designating business risk owners for key systems and applications to ensure shared accountability
- Introducing integration roles that span traditional boundaries, such as business information security officers assigned to specific business units

Communication frameworks that bridge the gap between technical and business perspectives might include:

- Risk reporting templates that include both technical details and business implications
- Regular translation sessions where security teams present risks in business terms
- Executive dashboards that connect security metrics to business objectives
- Shared risk assessment processes that incorporate multiple perspectives

Process changes to implement integrated risk management often include:

- Modifying risk assessment methodologies to incorporate business impact analysis
- Aligning security project prioritization with business priorities
- Integrating security considerations into business decision processes
- Developing shared metrics that connect security activities to business outcomes

When setting expectations for transformation, organizations should recognize that integration is a journey rather than a destination as depicted in Figure 1.5. Initial steps might focus on improving communication and

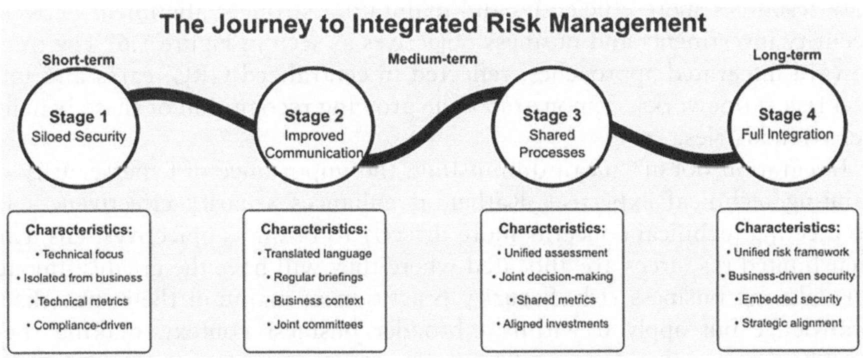

Figure 1.5 The journey to integrated risk management

developing shared understanding, while later stages address more fundamental changes to organizational structures, processes, and metrics.

Realistic expectations include:

- Short-term improvements in communication and coordination
- Medium-term alignment of priorities and investments
- Longer-term changes to organizational structures and incentives
- Ongoing refinement as the organization learns from experience

By starting with practical steps while maintaining a clear vision of the desired end state, organizations can begin to bridge the artificial divide between cyber and business risk, gradually moving toward a more integrated approach that delivers better protection at lower cost.

Downloadable Resource: Security-Business Integration Workshop

1.11 CONCLUSION

The concept of "cyber risk" as a distinct category separate from business risk has proven to be a costly and dangerous myth. Throughout this chapter, we've seen how this artificial separation creates communication barriers, fragments accountability, misaligns resources, and ultimately leaves organizations more vulnerable to the very threats they seek to mitigate.

This separation is not inevitable but a historical artifact. It stems from the technical origins of cybersecurity, reinforced by specialized language, organizational structures, and regulatory frameworks that treat security as a domain apart from broader business concerns. Despite its historical roots, this separation no longer serves organizations well in an environment where technology risks are inseparable from business risks.

The evidence is clear: organizations that integrate cyber risk into their broader business risk frameworks achieve better outcomes. They experience fewer breaches, respond more effectively when incidents occur, allocate resources more efficiently, and maintain a stronger alignment between security investments and business objectives as seen in Figure 1.6. The trend toward integrated approaches, reflected in centralized GRC teams and unified risk frameworks, demonstrates the growing recognition of these benefits across industries.

Integration doesn't mean diminishing the importance of cybersecurity or diluting technical expertise. Rather, it enhances security effectiveness by connecting technical concerns more directly to business objectives, ensuring that limited resources are allocated where they will have the greatest impact on reducing business risk. Security practitioners maintain their specialized knowledge but apply it within a broader business context, making their expertise more valuable and influential.

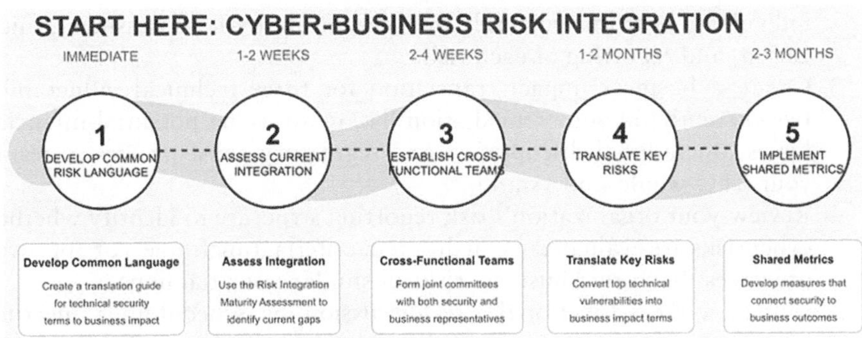

Figure 1.6 Cyber-business risk integration

Some may resist this integration, fearing loss of specialized status or resources. Yet the evidence suggests that integration typically enhances rather than diminishes security effectiveness. By connecting security concerns to business objectives, integration often increases executive support for security initiatives and ensures that resources are allocated based on business impact rather than on technical criteria alone.

In the next chapter, we'll explore specific methods for translating technical vulnerabilities into business impact, providing practical tools for organizations seeking to bridge the gap between security and business perspectives. This translation represents a first step toward more integrated risk management, enabling more effective communication, better decision-making, and ultimately stronger protection for organizational assets.

For now, we encourage readers to begin rethinking their own organization's approach to risk. Consider the language you use to describe security concerns. Examine how your organizational structure supports or hinders integration. Evaluate whether your risk assessment processes connect technical vulnerabilities to business impacts. These initial reflections can set the stage for meaningful change, moving your organization toward a more integrated approach that treats cybersecurity as an integral component of business risk management, rather than a separate technical domain.

1.12 ACTION ITEMS FOR READERS

1. Assess your organization's current risk language by reviewing the last three months of security-related communications to executives and identifying instances where technical terminology was used without business context translation.
2. Conduct a risk ownership mapping exercise by listing your organization's top 10 technology-related risks and documenting which specific

individuals or teams currently own responsibility for assessment, mitigation, and reporting of each risk.

3. Create a business impact translation for three technical vulnerabilities currently on your remediation list, quantifying potential financial losses, operational disruptions, and regulatory consequences in terms your CFO would understand.
4. Review your organization's risk reporting structure to identify whether cyber risks are evaluated using different criteria, timeframes, or approval processes than other business risks of similar potential impact.
5. Initiate a cross-functional risk discussion by scheduling a meeting between your security team and one business unit to jointly assess a shared technology risk using both technical severity and business impact criteria.

Chapter 2

Lost in translation

Why technical vulnerabilities don't resonate

Chapter in One Sentence: Security vulnerability reports fail to drive executive action not because of intelligence gaps but relevance gaps – requiring a structured translation approach that connects technical findings to business outcomes using language, context, and frameworks that resonate with decision-makers.

2.1 EXECUTIVE SUMMARY

This chapter examines the persistent gap between technical security findings and executive action. Despite diligent identification of vulnerabilities by technical teams, their warnings frequently fail to translate into business decisions. This disconnect stems from three primary factors: competing priorities, ineffective translation, and lack of confidence in decision-making. Executives face numerous urgent matters daily, with vulnerability reports representing just one of many demands for attention and resources. Within this context, technical reports often fail to break through because they use language that creates cognitive barriers and lacks business relevance.

The human brain processes risk information through distinct mechanisms that combine emotional and analytical responses. Cognitive biases systematically influence perception, including availability bias (overemphasizing recent or vivid risks), optimism bias ("it won't happen to us"), and status quo bias (preferring current conditions over change). These psychological factors significantly affect how vulnerability information is received and acted upon.

Technical reports typically miss the mark by using specialized jargon, failing to provide business context, and not connecting findings to business outcomes. The Capital One data breach case study illustrates how these communication failures can lead to catastrophic outcomes, with technical vulnerabilities identified but not effectively translated into business risks.

Effective security communication requires reframing technical issues through a business lens, connecting vulnerabilities to revenue impacts, cost implications, strategic objectives, compliance requirements, and reputation considerations. Communication strategies that drive decision-making include

DOI: 10.1201/9781003744146-2

using narratives to make abstract risks concrete, visual elements to simplify complex concepts, and analogies to build understanding. Timing communications to align with budget cycles, strategy sessions, and industry breach events increases their impact.

By implementing structured approaches to translate between technical and business domains, security professionals can significantly increase the likelihood that vulnerability reports will drive appropriate action. This doesn't require executives to become technical experts or security professionals to become business experts; it requires a systematic framework for making technical findings meaningful to business decision-makers.

2.2 KEY TAKEAWAYS

- Technical vulnerability reports fail to drive action due to competing priorities, ineffective translation into business language, and executives' lack of confidence in making technical decisions
- The human brain processes risk through both emotional and analytical systems, with cognitive biases systematically influencing how risk information is perceived
- Effective security communication connects vulnerabilities to business impacts (revenue, costs, strategy, compliance, reputation) rather than focusing on technical severity
- Using narratives, visual elements, and business-relevant metrics makes security communications more compelling and actionable for executives
- Strategic timing and structured templates that prioritize business relevance significantly improve the effectiveness of security communications

2.3 APPLICATION QUESTIONS

1. How do your current security communications account for the competing priorities and cognitive constraints facing your executives?
2. What specific business metrics could you use to quantify the impact of your top three security vulnerabilities?
3. How might you restructure your vulnerability reporting process to incorporate business context and executive-friendly language?

2.4 TOOLS REFERENCED IN THIS CHAPTER

All tools available at kaynemcgladrey.com/myth/

- Exercise: Cognitive Bias Identification
- Exercise: Risk Perception Assessment
- Risk-to-Value Mapping Framework
- Business Impact Translation Matrix

- Risk Communication Decision Tree
- Exercise: Vulnerability Translation Practice
- Business-Focused Vulnerability Translator

2.5 INTRODUCTION

Imagine this: A cybersecurity team discovers a critical vulnerability in your organization's customer database. They document it meticulously, complete with technical details, CVSS scores, and remediation recommendations. The report is sent to executive leadership with an urgent flag. Three months later, nothing has changed. The vulnerability remains unaddressed. Then it happens – a breach occurs through this exact vulnerability, affecting millions of customers and costing the organization millions of dollars in remediation, legal fees, and reputational damage.

This scenario plays out regularly across organizations worldwide. Despite the diligence of technical teams in identifying and reporting vulnerabilities, their warnings frequently fail to translate into executive action. The disconnect isn't about competence or commitment – it's about communication. Technical teams speak the language of CVEs, patches, and exploits, while executives think in terms of market share, quarterly targets, and shareholder value. When these languages don't align, critical security messages get lost in translation.

This chapter examines the persistent gap between technical security findings and business decision-making. We'll uncover why technical vulnerability reports often fail to drive executive action, how human psychology influences risk perception, and what approaches can bridge this critical divide. The questions we'll address include: Why don't technical reports motivate action from decision-makers? How does the human brain process different types of risk information? What communication strategies drive executive decision-making?

Building on the previous chapter's discussion of the separation between cybersecurity and business concerns, we'll now focus specifically on the communication challenges that prevent technical findings from becoming business priorities. By understanding these dynamics, security professionals can develop more effective approaches to translating technical concerns into business action.

2.6 THE EXECUTIVE'S DILEMMA: WHY TECHNICAL VULNERABILITY REPORTS FAIL TO DRIVE ACTION

Every day, executives make decisions that shape the future of their organizations. These decisions occur within the context of competing priorities, limited resources, and incomplete information. Understanding this decision-making context is essential for security professionals who want their vulnerability findings to drive meaningful action.

2.6.1 The competing priorities problem

Executives rarely lack the will to address security vulnerabilities. What they lack is the capacity to address every issue that crosses their desk with equal urgency. An average day for a C-suite executive might include reviewing quarterly financials, addressing pressing talent issues, evaluating market expansion opportunities, and responding to shareholder concerns – all before lunch.

Within this whirlwind of activity, vulnerability reports represent just one of many competing demands for attention and resources. As noted in Chapter 1, while CLOs recognize data breaches as a primary threat, they face significant budget pressures, with 42% reporting cost-cutting mandates over the past year. This creates a fundamental tension between recognizing cybersecurity importance and having resources to address it.

The cognitive load of processing detailed technical reports alongside other business demands further complicates matters. Research in cognitive psychology suggests that people have finite cognitive resources, and the complexity of technical vulnerability reports may exceed what busy executives can effectively process. When faced with information overload, decision-makers tend to focus on familiar problems with simple solutions rather than complex issues requiring specialized knowledge.

Many technical teams fail to recognize this reality. They assume that presenting comprehensive technical information is sufficient to drive action, without accounting for the competing priorities and cognitive constraints affecting executive decision-making. This disconnect often leads to frustration on both sides: security teams wonder why their urgent warnings go unheeded, while executives struggle to determine which of the many "urgent" matters on their desk truly require immediate attention.

Chapter 5 examines this executive mindset in depth, explaining how business leaders evaluate investment opportunities and what security leaders must understand to compete effectively for resources.

2.6.2 The translation gap

The format and language of typical vulnerability reports rarely align with executive decision-making needs. Consider a standard vulnerability report: it typically includes technical details about affected systems, vulnerability identifiers, technical impact assessments, and remediation steps. What it often lacks is a clear translation of these technical findings into business implications that resonate with executive priorities.

According to PwC's 2024 Global Digital Trust Insights (PwC, 2024), while investment in cybersecurity is increasing, actual improvements in security practices remain slow. This disconnect indicates that technical findings are not effectively translating into business action, likely because of communication gaps between technical and executive teams.

Common reporting formats that fail to drive action include:

- Vulnerability scan results with long lists of findings but no business context or prioritization
- Technical assessments that emphasize technical severity ratings without connecting to business impact
- Remediation recommendations that focus on technical fixes without addressing business constraints or opportunities

These approaches assume executives will independently connect technical details to business implications – an assumption that rarely holds true. Most executives lack the technical background to translate CVE numbers or CVSS scores into concrete business risks. Without this translation, vulnerability reports become noise rather than actionable intelligence.

In Chapter 3, we'll introduce Business Impact Analysis as a structured methodology for bridging this translation gap, enabling security professionals to convert technical findings into business impact terms.

This translation problem manifests directly in the security metrics challenges discussed in Chapter 6, where we'll examine how traditional technical metrics fail to communicate business value.

2.6.3 The confidence problem

When presented with technical decisions outside their domain expertise, many executives experience significant uncertainty. This uncertainty often leads to decision paralysis or deference to others who may not fully understand the business implications of technical vulnerabilities.

This confidence gap, discussed in Chapter 1, reflects how technical vulnerability reports fail to provide the business context needed for decisive action. This striking lack of confidence among senior legal executives suggests that technical vulnerability reports are not effectively communicating risk in a way that enables business leaders to act with certainty. Instead, the excessive technical detail and lack of business context create uncertainty that impedes decisive action.

For many executives, technical vulnerability reports trigger a series of challenging questions:

- How serious is this vulnerability compared to others?
- What's the likelihood it will be exploited?
- What business functions would be affected?
- What's the potential fiscal impact?

Without straightforward answers to these questions, taking action feels like a leap of faith rather than a calculated decision.

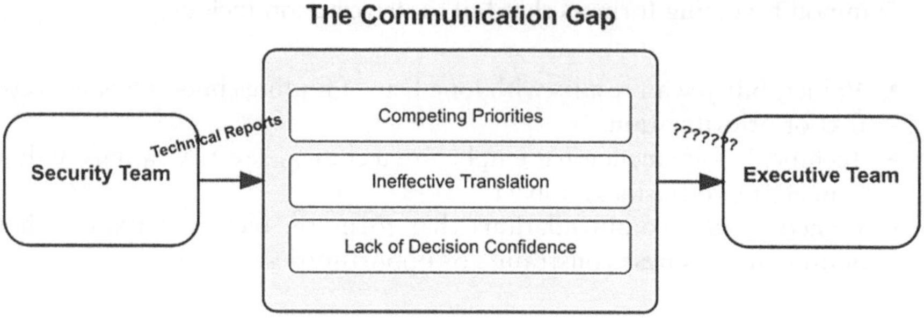

Figure 2.1 The communication gap.

This uncertainty creates a paralyzing effect that often results in delayed decisions or default to the status quo. When executives don't feel confident making decisions about technical vulnerabilities, they tend to:

- Defer to technical teams without providing clear business priorities
- Request additional information that may delay necessary action
- Approve partial measures that may not address the core risk
- Postpone decisions pending further review

These responses reflect not a lack of concern, but a lack of confidence in navigating technical security decisions with a limited business context as illustrated in Figure 2.1.

Executive inaction on vulnerability reports stems from three key factors: competing priorities that force difficult trade-offs, ineffective translation of technical findings into business terms, and a lack of confidence in making technical security decisions. These challenges are not insurmountable, but addressing them requires understanding how executives process risk information and make decisions – a topic we'll explore in the next section.

2.7 THE PSYCHOLOGY OF RISK PERCEPTION AND DECISION-MAKING

To effectively communicate security risks to executives, we must understand how the human brain processes risk information. By aligning our communication approaches with natural cognitive processes, we can significantly improve the likelihood that technical vulnerability reports will drive appropriate action.

2.7.1 How the human brain processes risk information

The human brain employs distinct mechanisms when processing risk information, with significant implications for security communications. These mechanisms combine emotional, intuitive responses with more deliberate analytical reasoning.

At a fundamental level, the brain processes risk through two complementary systems. The first – often called System 1 – operates quickly, automatically, and emotionally. It provides immediate gut reactions to potential threats based on previous experiences and evolutionary programming. The second – System 2 – engages in slower, more deliberate analysis, weighing evidence and calculating probabilities.

These systems process different types of risk information in distinct ways. Quantitative risk information – such as probability statistics or fiscal impact numbers – activates analytical processing. However, this type of information may feel abstract and fail to generate urgency without emotional context. Qualitative risk information – such as scenarios or narratives – typically triggers emotional processing, creating immediacy but potentially sacrificing precision.

The brain's emotional centers, particularly the amygdala, play a crucial role in risk perception. When security risks are presented in abstract, technical terms, they may fail to activate emotional processing. This may explain why detailed vulnerability reports often fail to generate the sense of urgency that security professionals expect. By contrast, vivid descriptions of breach scenarios or potential business consequences can trigger emotional responses that increase the importance of perceived risk.

Effective risk communication must engage both systems – providing analytical data for rational evaluation while also creating emotional resonance that drives action as shown in Figure 2.2. Understanding this dual processing mechanism helps explain why purely technical vulnerability reports often fail to motivate executive action.

2.7.2 Common cognitive biases affecting security decisions

Even the most rational executives are susceptible to cognitive biases that systematically distort risk perception and decision-making. These biases can significantly affect how vulnerability information is processed and acted upon.

Availability bias leads decision-makers to overemphasize risks that are easy to recall or imagine. Recent, vivid, or frequently discussed security incidents receive disproportionate attention, while equally important but less salient risks may be overlooked. This explains why many organizations implement significant security measures after experiencing a breach, even when the same vulnerabilities were previously identified but ignored.

Optimism bias manifests as the "it won't happen to us" mentality. Despite objective evidence of vulnerability, many executives maintain an unrealistic belief that their organization is less likely to experience negative events than similar organizations. This bias may contribute to the tendency to acknowledge

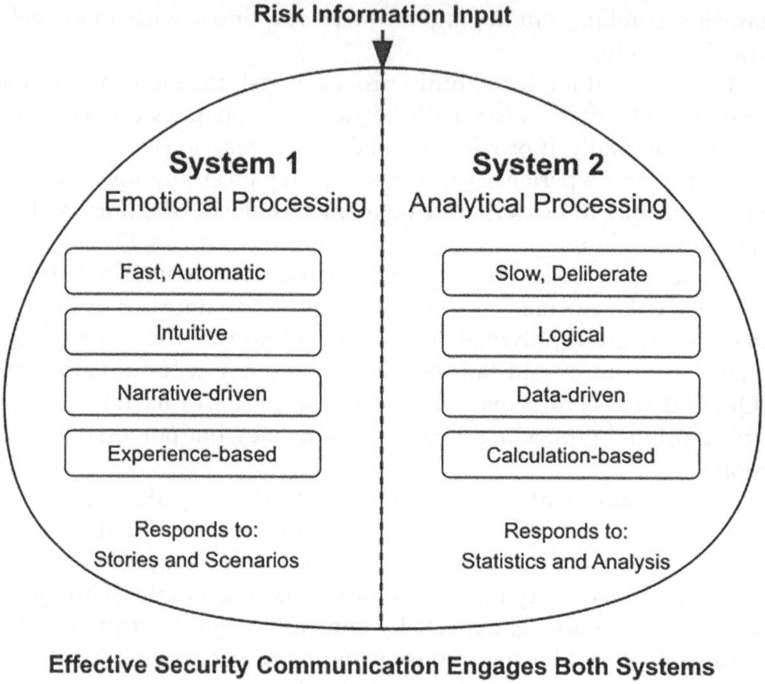

Figure 2.2 How the brain processes risk information.

security risks in principle while downplaying the likelihood of successful attacks against one's own organization.

Status quo bias creates a tendency to favor existing conditions over changes, even when changes would reduce risk. Executives may unconsciously weigh the potential downside of security changes (disruption, cost, complexity) more heavily than the benefits. This bias often manifests as reluctance to implement security measures that might interrupt business operations or require significant change management.

Framing effects demonstrate how the presentation of risk information significantly influences perception and decision-making. When identical risks are framed in terms of potential losses (e.g., "failure to address this vulnerability could cause $2 million in damages"), they typically generate stronger responses than when framed as foregone gains (e.g., "addressing this vulnerability could save $2 million"). Security communications that fail to leverage appropriate framing may unintentionally minimize perceived risk importance.

These psychological factors directly influence how business leaders evaluate security investment proposals, a topic we'll explore further in Chapter 5 when we discuss building business cases for security investments.

Downloadable Exercise: Cognitive Bias Identification

2.7.3 Different processing styles among executives

Executive decision-makers vary considerably in how they process and respond to risk information. Understanding these differences can help security professionals tailor communications more effectively.

Some executives primarily employ analytical decision-making approaches. These individuals prefer structured data, quantitative analysis, and logical arguments. They respond well to statistics, trend analyses, and probability assessments. When communicating with analytically oriented executives, effective security communications emphasize data-driven risk assessments and cost-benefit analyses.

Other executives rely more heavily on intuitive decision-making. They make judgments based on experience, pattern recognition, and gut feeling. These executives may respond better to security narratives, analogies, and scenarios that connect technical vulnerabilities to familiar business situations. They often prioritize the perspectives of trusted advisors over abstract data.

Professional background significantly influences how executives interpret risk information. Those with financial backgrounds may gravitate toward quantitative risk assessments and ROI calculations. Executives with legal backgrounds often focus on compliance implications and liability concerns. Those with marketing or sales experience may be particularly attuned to reputational risks. Effective security communications acknowledge these different frames of reference and adapt accordingly.

Time pressure and competing demands further affect risk processing. Under pressure, executives tend to rely more heavily on intuitive judgments and heuristics rather than detailed analysis. Complex, technical vulnerability reports that require significant cognitive effort may be set aside in favor of more immediately actionable items. This suggests that security communications should frontload key business implications and recommendations rather than starting with technical details.

Armed with this understanding of how the human brain processes risk information – through dual systems, influenced by predictable biases, and varying by individual decision-making styles – we can now examine specific ways technical reports miss their mark. The following examples demonstrate how security communications fail not because executives don't care, but because the messages don't align with how their brains naturally process and prioritize information. These failures follow predictable patterns that, once recognized, can be systematically addressed.

2.7.3.1 Exercise: Cognitive bias identification

- **PURPOSE:** Helps security professionals identify and counteract cognitive biases that affect how risk information is perceived and acted upon.
- **WHEN TO USE:** When preparing important security communications or after experiencing resistance to security recommendations.

Table 2.1 Potential biases affecting your security communications

Cognitive bias	*How it affects security decisions*	*Signs it may be present*	*Countermeasures*
Availability bias	Focus on recent or memorable security events rather than most significant risks	"We need to focus on ransomware because Company X was just hit" (while ignoring higher risks)	Provide objective data on actual threat frequency and impact in your environment
Optimism bias	Underestimating vulnerability to threats ("It won't happen to us")	"Our industry hasn't been targeted" or "We're too small to be a target"	Share specific examples of similar organizations affected; connect to actual vulnerabilities in your systems
Status quo bias	Preference for current state over potentially disruptive security changes	Repeated deferral of security improvements despite acknowledged risks	Highlight costs of inaction; frame security changes as enabling business rather than disrupting it
Framing effect	Different responses to identical information based on how it's presented	More concern about "losing $1M to a breach" than "failing to save $1M by preventing a breach"	Present both potential losses and potential savings in your communications

STEP 1: Identify potential biases affecting your security communications using the chart in Table 2.1.

STEP 2: Review recent security communications

- Examine a recent security report or presentation and answer:
- Did you rely heavily on technical metrics that executives may not understand? If so, rewrite with business metrics.
- Did you present risks in terms of potential losses or potential protection? Try reframing.
- Did you assume technical urgency would translate to business urgency? Add explicit business context.
- Did you provide concrete scenarios or only abstract possibilities? Add a specific scenario.

STEP 3: Create a bias-resistant communication plan

- What objective data will you include to counter availability bias?
- How will you overcome optimism bias by making threats concrete and relevant?
- How will you address status quo bias by making change seem less disruptive?
- How will you frame the information to maximize impact?

IMPLEMENTATION TIPS:

- Review this exercise with both technical and business colleagues to identify blind spots
- Use actual examples from your organization's history to make the biases more concrete

Revisit this exercise periodically, as biases can change based on recent experiences

2.8 WHEN TECHNICAL REPORTS MISS THE MARK

Even well-intentioned security reports often fail to drive executive action because of fundamental flaws in how they present information. By examining these common shortcomings, we can identify opportunities to improve the effectiveness of security communications significantly.

2.8.1 The language barrier: impact of technical jargon

Technical security reports frequently employ specialized language that creates substantial cognitive barriers for non-technical executives. Consider this example from an actual vulnerability report:

> CVE-2025-47657 presents a critical risk due to improper neutralization of special elements used in an SQL Command ('SQL Injection') vulnerability in Productive Minds Productive Commerce allows SQL Injection. This issue affects Productive Commerce: from n/a through 1.1.22. CVSS score: 9.3 (CVSS:3.1/AV:N/AC:L/PR:N/UI:N/S:C/C:H/I:N/A:L).
>
> (CVE-2025-47657, 2025)

To a security professional, this conveys essential information about vulnerability type, severity, and potential impact. To most executives, it might as well be written in a foreign language. The jargon creates cognitive friction that impedes understanding and action.

This language barrier goes beyond simple translation issues. Technical jargon activates what psychologists call "cognitive load" – the mental effort required to process information. When cognitive load is high, decision-makers have fewer mental resources available for evaluating importance and determining appropriate actions. In practical terms, this means that jargon-heavy reports are more likely to be deferred, delegated, or overlooked entirely.

More effective approaches focus on plain language descriptions that maintain technical accuracy while ensuring accessibility. Consider this alternative to the previous example:

> We discovered a severe security flaw in our customer authentication system that could allow attackers to bypass security controls and access sensitive customer data. Without addressing this issue, we risk unauthorized access to all customer information and potential system disruption.

This conveys the essential information in terms that connect to business concerns without sacrificing accuracy. It enables executives to focus on implications and decisions rather than decoding technical terminology.

2.8.2 The missing link: business context in vulnerability reports

Technical severity does not automatically translate to business priority – yet many vulnerability reports fail to make this critical connection. Security professionals often assume that a high technical severity rating (like a CVSS score of 9.8) inherently communicates business priority, but this assumption rarely holds true.

Without explicit business context, executives must independently determine:

1. Which business functions, services, or data are at risk
2. What customer, financial, or operational impacts might occur
3. How the vulnerability relates to strategic business objectives
4. What regulatory or contractual obligations might be affected

Making these connections requires specialized knowledge that spans both technical and business domains – a rare combination. When vulnerability reports don't explicitly provide this context, the burden of translation falls on busy executives who may lack the technical background to assess implications accurately.

This missing link becomes particularly problematic when organizations face numerous vulnerabilities. According to the Mandiant M-Trends 2025 Report (Mandiant, 2025), the global median dwell time for breaches increased to 11 days from 10 days in the prior year. Longer dwell times can result from delayed business action on technical vulnerability reports, often because of ineffective communication or lack of clarity in translating technical findings into business risk.

Without clear business context, prioritization becomes arbitrary or defaults to technical criteria that may not align with business priorities. The result is often misallocated resources, with significant effort directed toward technically severe vulnerabilities that pose limited business risk while more consequential issues remain unaddressed.

Downloadable Resource: Risk-to-Value Mapping Framework

2.8.3 Case study: Capital One data breach

2.8.3.1 Context

In 2014, Capital One embarked on a bold digital transformation strategy, positioning itself as a technology company that happened to be in banking. Under the leadership of CTO George Brady, the financial giant made several strategic decisions that set it apart from more conservative peers in the heavily regulated financial industry. These included commitments to open-source technology, agile development practices, public cloud adoption (specifically Amazon Web Services), and aggressive acquisition of technical talent.

Capital One was considered one of the most cloud-savvy enterprises at the time, serving as an early and vocal advocate for AWS. By 2018, their CIO Rob Alexander proudly stated, "We are a software shop. We build software." The bank's leadership intentionally distanced themselves from traditional banking approaches, with CEO Richard Fairbank noting just one month before the breach, "A lot of how we built our company is not by studying banking, but by forgetting about banking."

2.8.3.2 Challenge

This technology-forward strategy created a fundamental challenge: the pace of technology adoption outstripped the maturity of the organization's security practices. While Capital One's annual reports acknowledged increased risk exposure from cloud technologies, the company failed to establish adequate risk management processes for its cloud strategy.

Several key disconnects emerged:

First, a significant gap developed between technical assessments and business understanding. Cybersecurity staff identified vulnerabilities but struggled to translate them into business impacts that would motivate leadership action. As The Wall Street Journal reported after the breach, "Technology employees had at times been given free rein to write in many coding languages – so many that it made it harder for the cybersecurity unit to spot problems."

Second, the cybersecurity team experienced high turnover, with approximately one-third of employees leaving in 2018 alone. This created knowledge gaps and operational challenges; for example, a security software called Endgame purchased in 2017 remained uninstalled a year later.

Third, and most significantly, there was a misunderstanding of the shared responsibility model common to SaaS and IaaS environments. The assumption that AWS was primarily responsible for security created a false sense of protection. As security expert Evan Johnson noted, "There's a lot of specialized knowledge that comes with operating a service within AWS, and to someone without specialized knowledge of AWS, [certain vulnerabilities are] not something that would show up on any critical configuration guide."

2.8.3.3 *Approach*

Capital One's approach to addressing these challenges reveals important failures in risk communication:

The bank relied heavily on technical controls without effectively communicating their limitations. They deployed a Web Application Firewall (WAF) using open-source ModSecurity software to meet regulatory requirements, but the technical teams failed to articulate the specific business risks associated with misconfigurations.

A "checkbox" compliance mentality prevailed. Capital One technically satisfied regulatory requirements but treated them as bureaucratic exercises rather than substantive security measures. The company's board had established formal cyber risk management practices but lacked direct communication channels with the CISO, limiting their understanding of actual risk exposure.

The technical governance structure contributed to poor risk communication. Identity and access management – an area that proved catastrophic in the breach – was managed through complex permission systems that one cloud security engineer described as "weird inherited side effects... not obvious at all." This complexity made it difficult to convey risks clearly to business leaders.

Perhaps most telling was the absence of effective intrusion detection monitoring. When the breach occurred in March 2019, the attacker remained undetected for over 127 days, exfiltrating approximately 30GB of sensitive customer data. The breach was only discovered after an external party reported it to Capital One in July 2019.

2.8.3.4 *Outcome*

On July 29, 2019, Capital One announced a data security incident that exposed personal information of approximately 106 million individuals in the United States and Canada. The breach compromised credit card application data including names, addresses, phone numbers, email addresses, dates of birth, self-reported incomes, credit scores, and – for smaller percentages of customers – Social Security numbers and linked bank account numbers.

The technical failure stemmed from five distinct control failures, but the root causes were failures in risk communication and business understanding:

- A misconfigured reverse proxy
- Exploitation of cloud infrastructure that trusted API calls from compromised resources
- Over-provisioned IAM roles granting excessive permissions
- Ineffective encryption implementation
- Inadequate intrusion detection monitoring

The consequences were severe:

- A $190 million class action settlement (In Re: Capital One Customer Data Security Breach Litigation, 2022)

- An $80 million civil money penalty from the Office of the Comptroller of the Currency (OCC) (Office of the Comptroller of the Currency (OCC). Capital One, N.A., and Capital One Bank (USA), N.A., 2020)
- Mandated business practice changes regarding cybersecurity
- Reputational damage and loss of customer trust
- Required improvements in board oversight, risk assessment, cloud operations, and audit functions

The OCC specifically cited Capital One's "failure to establish effective risk assessment processes prior to migrating its information technology operations to the cloud operating environment." The consent order noted the bank "failed to establish appropriate risk management for the cloud operating environment, including appropriate design and implementation of certain network security controls, adequate data loss prevention controls, and effective dispositioning of alerts."

2.8.3.5 Lessons

The Capital One breach provides four key lessons about why technical vulnerability descriptions often fail to drive business action:

1. Risk Translation Failures Technical teams identified vulnerabilities but didn't effectively translate them into business impact. The misconfigured WAF was known, but its potential to compromise millions of customer records and result in nearly $300 million in direct costs wasn't conveyed in business terms. Security teams must move beyond technical descriptions to articulate business consequences.
2. Governance Disconnects Despite having formal cybersecurity governance structures, Capital One's board lacked direct communication with security leadership. After the breach, the OCC required Capital One to "reassess the quality and content of Board reporting and improve transparency into the materiality and status of known technology and cyber risk issues." Risk communications must reach decision-makers with authority to allocate resources.
3. Shared Responsibility Confusion Capital One misunderstood its responsibilities in the cloud shared responsibility model. As a financial institution regulated by the OCC, Capital One remained accountable for data security regardless of the cloud provider's role. Technical teams failed to communicate that AWS best practices alone were insufficient protection, and specialized knowledge was needed to secure configurations.
4. Cultural Blind Spots: The company's quest to be seen as a technology innovator rather than a bank created cultural blind spots about risk. Technical leaders must present security risks in the context of the organization's primary business purpose and regulatory requirements, not just its aspirational identity.

This case demonstrates that even when technical vulnerabilities are identified, they must be effectively communicated in business terms to drive appropriate action. When these connections are made effectively, executives can make informed decisions about resource allocation and risk acceptance. The focus on technological innovation without corresponding maturity in risk communication created the conditions for a catastrophic breach that could have been prevented with better translation between technical and business perspectives. We'll revisit Capital One and their progress since this case in chapter ten.

The Capital One breach and other examples demonstrate that identifying vulnerabilities is only half the battle – the other half is communicating them in ways that drive action. The gap between technical discovery and business response isn't insurmountable; it simply requires a structured approach to translation. The following framework provides practical principles and tools for bridging this gap, transforming technical findings into business intelligence that executives can understand, evaluate, and act upon. These aren't simplifications or dumbed-down versions of technical reports – they're translations that maintain technical integrity while adding the business context that enables decision-making.

2.9 BUILDING A TRANSLATION FRAMEWORK: PRINCIPLES OF EFFECTIVE RISK COMMUNICATION

Effective security communication requires a structured approach to translating technical findings into business-relevant information. The following framework provides practical principles and techniques for bridging the gap between technical vulnerability reports and executive decision-making.

2.9.1 The business lens: reframing technical issues

Successfully communicating security risks begins with reframing technical vulnerabilities in terms of business objectives and outcomes. This isn't about simplifying technical details; it's about providing the business context that makes those details meaningful to decision-makers.

An effective business framing connects security vulnerabilities to one or more of the following:

- Revenue Impact: How might the vulnerability affect the organization's ability to generate revenue? Could it disrupt sales channels, damage customer relationships, or create competitive disadvantages?
- Cost Implications: What potential costs are associated with the vulnerability? These might include remediation costs, potential regulatory fines, litigation expenses, or increased insurance premiums.

- Strategic Objectives: How does the vulnerability relate to key strategic initiatives or organizational goals? Could it impede digital transformation efforts, geographic expansion, or new product launches?
- Compliance Requirements: What regulatory or contractual obligations might be affected? Are there specific compliance deadlines or mandatory reporting requirements to consider?
- Reputation and Trust: How might exploitation of the vulnerability affect stakeholder trust and brand reputation? How would it look to the press if this vulnerability led to a public incident?

Quantifying technical risks in business terms significantly enhances their relevance to executive decision-makers. Instead of reporting that a system has "critical vulnerabilities requiring remediation," translate this into business metrics:

> The identified vulnerabilities in our payment processing system create a potential exposure of $3.2M based on average daily transaction volume and estimated downtime for recovery (4-6 days). Additionally, we estimate potential regulatory penalties of $500K-$1.5M based on recent enforcement actions for similar incidents.

This translation maintains technical accuracy while expressing impact in terms that directly connect to business metrics that executives regularly use for other decisions as seen in Figure 2.3.

Downloadable Resource: Business Impact Translation Matrix

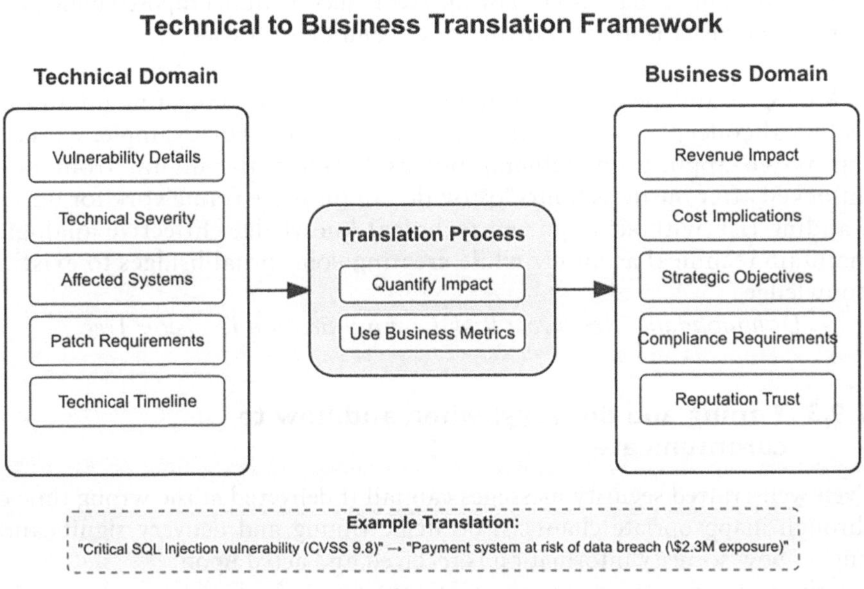

Figure 2.3 Technical to business translation framework.

2.9.2 Communication strategies that drive decision-making

Beyond reframing content, specific communication strategies can significantly enhance the effectiveness of security messages. These strategies leverage psychological principles of information processing to increase comprehension, retention, and action.

Narrative and context are powerful tools for making abstract risks concrete and memorable. Research in cognitive psychology suggests that information presented as a narrative is significantly more likely to be remembered and acted upon than the same information presented as abstract facts. Effective security communications often include brief scenarios that illustrate:

- How the vulnerability might be exploited
- What business processes would be affected
- What the direct and indirect consequences might be
- How suggested mitigations would reduce these risks

Visual communication approaches can dramatically simplify complex concepts and relationships. Decision-makers process visual information more quickly and remember it more accurately than text alone. Effective visual elements for security communications include:

- Heat maps that show risk concentration across business functions
- Simple flowcharts illustrating attack paths and business impacts
- Before/after comparisons showing risk reduction from proposed mitigations
- Trend visualizations showing risk evolution over time

Analogies and metaphors build understanding by connecting unfamiliar technical concepts to familiar business situations. For example, explaining a web application vulnerability as "leaving the digital front door unlocked after business hours" provides an intuitive framework for understanding risk without requiring technical knowledge. Effective analogies maintain technical accuracy while creating conceptual bridges to existing knowledge.

🔗 *Downloadable Resource: Risk Communication Decision Tree*

2.9.3 Timing and delivery: when and how to communicate

Even well-crafted security messages can fail if delivered at the wrong time or through inappropriate channels. Strategic timing and delivery significantly impact how security information is received and acted upon.

Critical decision moments represent opportunities when executives are particularly receptive to security information. These include:

- Budget planning cycles when resource allocations are being determined
- Strategy sessions where business initiatives are being evaluated
- Response to industry breach events that create heightened awareness
- Regulatory changes that affect compliance requirements
- Technology transformation initiatives that involve system changes

Aligning security communications with these moments increases the likelihood that vulnerability information will be incorporated into broader business decisions rather than treated as a separate "IT issue."

Right-sizing information for different organizational levels ensures each audience receives the information most relevant to their role and decisions. A tiered approach might include:

- Board level: Focus on risk trends, governance effectiveness, and strategic implications
- C-suite: Emphasize business impact, resource requirements, and strategic alignment
- Business unit leaders: Connect vulnerabilities to specific business functions and services
- Technology leaders: Provide technical details and specific implementation guidance

Each tier receives information appropriate to their decision-making authority and responsibility, with consistent messaging across levels.

Building communication pathways that maintain technical integrity while enhancing business relevance often requires structured collaboration between security and business teams. Formal processes might include:

- Joint review of significant findings by security and business stakeholders
- Defined templates that require both technical and business impact information
- Regular cross-functional risk reviews to align security and business priorities
- "Translators" who specialize in bridging technical and business perspectives

These structured approaches ensure that technical accuracy is maintained throughout the translation process while enhancing relevance for business decision-makers.

2.9.4 Practical communication templates and approaches

Implementing effective security communication requires practical tools and frameworks that security teams can adapt to their specific organizational context, such as the example seen in Figure 2.4.

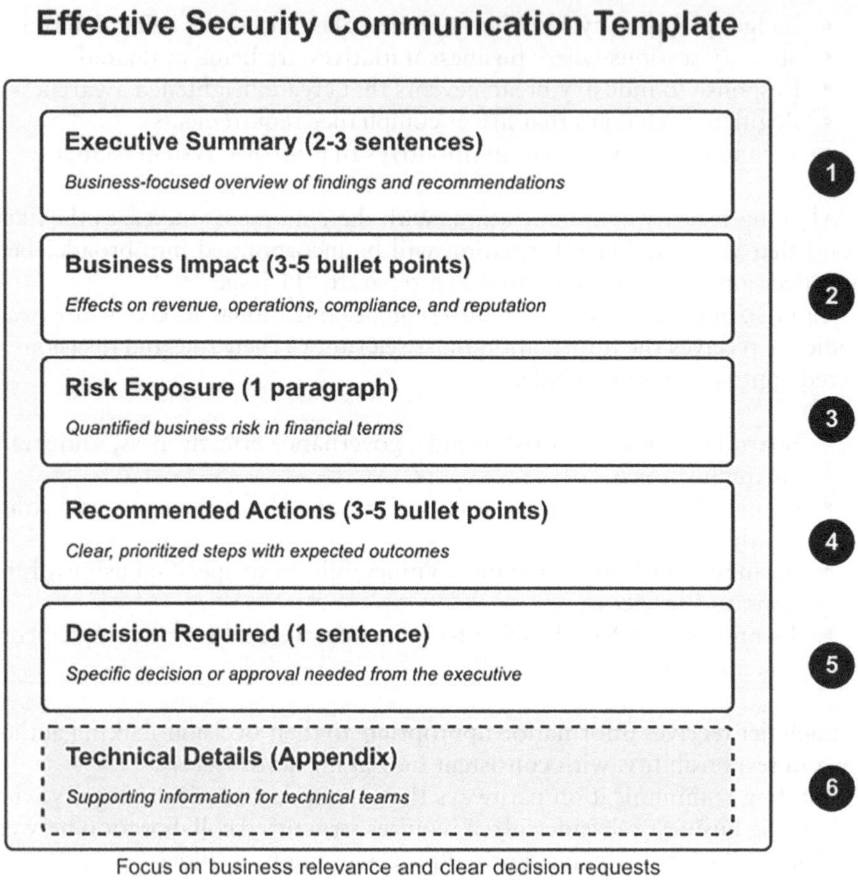

Figure 2.4 Effective security communication template.

A basic vulnerability translation template might include the following elements:

- Executive Summary (2–3 sentences): Business-focused overview of the most important findings and recommendations
- Business Impact (3–5 bullet points): Potential effects on revenue, operations, compliance, and reputation
- Risk Exposure (1 paragraph): Quantified business risk in financial terms whenever possible
- Recommended Actions (3–5 bullet points): Clear, prioritized steps with expected outcomes
- Decision Required (1 sentence): Specific decision or approval needed from the executive
- Technical Details (Appendix): Supporting technical information for technical teams

This structure ensures that executives receive the most valuable information first, with supporting details available as needed.

Effective executive summaries follow a consistent pattern:

1. Start with the business context or affected function
2. Clearly state the risk or opportunity
3. Provide a concise recommendation
4. Indicate required decision or next steps

For example: "Our customer data platform, which manages information for 2.3M active customers, contains vulnerabilities that could allow unauthorized access to personal and payment information. We recommend implementing enhanced access controls and encryption at an estimated cost of $120K to prevent potential regulatory penalties and reputational damage. Your approval is needed for this unbudgeted expenditure."

Methods for presenting options and recommendations should acknowledge business constraints while providing clear guidance. An effective approach is to present a limited set of options (typically 2–3) with explicit trade-offs:

Option 1: Full Remediation

- Benefits: Eliminates vulnerability, ensures compliance, protects all affected data
- Drawbacks: Requires $120K investment, 2-week implementation timeline
- Residual risk: Minimal (reduces risk exposure by approximately 95%)

Option 2: Partial Remediation

- Benefits: Addresses highest-risk components, lower initial cost ($45K)
- Drawbacks: Leaves some vulnerabilities unaddressed, requires follow-up project
- Residual risk: Moderate (reduces risk exposure by approximately 60%)

Option 3: Compensating Controls

- Benefits: Lowest immediate cost ($25K), minimal operational disruption
- Drawbacks: Doesn't address root causes, requires ongoing monitoring
- Residual risk: Substantial (reduces risk exposure by approximately 40%)

Recommendation: Option 1 provides the best risk reduction and long-term value.

This approach acknowledges business realities while providing clear security guidance, empowering executives to make informed decisions that balance security requirements with business constraints.

Chapter 6 expands on this translation approach with specific metrics and measurement techniques that demonstrate security's business contributions in quantifiable terms.

2.9.4.1 *Exercise: vulnerability translation practice*

Take a recent technical vulnerability report from your organization and translate it using the following steps:

1. Identify the affected business functions, services, or data
2. Determine potential business impacts in terms of:
3. Financial consequences (direct and indirect)
4. Operational disruption
5. Compliance implications
6. Reputational effects
7. Quantify the business risk exposure to the extent possible
8. Develop 2–3 response options with explicit trade-offs
9. Create an executive summary following the template above
10. Review your translation with both technical and business colleagues for accuracy and relevance

This exercise builds the translation skills needed to effectively communicate technical vulnerabilities in business terms, increasing the likelihood of appropriate executive action.

2.10 CONCLUSION

Throughout this chapter, we've explored the fundamental disconnect between technical vulnerability reports and executive action. We've seen that this gap isn't primarily about technical competence or executive indifference – it's about communication. Technical reports often fail to resonate with executives because they don't account for the competing priorities that constrain executive attention, don't translate technical findings into business terms, and don't provide the confidence executives need to make security decisions.

Understanding the psychology of risk perception provides valuable insight into this challenge. The human brain processes different types of risk information through distinct mechanisms, with cognitive biases systematically influencing how we perceive and respond to potential threats. Executives vary in their decision-making styles and preferences, requiring tailored approaches to security communication.

Common shortcomings in technical reports include excessive jargon that creates cognitive barriers, missing business context that forces executives to make connections they're ill-equipped to make, and failure to connect technical findings to business outcomes that drive decisions. These aren't simply stylistic issues; they fundamentally undermine the effectiveness of security communications.

The translation framework presented in this chapter provides practical principles for bridging this gap. By reframing technical issues through a business lens, employing communication strategies that enhance understanding, timing communications strategically, and using structured templates that prioritize business relevance, security professionals can significantly increase the likelihood that vulnerability reports will drive appropriate executive action.

The key message is that effective security communication isn't about simplifying technical details; it's about providing the business context that makes those details meaningful to decision-makers. This requires recognizing that communication failures stem from relevance gaps, not intelligence gaps. Executives don't need to become technical experts, and security professionals don't need to become business experts. What's needed is a structured approach to translating between these domains.

In the next chapter, we'll explore Business Impact Analysis as a formal mechanism for systematically connecting technical vulnerabilities to business consequences. This structured approach builds on the communication principles discussed here, providing a repeatable process for ensuring that security priorities align with business objectives.

Security professionals seeking to drive meaningful action must adopt alternative communication approaches that bridge the gap between technical findings and business decisions. By understanding the executive perspective, adapting to how humans process risk information, and consistently translating technical details into business terms, you can transform vulnerability reports from ignored documents into drivers of effective security decisions.

2.11 ACTION ITEMS FOR READERS

1. Audit your organization's last five vulnerability reports to identify instances of technical jargon, missing business context, and failure to connect technical findings to business outcomes that executives care about.
2. Interview three executives in your organization to understand their decision-making styles, competing priorities, and preferred information formats when evaluating security investments and risk mitigation options.
3. Create a standardized vulnerability translation template that includes executive summary, business impact assessment, quantified risk exposure, and decision options with explicit trade-offs for your organization's reporting process.

4. Collaborate with business stakeholders to map your organization's most important systems and data to specific business functions, revenue streams, and compliance requirements to improve future business impact assessments.
5. Implement the new communication framework on your next significant vulnerability or security initiative by presenting both technical details and business-focused executive summary to measure the difference in stakeholder engagement and decision speed.

Downloadable Resource: Business-Focused Vulnerability Translator

Chapter 3

Business Impact Analysis

The essential translation tool

Chapter in One Sentence: Business Impact Analysis serves as the essential translation methodology connecting technical security vulnerabilities to business consequences, enabling informed decision-making and proper resource allocation to protect what matters most to the organization.

3.1 EXECUTIVE SUMMARY

This chapter introduces Business Impact Analysis (BIA) as the essential methodology for bridging the communication gap between security professionals and business executives. This disconnect represents more than a communication problem; it's a fundamental business risk, as illustrated by the 2013 Target breach where technical warnings weren't translated into business terms, resulting in costs exceeding $300 million. BIA provides a structured framework for connecting technical vulnerabilities to potential business consequences, enabling informed decision-making at all organizational levels.

The chapter outlines a comprehensive BIA framework that begins with mapping technical infrastructure to business functions, revealing dependencies between business operations and supporting technical components. This mapping process uncovers how vulnerabilities in technical systems can impact business objectives, operations, and financial performance. Through systematic analysis, organizations can quantify potential impacts across multiple categories: financial losses, operational disruption, reputational damage, and regulatory consequences.

Moving beyond technical severity scores like CVSS, BIA enables prioritization based on business relevance. This approach ensures resources address vulnerabilities that pose the greatest business risk rather than those with the highest technical severity scores alone. The chapter provides methodologies for risk exposure calculation, weighted scoring approaches, and decision frameworks to systematize prioritization.

Documentation proves equally important through risk registers that present security risks in language resonating with non-technical stakeholders.

DOI: 10.1201/9781003744146-3

Effective visualization and scenario-based stories can help clarify potential impacts, avoiding technical jargon while maintaining accuracy.

The ultimate purpose of BIA is to drive action – ensuring security investments align with business priorities and address the organization's most significant risks. By quantifying potential impacts in financial terms and demonstrating how security risks affect business objectives, security professionals position themselves as strategic partners rather than technical specialists.

When organizations fail to translate technical risks effectively, they remain vulnerable to considerable damage despite investments in security controls. BIA allows security professionals to connect technical vulnerabilities to the business consequences that executives and board members care about most.

3.2 KEY TAKEAWAYS

- BIA bridges the technical-business gap by translating security vulnerabilities into business consequences and financial terms
- Effective BIA requires mapping technical infrastructure to business functions and understanding their interdependencies
- Prioritization should balance technical severity with business relevance, focusing resources on vulnerabilities with the greatest potential business impact
- Quantifying impacts across financial, operational, reputational, and regulatory dimensions provides comprehensive risk understanding
- Communication through risk registers and visualization techniques eliminates technical jargon while maintaining accuracy

3.3 APPLICATION QUESTIONS

1. How well does your organization currently map its technical infrastructure to business functions, and what hidden dependencies might you discover through a more thorough mapping process?
2. What metrics and methods could you implement to better quantify the potential business impacts of security vulnerabilities in financial terms?
3. How might your organization's prioritization of security risks change if you balanced technical severity scores with business impact assessments?

3.4 TOOLS REFERENCED IN THIS CHAPTER

All tools available at kaynemcgladrey.com/myth/

- Vulnerability-to-Business Impact Mapping Framework
- Business Impact Quantification Calculator
- Risk Register Template
- Cross-Functional Risk Translation Workshop
- Business Impact Analysis Maturity Assessment Checklist

3.5 INTRODUCTION

In many organizations, a significant communication gap exists between technical security teams and business executives. Security professionals often speak in terms of vulnerabilities, threats, and exploits, while business leaders think in terms of revenue, costs, and market share. Building on the communication challenges outlined in Chapter 2, this chapter provides a structured methodology for bridging the gap between technical vulnerabilities and business consequences.

Consider what happened at Target in 2013. The retailer's technical systems detected suspicious activity indicative of a breach, but these warnings weren't translated into business impact terms that would have triggered immediate executive action. The resulting data breach affected 41 million customer payment card accounts and led to costs exceeding $300 million.

BIA serves as a translation methodology to bridge this gap. Traditionally used in disaster recovery planning, BIA can be a powerful tool for communicating security risks in business terms. It provides a structured framework for connecting technical vulnerabilities to potential business consequences, enabling informed decision-making at all levels of the organization.

The stakes of this translation process are substantial. Organizations that fail to translate technical vulnerabilities into business impacts consistently struggle to make appropriate resource allocation decisions. They either underinvest in security controls for significant risks or overspend on addressing technical issues with minimal business relevance. Neither scenario serves the organization's interests effectively.

This disconnect is often most impactful in the boardroom, where security leaders may present technical metrics that leave business executives confused about the actual business implications. Meanwhile, business leaders might make decisions that unknowingly increase technical risk because they lack a clear understanding of how technical vulnerabilities translate to business impacts.

This chapter provides a comprehensive framework for implementing BIA as your translation tool. We'll examine:

- The framework for BIA, including its definition, application, and integration with existing risk processes
- Systematic methods for connecting technical vulnerabilities to business processes
- Techniques for quantifying potential business impacts in financial and operational terms
- Approaches for prioritizing risks based on their business relevance rather than technical severity alone
- Effective documentation and communication strategies that resonate with business stakeholders

By mastering the BIA methodology, security professionals can fulfill their organizational duty to translate complex technical risks into simple business terms. Simultaneously, business executives gain the insights needed to make informed risk management decisions. The result is a more resilient organization where security investments align with business priorities and both technical and business stakeholders share a mutual understanding of risk.

3.6 THE BUSINESS IMPACT ANALYSIS FRAMEWORK

Organizations consistently struggle to communicate security risks in terms that resonate with business executives. BIA provides a structured methodology that appears to bridge this communication gap by connecting technical vulnerabilities to potential business consequences as shown in Figure 3.1. This foundational framework enables security professionals to translate complex technical issues into the financial and operational terms that drive executive decision-making.

3.6.1 Defining Business Impact Analysis

BIA in the security context represents a structured methodology for identifying, assessing, and communicating how security vulnerabilities and threats may affect an organization's business objectives, operations, and financial

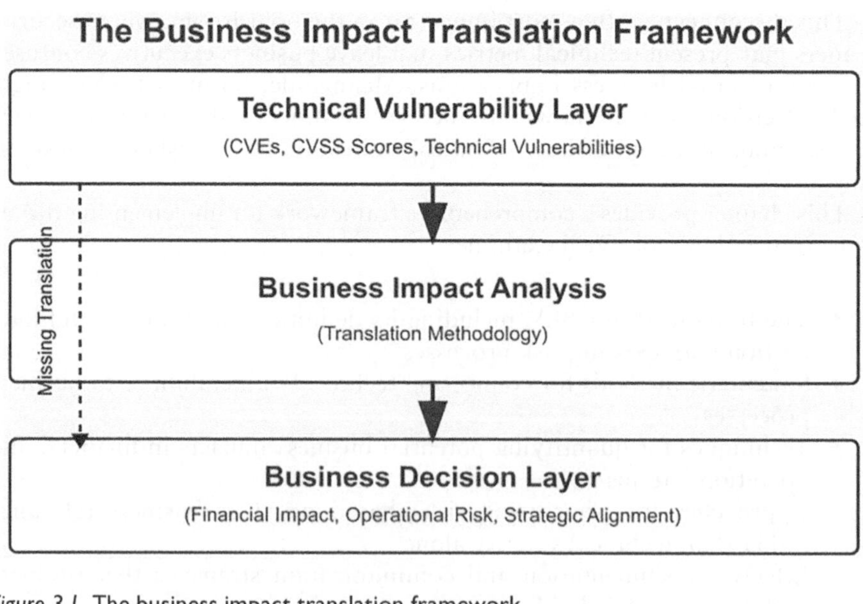

Figure 3.1 The business impact translation framework.

performance. Unlike purely technical risk assessments, BIA focuses on the business consequences of security incidents, providing crucial context for decision-makers.

Historically, BIA developed as a component of IT disaster recovery planning, where it helped organizations identify their most business-critical systems and determine appropriate recovery timeframes. Over time, its application expanded beyond recovery planning to become an integral part of security risk assessment. This evolution reflects the growing recognition that security risks must be evaluated based on their potential business impact rather than technical severity alone.

Several key principles underpin effective BIA:

- Business-centricity: BIA starts with the business function rather than the technology. It asks, "What business activities are most essential to achieving our objectives?" and works backward to identify supporting technical assets.
- Interdependency recognition: BIA acknowledges that business functions rarely operate in isolation. It maps the complex web of dependencies between business processes, supporting applications, and infrastructure components.
- Stakeholder inclusion: Effective BIA requires input from diverse stakeholders across the organization, including business unit leaders, IT personnel, security professionals, and executives. Each brings unique perspectives on what constitutes a significant business impact.
- Quantification emphasis: Wherever possible, BIA seeks to quantify potential impacts in financial terms to enable more objective prioritization and decision-making.

To understand the practical application of BIA, consider this simple exercise: Identify three essential business functions in your organization, then list the IT systems that support each function. For a financial services company, these might include:

1. Customer account management
    - Core banking system
    - Customer Relationship Management (CRM) platform
    - Identity and access management system
2. Trade execution
    - Trading platform
    - Market data feeds
    - Risk management system
3. Regulatory compliance reporting
    - Transaction monitoring system
    - Reporting database
    - Document management system

This exercise begins to uncover the critical dependencies between business functions and IT systems, which is a foundational element of effective BIA.

3.6.2 When and how to conduct a BIA

BIA should not be viewed as a one-time activity but as an ongoing process triggered by various organizational changes and external factors. Key triggers for conducting or updating a BIA include:

- Discovery of significant new vulnerabilities that may affect critical systems
- Implementation of new systems or major changes to existing ones
- Organizational changes such as mergers, acquisitions, or restructuring
- Shifts in the regulatory landscape affecting your industry
- Changes in business strategy or the introduction of new products and services
- Emerging threat intelligence indicating new attack vectors relevant to your organization

A comprehensive BIA requires participation from various stakeholders, typically organized into a cross-functional team. This team might include:

- Business process owners who understand operational requirements
- IT personnel familiar with technical dependencies and configurations
- Security professionals who can assess vulnerabilities and controls
- Risk management specialists to facilitate risk assessment
- Executive sponsors to ensure appropriate resources and attention

The timeframe for conducting a BIA varies based on organizational complexity, but generally requires several weeks to complete properly. A mid-sized organization might allocate 4-6 weeks for the initial assessment, with subsequent updates requiring 1–2 weeks depending on the scope of changes.

Organizations often face several challenges when conducting BIA:

- Knowledge gaps: Many organizations lack comprehensive documentation of business processes and their supporting technical components.
- Stakeholder availability: Business leaders may resist taking part due to competing priorities.
- Quantification difficulties: Estimating potential financial impacts often requires assumptions that stakeholders may hesitate to commit to.
- Scope management: Without clear boundaries, BIA efforts can expand indefinitely.

These challenges can be addressed through careful planning, executive sponsorship, clear scope definition, and incremental improvement of the BIA process over time.

This business alignment extends the reframing techniques we introduced in Chapter 2, where we examined how to translate technical security issues into business language.

3.6.3 BIA as a communication tool

The communication gap between security and business teams, explored in Chapter 1, manifests most clearly in vulnerability discussions. BIA serves as the essential translation methodology that bridges this divide, establishing a common language focused on business outcomes rather than technical details.

The BIA communication framework:

1. Audience-Specific Translation: BIA provides the structure to translate technical vulnerabilities into terms meaningful to various stakeholders:
   - Executive leadership: Strategic implications and financial exposure
   - Business unit leaders: Operational impacts and resource requirements
   - Technical teams: Implementation requirements and dependencies
   - Compliance and legal: Regulatory implications and documentation needs
2. Visualization Tools: BIA enables effective visualization of risk information:
   - Heat maps showing risks by likelihood and business impact
   - Trend charts tracking risk exposure over time
   - Dependency diagrams linking vulnerabilities to business processes
3. Narrative Development: BIA creates the foundation for compelling risk stories that illustrate:
   - How vulnerabilities might be exploited
   - Which business processes would be affected
   - What the operational, financial, and reputational impacts would be
   - Why specific security investments would mitigate these risks

Rather than simply identifying communication barriers, BIA provides a practical solution. It transforms abstract technical vulnerabilities into concrete business scenarios that stakeholders can evaluate and act upon. When a SQL injection vulnerability is presented as "a potential $2.3 million exposure from customer data compromise, including $400,000 in notification costs and $1.9 million in projected customer churn," business executives suddenly have the context they need to make informed decisions.

Implementing BIA as a communication framework delivers measurable improvements:

- Technical teams gain business context for security alerts, improving response prioritization

- Business executives receive risk information in terms that they can evaluate and act upon
- Shared responsibility for security risks emerges across functions
- Clear escalation paths develop based on business impact thresholds rather than technical severity alone

This communication framework extends the reframing techniques introduced in Chapter 2 and provides the foundation for the documentation and reporting approaches we'll explore in Section 5.1.

3.6.4 Case study: Target data breach – when technical alerts don't translate to business risk

3.6.4.1 *Context*

Target, the second-largest retailer in the United States with nearly 1,800 store locations, suffered one of the largest data breaches in retail history during the 2013 holiday shopping season between November 15 and December 15, 2013. At the time, Target had implemented what appeared to be reasonable security measures, including firewalls, malware detection software, and a recently deployed advanced security monitoring system from FireEye which was installed and functional prior to the date of the Target data breach. The company had even obtained certification in September 2013 that it was compliant with all "payment industry requirements," including the Payment Card Industry Data Security Standards (PCI DSS) for protecting credit card data.

Despite these investments in security technology, Target's security team failed to recognize the business significance of technical security alerts, leading to one of the most consequential data breaches in history.

3.6.4.2 *Challenge*

Target's primary challenge wasn't a lack of security technology – it was a failure to connect technical alerts to potential business impacts. The company's security systems detected the attack multiple times, but the warnings were not properly understood or prioritized from a business risk perspective.

The breach began when attackers stole credentials from Fazio Mechanical Services, a Pennsylvania HVAC contractor that worked for Target. The attackers used these stolen vendor credentials to access Target's network and install malware on point-of-sale (POS) terminals that captured customer payment card data.

Target's newly implemented FireEye security system detected suspicious activity and generated alerts, but these warnings weren't translated into an understanding of potential business consequences. On November 30, 2013, FireEye, Target's malware detection system, spotted the hackers uploading malware and alerted Target's security team, but they took no action. Even more telling, Target's antivirus system, Symantec Endpoint Protection ("SEP"), also identified the same suspicious behavior. Target again took no action.

A Bloomberg Businessweek investigation later revealed that FireEye's malware detection program "worked beautifully. But Target stood by as 40 million credit card numbers – and 70 million addresses, phone numbers, and other pieces of personal information – gushed out of its mainframes." Most significantly, "the alerts went off early enough that the hackers hadn't begun transmitting the stolen card data out of Target's network."

The security technology did its job by identifying the technical risk, but the organization lacked a process to translate those alerts into business impact terms that would drive appropriate prioritization and response.

3.6.4.3 Approach

In this case, Target's approach represents what not to do – a failure to implement BIA as part of their security operations. Without this crucial translation mechanism, technical alerts remained just that – technical notifications without business context.

When FireEye detected the malware on November 30, 2013, the system had an option to automatically delete the malware as it was detected, but Target's security team had turned that function off. On December 2, Target received the exact same alert from FireEye that it had received on November 30, and again failed to respond.

The U.S. Senate Committee on Commerce, Science and Transportation later conducted an investigation and found that Target "appears to have failed to respond to multiple automated warnings from the company's anti-intrusion software that the attackers were installing malware on Target's system" and "appears to have failed to respond to multiple warnings from the company's anti-intrusion software regarding the escape routes the attackers planned to use to exfiltrate data from Target's network."

Instead of recognizing these alerts as indicators of significant business risk requiring immediate action, Target's security team did not act until December 12, 2013, when the U.S. Justice Department contacted Target about the breach. By that time, the attackers had already exfiltrated millions of customers' data.

A proper BIA would have helped Target's security team:

- Understand which systems hold critical business data
- Establish the potential financial and reputational costs of a breach
- Create escalation procedures for alerts based on business impact rather than just technical severity
- Prioritize response actions based on potential business consequences

3.6.4.4 Outcome

The results of Target's failure to connect technical alerts to business impact were devastating:

Financial Impact:

- $10 million settlement with affected consumers (In re: Target Corporation Customer Data Security Breach Litigation, 2015)
- $39 million settlement with affected banks and credit unions (In re: Target Corporation Customer Data Security Breach Litigation, 2014)
- $18.5 million to settle a multi-state lawsuit
- Approximately $1 billion in estimated total costs from the attack
- Only a small fraction of the costs were covered by cyber insurance

Operational and Leadership Impact:

- Target's share price fell 2.2% immediately after the announcement
- Both CEO Gregg Steinhafel and Chief Information Officer Beth Jacob resigned in the aftermath
- Damaged customer confidence and brand reputation

Customer Impact:

- 40 million credit and debit card numbers stolen
- 70 million records of personal information compromised

The breach dramatically raised awareness of the cybersecurity landscape, with one analyst noting that, "For many Americans, the scope and prominence of the Target attack brought cyber risk out of the realm of abstraction and made it a concrete reality."

3.6.4.5 Lessons

The Target breach offers several crucial lessons about BIA as a translation tool:

1. Technical Alerts Are Not Business Decisions: Target had the technical capability to detect the breach but lacked the process to translate alerts into business risk terms. A BIA framework would have helped security professionals communicate the potential consequences in language that drives action.
2. Prioritization Requires Business Context: Without understanding how security incidents affect business operations, organizations struggle to prioritize responses appropriately. Target's security team received multiple alerts but didn't recognize their significance from a business perspective.
3. Integration of Security Into Business Processes: The breach demonstrates the importance of integrating security operations with business operations. As cybersecurity expert Stephen Cobb noted after the breach, "Just going through the motions, like buying security products

and getting your security tested, was not going to cut it: you need to architect for security, skill up for security, and train for security... If the C-suite is not making security a priority for all departments and all employees, you are at higher risk than your competitors that do prioritize security" (Myers, 2018).

4. Third-Party Risk Requires Business Impact Assessment: The initial compromise came through an HVAC vendor, demonstrating how the Target breach became "a primary driver of two key expectations with cyber risk management. First was that cybersecurity programs must include understanding and minimizing vulnerabilities posed by network and data access by vendors and the greater supply chain, not just the protection of the corporate network and data itself" (Sean Steinberg, 2021).
5. Security Investments Need Business Justification: Target had invested in advanced security technology but failed to implement the processes and people components needed to utilize it effectively. BIA helps justify the full range of investments needed for effective security.

The Target breach serves as a powerful example of why technical security controls alone are insufficient. Without BIA as a translation mechanism, organizations risk missing critical security alerts even when their technical systems detect them. By implementing a structured BIA process, security professionals can ensure that technical security information is translated into business risk terms that drive appropriate action at all levels of the organization.

The Target breach highlights operational governance failures, while in Chapter 7, we'll examine the Marriott case which focuses on board-level governance responsibilities for security oversight.

3.6.5 Integrating BIA with existing risk processes

To maximize its value, BIA must be strategically integrated with broader organizational processes rather than operating as an isolated security activity. This integration framework ensures BIA findings inform enterprise-wide risk governance and decision-making.

Strategic Integration Framework Components:

1. Governance Alignment
   - BIA outputs should directly feed executive risk committees
   - Security risk assessments should follow the same methodology as enterprise risks
   - Common risk terminology should be established across functions
   - Risk ownership and acceptance thresholds should be harmonized
2. Process Synchronization
   - BIA should operate on the same assessment cycle as ERM
   - Security planning should align with business planning calendars

- Incident response scenarios should connect to business continuity plans
- Risk register updates should trigger enterprise risk updates

3. Shared Tooling and Information Flows
   - BIA should leverage the organization's Enterprise Risk Management software
   - Vulnerability scans should automatically map to business process inventories
   - Business impact data should flow into security operations dashboards
   - Security metrics should appear on business performance scorecards

The PwC research discussed in Chapter 1 further confirms that most organizations are not effectively integrating security with business priorities.

The integration benefits outlined in Chapter 1 become tangible when organizations implement BIA within broader risk frameworks.

In Chapter 4, we'll explore how the outputs of BIA become core inputs to integrated security risk registers, creating a unified view of security risks alongside other enterprise risks. Later chapters will build upon this integration framework with specific metrics (Chapter 6) and governance structures (Chapter 7) that reinforce the business-security alignment.

With the BIA framework established, the next step involves systematically identifying and mapping the relationships between technical infrastructure and business functions. This mapping process forms the foundation for understanding how technical vulnerabilities might affect business operations.

3.7 SYSTEMATICALLY CONNECTING TECHNICAL VULNERABILITIES TO BUSINESS PROCESSES

Effective BIA requires a clear understanding of how technical systems support business operations. This systematic approach reveals the often-hidden dependencies between infrastructure components and revenue-generating activities. By mapping these relationships, organizations can identify which technical vulnerabilities pose the greatest threat to their business objectives.

3.7.1 Mapping the technical infrastructure to business functions

Creating a clear map of relationships between technical infrastructure and business functions forms the foundation for effective BIA. This mapping process illustrated in Figure 3.2, shows how technical vulnerabilities might translate into business impacts by illustrating the dependencies between business operations and their supporting technical components.

Begin by identifying your organization's key business functions, those activities that directly support core business objectives and revenue generation. For a healthcare organization, these might include patient care delivery, medical records management, billing operations, and regulatory compliance activities.

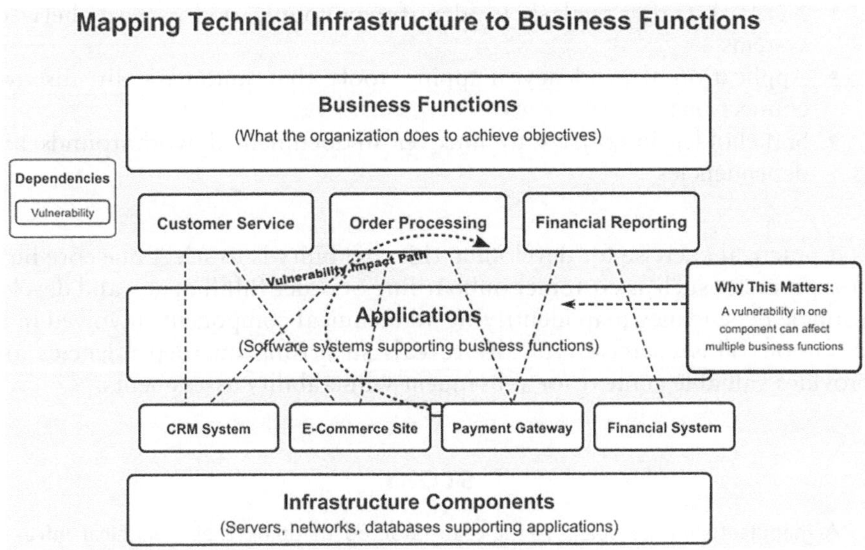

Figure 3.2 Mapping technical infrastructure to business functions.

Next, document the applications and systems that support each business function. For patient care delivery, these might include:

- Electronic health record (EHR) system
- Clinical decision support systems
- Laboratory information systems
- Pharmacy management systems
- Medical device networks

Then extend this mapping to include the underlying infrastructure components that support these applications, such as:

- Database servers
- Application servers
- Network infrastructure
- Authentication systems
- Storage systems

This mapping process often reveals previously undocumented dependencies that might otherwise be overlooked in security planning. For example, many organizations discover that supposedly non-critical systems support essential business functions through hidden integrations or data flows.

Techniques for discovering these hidden dependencies include:

- Process tracing exercises that follow information flows from initiation to completion

- Network traffic analysis to identify communication patterns between systems
- Application dependency mapping tools that automatically discover connections
- Stakeholder interviews to uncover undocumented workarounds and dependencies

A practical exercise for developing this capability is to select one core business process – such as customer onboarding or order fulfillment – and develop a simple dependency map identifying all technical components involved in its execution. This exercise typically reveals surprising interdependencies and provides valuable context for subsequent vulnerability assessments.

STORY

A manufacturing company's risk team started mapping their technical infrastructure to business functions following a minor security incident. During a workshop with the production floor manager, the security lead asked about systems supporting the assembly line operations.

"Just our main production management system," the manager replied confidently. "It controls everything from components to scheduling."

But as the security team traced network connections and data flows, they discovered something unexpected. A small, forgotten server tucked in a corner of the IT room was processing quality control metrics and feeding them directly into the production system. This server, running outdated software and missing months of security patches, had been installed years earlier as a "temporary solution."

Further investigation revealed that without this overlooked server, the entire quality verification process would fail, potentially allowing defective products to ship to customers. The team was stunned to realize that this neglected system – absent from every official infrastructure diagram and security scan – represented a single point of failure for product safety compliance and the company's quality certification.

The manufacturing firm's leadership had allocated substantial resources to protecting their "mission-critical" production management system while leaving this essential dependency completely exposed. In their BIA, they calculated that a failure of this quality control server could trigger regulatory violations, customer returns, and warranty claims potentially exceeding $5 million.

This discovery transformed the company's approach to infrastructure mapping. They now require physical walkthroughs and live process tracing exercises that follow actual business workflows rather than relying solely on official documentation and stakeholder interviews.

3.7.2 Vulnerability context analysis

As we discussed in chapter two, traditional vulnerability management often focuses narrowly on identifying and patching technical vulnerabilities without sufficient consideration of their business context. BIA enhances this approach by evaluating vulnerabilities based on:

- Which business functions would be affected if the vulnerability were exploited
- How significant those functions are to overall business operations
- What the potential financial and operational impacts would be

Moving beyond vulnerability scanners requires developing a contextual vulnerability assessment process. This process begins with standard vulnerability identification but extends to analyze each vulnerability in its specific business context.

For example, a critical vulnerability in a development server might pose minimal business risk if that server contains no production data and has no connection to production systems. Conversely, even a medium-severity vulnerability could represent significant business risk if it exists in a system supporting core revenue-generating activities.

Methods for determining which vulnerabilities affect which business functions include:

- Overlay vulnerability scan results onto your infrastructure-to-business function dependency map
- Conduct threat modeling sessions that trace potential attack paths through business-critical systems
- Engage business process owners to assess potential operational impacts
- Review incident history to identify patterns of vulnerability exploitation and resulting business impacts

Developing this contextual understanding requires close collaboration between security, IT, and business teams. Security teams bring technical expertise regarding vulnerabilities and potential exploitation scenarios. IT teams contribute knowledge of system configurations and dependencies. Business teams provide insights into operational requirements and potential business impacts.

3.7.3 Threat modeling with a business impact lens

Traditional threat modeling focuses primarily on identifying potential vulnerabilities and attack vectors from a technical perspective. Adapting this approach to include business impacts as seen in Figure 3.3, adds context for prioritization and decision-making.

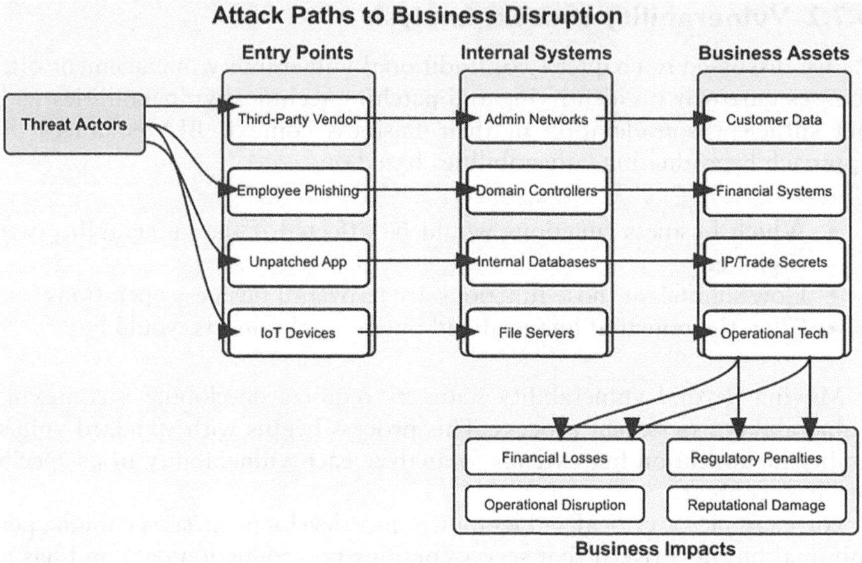

Figure 3.3 Threat modeling with a business lens.

Business-focused threat modeling begins with identifying critical business assets – the crown jewels that, if compromised, would most significantly impact the organization. These might include:

- Customer data
- Intellectual property
- Financial systems
- Operational technology
- Business-critical applications

For each asset, the threat modeling process explores:

- Who might target this asset (threat actors)
- How they might attempt to compromise it (attack vectors)
- What vulnerabilities might they exploit
- What business impacts would result from successful compromise

Understanding attack paths to business disruption requires tracing the sequence of steps an attacker might take to reach high-value business assets. This analysis often reveals that seemingly low-priority systems can serve as entry points for attacks that ultimately target business-critical assets.

The Target breach again shows how seemingly unrelated systems can serve as entry points for attacks targeting business-important assets. This illustrates why vulnerability context analysis must consider not just the affected system itself, but its potential role in broader attack scenarios.

Incorporating business stakeholders in threat modeling exercises ensures technical scenarios are considered in a proper business context. Business leaders can provide insights into which scenarios would most significantly disrupt operations, while security professionals can assess the technical feasibility of various attack paths.

3.7.4 Creating a vulnerability-to-business impact matrix

A structured vulnerability-to-business impact matrix provides a systematic tool for documenting and communicating the connections between technical vulnerabilities and potential business consequences. This matrix serves as a reference for prioritization discussions and helps ensure consistent evaluation across the organization.

A basic matrix structure might include the following elements:

- Vulnerability identifier and description
- Technical severity rating (e.g., CVSS score)
- Affected systems and infrastructure components
- Connected business functions and processes
- Potential business impacts (financial, operational, reputational, regulatory)
- Business impact rating (e.g., low, medium, high, critical)
- Combined risk rating (considering both technical severity and business impact)

The process for populating this matrix involves:

1. Starting with vulnerability scan results and technical severity ratings
2. Identifying which systems are affected by each vulnerability
3. Using the infrastructure-to-business function mapping to determine which business functions rely on those systems
4. Assessing potential business impacts if those functions were disrupted
5. Assigning a business impact rating based on standardized criteria
6. Calculating a combined risk rating that reflects both technical and business dimensions

To maintain this matrix over time, establish a regular review cycle aligned with your vulnerability management process. Update the matrix whenever:

- New high-impact vulnerabilities are discovered
- Business functions or their technical dependencies change
- New business impact information becomes available
- Remediation actions change the risk landscape

A well-maintained vulnerability-to-business impact matrix becomes a valuable tool for risk discussions with both technical and business stakeholders. It provides clear documentation of how technical issues translate to business concerns, facilitating more informed prioritization and resource allocation decisions.

Once organizations understand the connections between technical systems and business processes, they need practical methods to quantify the potential financial and operational impacts of security incidents. This quantification enables more objective risk assessment and resource allocation decisions.

Downloadable Resource: Vulnerability-to-Business Impact Mapping Framework

3.8 TECHNIQUES FOR QUANTIFYING BUSINESS IMPACTS

Moving beyond qualitative assessments, organizations need practical methods to quantify potential business consequences in financial terms. This quantification process enables objective comparison between different risks and supports data-driven resource allocation decisions. Multiple approaches can help translate security risks into the financial metrics that business leaders understand and act upon.

3.8.1 Categories of business impact

Comprehensive BIA requires consideration of multiple impact categories, each affecting the organization in different ways. Understanding these distinct categories helps ensure that all potential consequences are properly evaluated. The four categories and their relationships are shown in Figure 3.4.

Financial losses represent the most direct and often most compelling category for business stakeholders. These include:

- Direct costs: Immediate expenses resulting from a security incident, such as incident response services, forensic investigations, customer notification, credit monitoring services, and legal fees
- Recovery costs: Expenses associated with restoring systems and data, including potential technology replacement and consulting services
- Revenue loss: Income forfeited because of business disruption, including canceled orders, contract penalties, and customer attrition
- Long-term financial impacts: Decreased valuation, increased insurance premiums, and higher borrowing costs

Operational disruption impacts include:

- Productivity losses: Work hours lost when employees cannot access essential systems

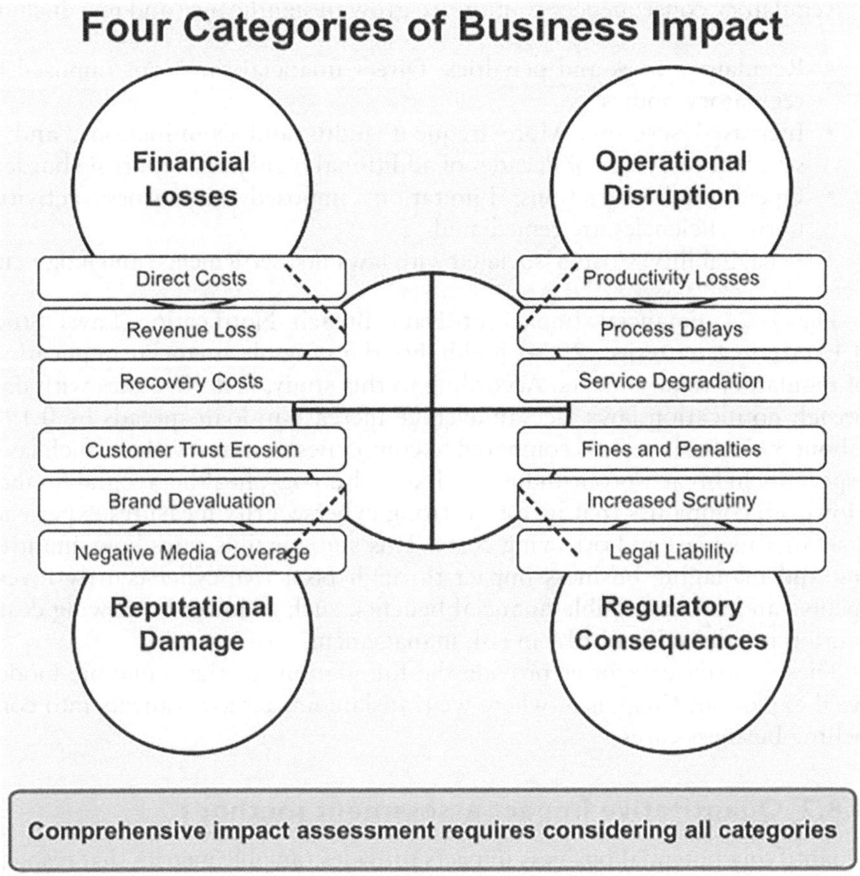

Figure 3.4 Four Categories of business impact.

- Process delays: Increased time to complete critical business activities
- Service degradation: Reduced quality or availability of customer-facing services
- Missed deadlines: Failure to meet contractual or regulatory timeframes

Reputational damage, while often difficult to quantify precisely, can include:

- Customer trust erosion: Reduced customer confidence leading to business loss
- Brand devaluation: Diminished brand equity and market positioning
- Media coverage: Negative publicity affecting public perception
- Recruiting challenges: Difficulty attracting and retaining talent

Regulatory consequences continue to grow in significance and may include:

- Regulatory fines and penalties: Direct financial sanctions imposed by regulatory bodies
- Increased scrutiny: More frequent audits and examinations, and in severe cases, years or decades of additional regulatory reporting burdens
- Operational restrictions: Limitations imposed on business activities until deficiencies are remediated
- Legal liability: Costs associated with lawsuits, settlements, and judgments

The 2024 Financial Impact of Data Breach Notification Laws Study (Chandrani Chatterjee, 2024) highlights the tangible financial implications of regulatory requirements. According to this study, firms in states with data breach notification laws face an average increase in loan spreads by 0.19% (about 39.79 basis points) compared to companies in states without such laws, especially in breach-prone industries like technology, healthcare, and finance. However, companies that invest in strong cybersecurity measures experience a smaller increase in borrowing costs. This statistic illustrates how quantifying and managing business impact through proactive cybersecurity investments can lead to tangible financial benefits, such as lower borrowing costs, reinforcing the value of BIA in risk management.

These impact categories provide the foundation for the economic models we'll explore in Chapter 5, where we translate impact assessments into compelling business cases.

3.8.2 Quantitative impact assessment methods

Quantifying potential business impacts provides tangible metrics that resonate with business stakeholders and enables more objective prioritization decisions. Several approaches can help translate security risks into financial terms.

Direct cost calculation represents the most straightforward approach, focusing on estimating the immediate, known costs that would result from a security incident:

- Response team costs: Internal labor hours and external consultant fees
- Technology recovery costs: System rebuilding and data restoration expenses
- Customer notification expenses: Communication, call center operation, and credit monitoring
- Legal and public relations services: External professional support costs

For these direct costs, organizations can develop standardized cost models based on:

- Historical incident data from their own experience
- Industry benchmarks and research reports

- Vendor quotes for incident response and recovery services
- Regulatory requirements for notification and remediation

Statistical models provide more sophisticated approaches for estimating financial impact, particularly when historical data is available. These might include:

- Regression analysis to identify patterns and relationships between incident characteristics and resulting costs
- Monte Carlo simulation to model a range of possible outcomes based on probability distributions
- Decision tree analysis to evaluate different scenarios and their associated probabilities and costs

When limited historical data are available, organizations can supplement their analysis with:

- Industry benchmarks and reports, such as the annual IBM Cost of Data Breach Study
- Peer comparison data from similar organizations
- Expert judgment from security and business leaders
- Scenario-based workshops that explore potential incident paths and consequences

A practical exercise for building this capability is to calculate the potential financial impact of a common vulnerability affecting a business-critical system. Begin with direct costs, then layer in operational disruption costs, potential regulatory penalties, and an estimate of reputational impact to develop a comprehensive view.

3.8.2.1 Direct cost calculation example: Data breach scenario

Consider a healthcare organization with 25,000 patient records assessing the potential financial impact of a database vulnerability. A direct cost calculation might include:

- Forensic investigation: $75,000 ($250/hour × 300 hours)
- Patient notification: $125,000 ($5 per record × 25,000 records)
- Credit monitoring: $375,000 ($50 per affected individual × 7,500 individuals accepting the service)
- Call center operations: $35,000 ($5,000 per day × 7 days)
- Legal consultation: $120,000 ($400/hour × 300 hours)
- Total direct costs: $730,000

3.8.2.2 *Revenue impact calculation example: E-Commerce scenario*

For an online retailer assessing the impact of a vulnerability in their payment processing system:

- Average daily revenue: $450,000
- Estimated outage duration: 4–8 hours (0.5–1 business day)
- Revenue impact multiplier: 2.5× (accounts for rush orders diverted to competitors)
- Immediate revenue loss: $450,000 × 0.5–1 day × 2.5 = $562,500–$1,125,000
- Customer churn impact:
  - 2% of affected customers ($9M annual revenue) × 35% retention risk = $63,000 monthly recurring revenue loss
  - 12-month impact: $756,000 ($63,000 × 12 months)
- Total revenue impact range: $1.32M–$1.88M

Organizations can develop standardized cost models using:

- Historical incident data from their own experience
- Industry benchmarks like IBM's Cost of Data Breach Report
- Vendor quotes for incident response and recovery services
- Regulatory fine schedules and enforcement precedents

These quantification techniques provide essential inputs to the economic models we'll explore in Chapter 5, where we develop comprehensive business cases for security investments.

Downloadable Resource: Business Impact Quantification Calculator

3.8.3 Qualitative and semi-quantitative approaches

While quantitative approaches are ideal for financial decision-making, qualitative and semi-quantitative methods often provide valuable complementary perspectives, particularly for impacts that resist precise estimation without excessive effort.

Qualitative impact scales typically use categorical classifications such as:

- Low: Minimal effect on business operations, no significant financial impact
- Medium: Noticeable disruption to some business operations, moderate financial impact
- High: Significant disruption to important business functions, substantial financial impact
- Critical: Severe disruption to core business operations, major financial consequences

These classifications should be accompanied by descriptive criteria that ensure consistent application across the organization. For example, "critical" might be defined as "disruption that would prevent execution of core business functions for more than 24 hours and result in financial losses exceeding $500,000." This definition should be agreed up on and signed off by all key stakeholders.

Semi-quantitative approaches bridge the gap between purely qualitative assessments and fully quantified financial estimates. These approaches typically assign numerical values to qualitative ratings to enable more sophisticated analysis while avoiding false precision (or requiring full quantitative data). For example, a 1–5 scale might be used where:

1 = Negligible impact (less than $10,000)
2 = Minor impact ($10,000–$100,000)
3 = Moderate impact ($100,000–$500,000)
4 = Major impact ($500,000–$1,000,000)
5 = Severe impact (over $1,000,000)

Business stakeholder input is essential for both qualitative and semi-quantitative approaches as senior security leaders cannot ethically estimate the impacts of business systems that they do not operate or fully comprehend. Structured methods for gathering this input include:

- Facilitated workshops with business and technical stakeholders
- Structured interviews with business process owners
- Delphi method surveys to gather expert opinions
- Scenario-based exercises that explore potential impact pathways

Organizations should consider qualitative approaches when:

- Precise financial data is unavailable or would require excessive data gathering and an analysis at a cost greater than the risk if it were realized
- Impacts include significant intangible elements such as reputational damage
- The assessment must accommodate varying risk perceptions among stakeholders
- The organization is in early stages of developing its impact assessment capabilities

Quantitative approaches are more appropriate when:

- Reliable financial data is readily available
- Objective comparisons between different risks are required
- Resource allocation decisions demand financial justification
- The organization has mature impact assessment capabilities

Many organizations find that a hybrid approach – using quantitative methods for readily quantifiable impacts and qualitative methods for others – provides the most comprehensive view.

3.8.4 Time dimension of business impact

The time dimension of business impact represents a critical but often overlooked aspect of comprehensive impact analysis. Business consequences rarely manifest as one-time events, but instead unfold over time with varying intensity and duration; an example is shown in Figure 3.5.

Immediate impacts typically include:

- System and service unavailability
- Initial response costs
- Productivity losses during the incident
- Immediate customer dissatisfaction

However, long-term impacts often exceed these initial consequences and may include:

- Ongoing customer attrition
- Brand reputation recovery costs
- Increased regulatory scrutiny
- Elevated insurance premiums
- Litigation and settlement costs

The escalating nature of costs over time is particularly evident in data breaches, where initial response expenses may represent only a fraction of total costs. This aligns with the PwC findings mentioned earlier.

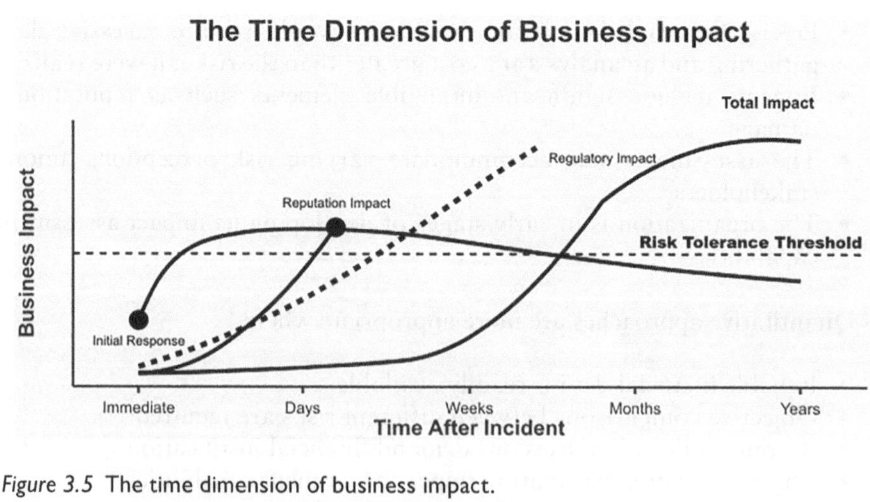

Figure 3.5 The time dimension of business impact.

Recovery time considerations play a central role in impact assessment. Organizations should determine:

- Recovery Time Objective (RTO): The maximum acceptable time to restore a business function after disruption
- Recovery Point Objective (RPO): The maximum acceptable data loss measured in time
- Time to Detection (TTD): How quickly an incident would likely be discovered
- Time to Containment (TTC): How long it would take to stop an incident from spreading

The relationship between impact and time is rarely linear. Instead, many business functions exhibit impact thresholds – points at which the severity of impact increases dramatically. For example:

- A one-hour system outage might cause minimal disruption
- A four-hour outage might trigger contract penalties
- A 24-hour outage might cause significant customer defection
- A week-long outage might threaten the organization's viability

BIA should consistently document these thresholds for critical business functions to inform recovery priorities and control investments. Functions with rapidly escalating impacts typically warrant more robust preventive and recovery controls than those with more gradual impact curves.

With quantified business impacts at hand, organizations can move beyond technical severity scores to prioritize risks based on their potential business consequences. This business-informed approach to prioritization helps ensure that security investments address the most significant organizational risks.

STORY

A mid-sized healthcare provider experienced what initially seemed like a minor security incident when an employee's email account was compromised through a phishing attack. The security team responded within hours, resetting the account and implementing additional authentication measures. In their initial assessment, they logged the incident as "contained" with minimal impact – approximately $2,000 in staff time and operational delay.

What emerged over subsequent weeks, however, told a different story of cascading business consequences across multiple time horizons:

Day 3: The compliance team determined that the compromised inbox contained protected health information for 240 patients, triggering legal notification requirements and initial costs of $15,000 for legal consultation and preparing notification letters.

Week 2: Patient notifications led to concerned calls overwhelming the provider's service center, requiring temporary staffing increases costing $30,000 and delaying routine appointment scheduling.

Month 1: Local media reported the breach, leading to appointment cancellations and a 15% drop in new patient registrations, representing approximately $120,000 in deferred revenue.

Month 3: The state healthcare regulatory body launched a compliance investigation, requiring extensive documentation preparation and executive time valued at $85,000.

Month 6: The organization's cyber insurance premiums increased by 30% during policy renewal, an unanticipated $200,000 annual expense attributed directly to the breach.

Year 1: Total quantifiable impact reached $595,000 – nearly 300 times the initial impact estimate – with lingering effects on patient acquisition rates.

The organization now incorporates explicit time-based impact analysis into their security risk assessment, evaluating potential consequences at 24 hours, one week, one month, three months, and one year post-incident. This temporal framework helps security and business leaders understand not just immediate disruption but the full business impact curve of security events.

3.9 PRIORITIZING RISKS BASED ON BUSINESS RELEVANCE

Technical severity scores alone may not reflect the true business risk that vulnerabilities represent to an organization. Business-informed prioritization considers both technical factors and potential business impact to guide resource allocation decisions. This approach appears to help organizations focus their limited security resources on addressing the risks that matter most to their business operations.

3.9.1 Beyond technical severity scores

While technical severity scores like CVSS have their place in vulnerability management, they suffer from the same business disconnect we explored in

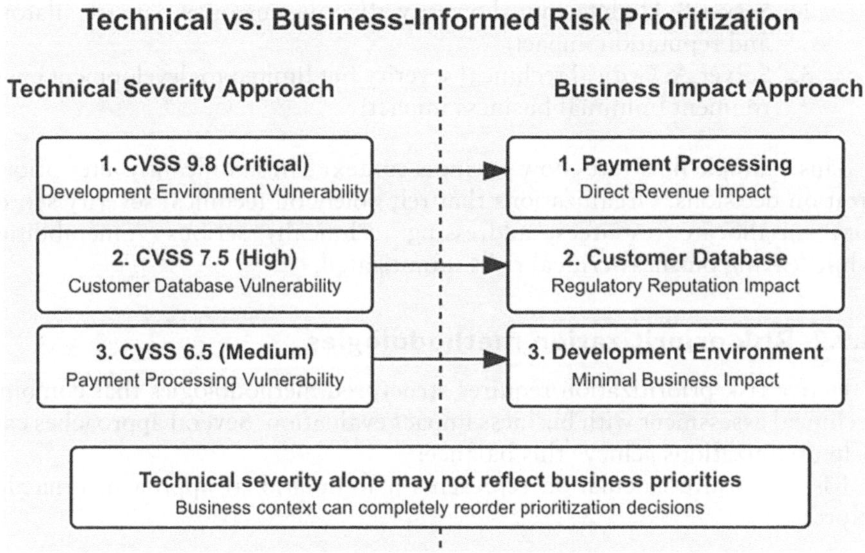

Figure 3.6 Technical vs. business-informed risk prioritization.

Chapter 1. These scores focus on technical exploitability rather than business impact, and don't account for:

- The business criticality of affected systems
- The sensitivity of data involved
- The existence of compensating controls
- The organization's specific threat landscape
- Potential business consequences if the vulnerability were exploited

For example, a vulnerability with a high CVSS score might affect a development system with no production data, resulting in minimal business risk. Conversely, a vulnerability with a moderate CVSS score could pose significant business risk if it exists in a system supporting critical revenue-generating activities.

Consider this comparison (shown in Figure 3.6) between technical and business-informed prioritization:

Technical Prioritization:

1. Server A: CVSS 9.8 (Critical) – Remote code execution in development environment
2. Server B: CVSS 7.5 (High) – SQL injection in customer database
3. Server C: CVSS 6.5 (Medium) – Denial of service in payment processing system

Business-Informed Prioritization:

1. Server C: Medium technical severity but affects payment processing (revenue impact)

2. Server B: High technical severity affecting customer data (regulatory and reputation impact)
3. Server A: Critical technical severity but limited to development environment (minimal business impact)

This example illustrates how business context can significantly alter prioritization decisions. Organizations that rely solely on technical severity scores may misallocate resources, addressing technically serious vulnerabilities while leaving business-critical risks unmitigated.

3.9.2 Risk prioritization methodologies

Effective risk prioritization requires structured methodologies that combine technical assessment with business impact evaluation. Several approaches can help organizations achieve this balance:

Risk exposure calculation represents a foundational approach, typically expressed as:

Risk Exposure XE "risk exposure" = Likelihood × Business Impact

This formula accounts for both the probability of successful exploitation and the potential business consequences. Likelihood factors might include:

- Technical exploitability of the vulnerability
- Threat intelligence regarding active exploitation
- Exposure of the vulnerable system
- Existence of compensating controls

Business impact factors would include those discussed in Section 3.1, such as financial losses, operational disruption, reputational damage, and regulatory consequences.

Weighted scoring approaches offer more sophisticated prioritization by:

- Assigning different weights to various impact categories based on organizational priorities
- Incorporating multiple factors beyond simple likelihood and impact
- Allowing for customization to reflect industry-specific concerns
- Enabling sensitivity analysis to test different weighting scenarios

Risk appetite and tolerance thresholds provide essential context for prioritization by establishing:

- The level of risk the organization is willing to accept
- Specific thresholds requiring escalation or immediate action
- Different tolerance levels for different business functions or risk categories
- Time-based expectations for risk remediation

Decision frameworks help systematize the prioritization process, providing clear guidance for different risk scenarios. A simple framework might categorize risks as:

- Critical: Require immediate remediation (within 24-48 hours)
- High: Remediation required within one week
- Medium: Require remediation within one month
- Low: Remediate during next maintenance cycle

The Target case illustrates how prioritization failures can lead to missed warning signals despite technical detection. As noted earlier, technical alerts indicating a potentially catastrophic breach did not receive urgent attention because they weren't properly prioritized based on business impact.

This example underscores the importance of prioritization methodologies that consider both technical indicators and potential business impacts.

Chapter 6 builds on this prioritization approach by introducing specific metrics that help organizations measure and communicate risk reduction in business terms.

3.9.3 Stakeholder input in prioritization

Effective risk prioritization requires structured input from diverse stakeholders across the organization. This input ensures that prioritization decisions reflect both technical realities and business concerns.

Structured methods for gathering stakeholder input include:

1. Risk assessment workshops that bring together technical and business stakeholders to evaluate specific risks. These workshops typically:
   - Present technical vulnerability information in business context
   - Facilitate discussion of potential business impacts
   - Capture diverse perspectives on likelihood and consequence
   - Build consensus on risk ratings and prioritization
2. Business impact interviews with process owners and subject matter experts to gather detailed insights on:
   - Critical time periods for business functions
   - Financial implications of disruption
   - Upstream and downstream dependencies
   - Regulatory and contractual requirements
3. Executive prioritization sessions that engage senior leaders in:
   - Reviewing high-impact risks
   - Establishing risk tolerance thresholds
   - Aligning risk priorities with strategic objectives
   - Allocating resources for risk treatment

Facilitation techniques for productive prioritization workshops include:

- Using standardized templates and rating scales
- Providing pre-workshop information packages
- Establishing clear decision-making processes
- Documenting assumptions and rationales
- Focusing discussion on business outcomes rather than technical details

Conflicts between technical and business priorities inevitably come up during these discussions. Common examples include:

- Technical teams prioritizing vulnerabilities with high exploitation potential, while business teams focus on systems with high revenue impact
- Disagreements about the likelihood of specific threat scenarios
- Different perspectives on the value of security investments versus business initiatives
- Varying time horizons for risk consideration

Resolving these conflicts requires:

- Focusing on objective evidence where available
- Documenting different perspectives for transparency
- Using structured decision-making frameworks
- Escalating unresolved conflicts to appropriate governance bodies
- Maintaining respectful dialogue focused on organizational interests

A practical exercise for developing this capability is a stakeholder prioritization workshop simulation. Select several sample vulnerabilities affecting different systems, then bring together representatives from security, IT, and business teams to evaluate and prioritize them. This exercise typically reveals different risk perspectives and provides practice in building consensus.

3.9.4 Dynamic prioritization for changing conditions

Risk prioritization cannot be a static, one-time activity. Business conditions, threat landscapes, and technical environments constantly change, requiring dynamic approaches to risk prioritization.

Key triggers for re-prioritization include:

- Emerging threat intelligence indicating increased likelihood of exploitation
- Changes in business strategy or operations affecting the criticality of systems
- New regulatory requirements introducing compliance obligations
- Discovery of previously unknown dependencies between systems

- Incidents or near-misses revealing new risk information
- Changes in the organization's risk appetite or tolerance

Monitoring business context changes requires ongoing communication between security and business teams. Mechanisms for maintaining this awareness include:

- Regular business review meetings
- Participation in change management processes
- Business stakeholder representation in security governance
- Periodic reassessment of critical business functions
- Alignment with strategic planning cycles

Incorporating threat intelligence enables timely adjustments to prioritization based on the modern threat landscape. Organizations should establish processes to:

- Monitor threat intelligence feeds for relevant indicators
- Assess how newer threats may affect existing vulnerabilities
- Adjust risk ratings and priorities accordingly
- Communicate changing priorities to stakeholders

Maintaining prioritization as a continuous process requires:

- Defined reassessment intervals for different risk categories
- Clear responsibilities for monitoring and reassessment
- Established escalation paths for significant changes
- Documentation of prioritization decisions and their rationale
- Regular reporting on the organization's risk posture and prioritization adjustments

Organizations that implement dynamic prioritization are better positioned to adapt to changing conditions and maintain focus on the risks that most threaten their business objectives.

Effective prioritization provides the foundation for clear risk communication, but organizations need structured approaches to document and present these findings to various stakeholder groups. The last step involves translating BIA results into formats that drive appropriate organizational action.

3.10 DOCUMENTING AND COMMUNICATING TRANSLATED RISKS

Effective risk communication requires documentation formats and messaging strategies that resonate with different stakeholder groups. The risk register serves as the central tool for presenting security risks in business terms that non-technical executives can understand and act upon. Clear communication strategies can help ensure that BIA results drive appropriate organizational action.

3.10.1 The risk register

The risk register serves as the central documentation tool for business and security risks, providing a structured format for communicating risks to stakeholders across the organization. Unlike technically oriented vulnerability reports, the risk register presents security risks in business terms that resonate with non-technical stakeholders.

A well-designed risk register typically includes the following components:

- Risk identifier: Unique reference code for tracking purposes
- Risk description: Clear statement of the risk in business terms
- Affected business functions: Business processes that could be impacted
- Potential business impacts: Consequences in financial, operational, reputational, and regulatory terms
- Current risk rating: Assessment of likelihood and business impact
- Risk owner: Business stakeholder responsible for accepting or addressing the risk
- Mitigation strategy: Planned approach for risk treatment
- Current status: Implementation progress and residual risk

Translating technical details into business language requires focusing on consequences rather than technical mechanisms.

For example, instead of: "Server X has an unpatched vulnerability that could allow buffer overflow attacks through the TCP port 445."

Use: "The customer database server has a security weakness that, if exploited, could allow unauthorized access to customer credit card data, potentially resulting in regulatory penalties, notification costs, and reputational damage."

While maintaining this business focus, the risk register should provide traceability to underlying technical vulnerabilities. This can be accomplished through:

- Reference codes linking to technical vulnerability databases
- Attachment of supporting technical documentation
- Relationships to specific findings in vulnerability scans
- Connections to specific security control deficiencies

Risk registers should be tailored to the organization's needs while maintaining consistency in format and terminology. Many organizations develop tiered documentation approaches, with summary-level information for executive audiences and more detailed information for operational stakeholders.

Downloadable Resource: Risk Register Template

3.10.2 Risk communication strategies

Effective risk communication requires tailoring messages to different stakeholder groups while maintaining consistency in the underlying risk information. Key stakeholder groups typically include:

- Executive leadership: Focused on strategic implications, financial impact, and alignment with enterprise risk
- Business unit leaders: Concerned with operational impacts, resource requirements, and business continuity
- Technical teams: Interested in implementation details, technical requirements, and operational feasibility
- Compliance and legal: Focused on regulatory implications and documentation requirements

Effective visualization of business risk information can significantly enhance communication. Visual formats might include:

- Heat maps showing risks plotted by likelihood and impact
- Trend charts showing risk levels over time
- Comparison charts illustrating risk levels before and after proposed mitigations
- Dependency diagrams showing relationships between risks and business functions

Stories and scenarios help clarify potential impacts by providing concrete examples of how risks might materialize. For instance, instead of simply stating "potential data breach," develop a scenario that describes:

- How the breach might occur
- What data might be compromised
- How customers would be affected
- What the response process would entail
- What financial and reputational consequences might result

Avoiding technical jargon while maintaining accuracy requires:

- Developing a glossary of business-friendly terms for common security concepts
- Using analogies that relate security concepts to familiar business situations
- Focusing on outcomes rather than technical mechanisms
- Providing technical details as supplementary information rather than the primary message

3.10.3 From analysis to action

The ultimate purpose of BIA is to drive action – to ensure that security investments align with business priorities and effectively address the organization's most significant risks.

Developing action plans based on BIA involves:

- Identifying potential risk treatment options (accept, mitigate, transfer, avoid)
- Evaluating the costs and benefits of different treatment approaches
- Determining implementation requirements and timeframes
- Assigning clear responsibility for implementation
- Establishing metrics for measuring effectiveness

Resource allocation recommendations should flow directly from the prioritization process, focusing investments on addressing the risks that pose the greatest potential business impact. These recommendations should include:

- Specific resource requirements (budget, personnel, technology)
- Expected risk reduction from proposed investments
- Implementation timeline and milestones
- Dependencies on other initiatives

Tracking and reporting on risk treatment progress provides accountability and visibility into risk management efforts. Key elements include:

- Regular status updates on implementation progress
- Reassessment of risk levels as controls are implemented
- Identification of implementation challenges or delays
- Adjustments to plans based on changing conditions

Measuring effectiveness in business terms ensures that security investments deliver the expected value. Metrics might include:

- Reduction in risk exposure for key business processes
- Decrease in incident frequency or severity
- Improvements in recovery capabilities
- Enhanced compliance with regulatory requirements

Target's experience, detailed in our case study, provides a compelling illustration of these translation failures. Had the company effectively applied the BIA principles outlined in this chapter, this costly breach might have been prevented or significantly mitigated.

🔗 *Downloadable Resource: Cross-Functional Risk Translation Workshop*

3.11 CONCLUSION

BIA serves as a translation methodology for connecting technical security risks to the business consequences that executives and board members care about most. By systematically mapping technical vulnerabilities to business functions and quantifying potential impacts, BIA bridges the communication gap between security professionals and business leaders.

The value of this translation cannot be overstated. When security professionals speak the language of business – discussing risks in terms of financial impact, operational disruption, and strategic consequences – they position themselves as business partners rather than technical specialists. This shift in communication enables more informed decision-making about security investments and resource allocation.

Throughout this chapter, we've explored how BIA provides a structured framework for identifying, quantifying, prioritizing, and communicating security risks in business terms. We've examined techniques for systematically connecting technical vulnerabilities to business processes, quantifying potential impacts, and prioritizing risks based on their business relevance rather than technical severity alone.

The case study of the Target breach underscores the potential consequences of failing to translate technical warnings into business impact terms. When organizations lack effective translation mechanisms, they remain vulnerable to significant financial and reputational damage despite investments in technical security controls.

As we'll explore in the next chapter, these translated risks become valuable inputs to Enterprise Risk Management processes. By integrating security risks with other enterprise risks, organizations can develop comprehensive risk management strategies that align with business objectives and optimize resource allocation.

Security professionals have an obligation to translate technical risks into business terms – not just as a communication strategy, but as a fundamental aspect of their organizational duty. By mastering the BIA methodology, security leaders can fulfill this obligation while positioning themselves as strategic business partners in protecting the organization's most valuable assets.

3.12 ACTION ITEMS FOR READERS

1. Identify your organization's three most important business functions and document the technical systems, applications, and infrastructure components that support each one, revealing hidden dependencies that could affect risk prioritization.
2. Calculate the potential business impact of one current vulnerability in your environment using the direct cost and revenue impact methodologies

presented in the chapter, creating a concrete example of financial risk quantification.

3. Facilitate a cross-functional workshop with business and technical stakeholders to evaluate and prioritize five existing security risks using business impact criteria rather than technical severity scores alone.
4. Create a business-focused risk register entry for one significant security risk, translating technical vulnerability details into clear business language that describes potential financial, operational, and reputational consequences.
5. Establish a process for regularly updating risk prioritization based on changing business conditions and threat intelligence, including defined triggers for reassessment and clear responsibilities for monitoring business context changes.

Downloadable Resource: Business Impact Analysis Maturity Assessment Checklist

Chapter 4

Integrating security into Enterprise Risk Management

Chapter in One Sentence: Integrating security into Enterprise Risk Management transforms security from an isolated technical function into a business-aligned discipline that enables organizations to make informed decisions about security investments, risk acceptance, and control implementation based on business impact.

4.1 EXECUTIVE SUMMARY

This chapter addresses the critical challenge many organizations face: treating security risks as isolated technical problems rather than business issues that threaten strategic objectives. This disconnected approach creates blind spots where vulnerabilities go unaddressed, security investments compete for resources without clear business alignment, and risk acceptance decisions occur without proper context. The chapter provides a framework for integrating security risks into Enterprise Risk Management (ERM) processes, transforming security from a technical silo into a business-aligned function.

The chapter examines how established ERM frameworks like COSO, ISO 31000, and NIST can be applied to security contexts by translating technical vulnerabilities into business impacts. Organizations typically progress through maturity stages – from siloed to coordinated, integrated, and finally strategic risk management – as they embed security into enterprise processes. Risk registers emerge as the central tool for this integration, documenting security risks alongside other enterprise risks and enabling consistent assessment, prioritization, and monitoring.

Effective organizational structures support integrated risk management through clear governance models. The Three Lines of Defense model clarifies roles across operational management, risk oversight functions, and independent assurance. Organizations must determine whether to centralize or distribute security risk management functions, often adopting hybrid approaches that balance consistency with business alignment.

Establishing clear risk ownership is foundational to effective security risk management. Whether using business ownership models, security oversight

DOI: 10.1201/9781003744146-4

models, or hybrid approaches, organizations need explicit accountability for risks. Formal risk acceptance protocols ensure that decisions to accept risks are made consciously, with appropriate documentation and approval based on risk level.

By integrating security into ERM, organizations can make more informed decisions about security investments, risk acceptance, and control implementation. This approach ensures security considerations are factored into strategic planning and business decisions, reducing the likelihood and impact of security incidents while supporting business objectives.

4.2 KEY TAKEAWAYS

- Security risks must be translated from technical terms into business impact language to enable effective integration with ERM processes
- Risk registers serve as the bridge between security and ERM by documenting security risks in consistent formats similarly to other business risks
- Breaking down organizational silos requires clear governance models, communication channels, and shared metrics between security and business teams
- Establishing explicit risk ownership and accountability ensures security risks receive appropriate attention from stakeholders with the authority to address them
- Security risk acceptance decisions should follow formal procedures with documentation requirements proportional to the level of risk

4.3 APPLICATION QUESTIONS

1. How do your organization's security risks appear in the enterprise risk register, and what improvements could you make to ensure security risks are documented consistently with other business risks?
2. Which elements of your organizational structure support or hinder the integration of security into ERM, and what changes might address existing barriers?
3. How clear is risk ownership for your top security risks, and what processes could you implement to strengthen accountability for security risk management?

4.4 TOOLS REFERENCED IN THIS CHAPTER

All tools available at kaynemcgladrey.com/myth/

- Security-ERM Integration Maturity Assessment Framework
- Cross-Functional Risk Assessment Workshop
- Risk Acceptance Decision Framework

4.5 INTRODUCTION

Many organizations continue to treat security risks as technical problems rather than business issues that threaten strategic objectives. This disconnect stems from a fundamental misalignment: security risks remain isolated in technical silos while other business risks are managed through established enterprise frameworks.

Many organizations maintain separate processes for managing security risks and enterprise risks, creating blind spots where critical vulnerabilities go unaddressed. Security teams often speak in technical terms that fail to resonate with executive leadership, while business leaders may not fully comprehend how security vulnerabilities translate to financial, operational, and reputational risks.

This fragmented approach creates several important challenges. First, security investments compete for limited resources without clear alignment with business priorities. Second, risk acceptance decisions often occur without proper business context, leading to either excessive caution or dangerous complacency. Third, accountability becomes diffused when security risks cross organizational boundaries, creating confusion about who ultimately owns these risks.

The consequences of this disconnected approach are substantial. Organizations may focus on compliance rather than true risk reduction, waste resources on security controls that don't address priority business risks, or fail to identify systemic vulnerabilities until after a breach occurs. When security risks remain trapped in technical silos, the organization cannot effectively leverage its ERM processes to address them.

This chapter explores how to bridge these divides by integrating security risks into ERM frameworks. We will examine how established ERM frameworks can be applied to security risks, how risk registers serve as a crucial integration tool, how organizational structures can support integrated risk management, and how to establish clear ownership and accountability for security risks.

By reframing security risks within business contexts and leveraging ERM practices, organizations can make more informed decisions about resource allocation, risk acceptance, and control implementation. The goal is not to create a separate security risk management function, but to embed security considerations into the organization's existing approach to managing risk across all domains.

As we explore these topics, we'll provide practical guidance for both security leaders seeking to align their work with enterprise objectives and financial executives looking to make informed decisions about security investments. The approaches described will help organizations move beyond technical compliance to true risk management that supports business objectives.

4.6 ENTERPRISE RISK MANAGEMENT FRAMEWORKS FOR SECURITY

Most organizations appear to treat security risks as isolated technical problems rather than business issues that threaten strategic objectives. This disconnects stems from a fundamental misalignment where security risks remain trapped in technical silos while other business risks benefit from established enterprise frameworks. Applying proven ERM frameworks to security contexts can bridge this gap, transforming security from a cost center into a business-aligned function that supports informed decision-making about investments, risk acceptance, and control implementation.

4.6.1 Overview of major ERM frameworks

ERM frameworks provide a structured approach to identifying, assessing, and addressing risks across an organization. These frameworks can be applied to security risks once we understand their core principles and processes.

The Committee of Sponsoring Organizations of the Treadway Commission (COSO) Enterprise Risk Management Framework offers a comprehensive approach to risk management that is widely adopted across industries. COSO defines ERM as "not a function or department. It is the culture, capabilities, and practices that organizations integrate with strategy-setting and apply when they carry out that strategy, with the purpose of managing risk in creating, preserving, and realizing value" (COSO, 2017).

The COSO framework emphasizes several principles relevant to security risk integration:

1. Risk management must be aligned with organizational strategy and objectives
2. Risk appetite should guide risk decisions across the enterprise
3. Risk assessment should consider potential impact on business objectives
4. Risk reporting should flow to appropriate governance bodies

For security risks, COSO provides a structure to connect technical vulnerabilities to enterprise impacts. Rather than focusing on vulnerabilities in isolation, security teams can use COSO to demonstrate how these vulnerabilities might affect strategic, operational, reporting, and compliance objectives.

The International Organization for Standardization (ISO) 31000 framework offers another widely adopted approach to risk management. ISO 31000 defines risk as "the effect of uncertainty on objectives" (ISO, 2018) and provides a process for managing risks that includes:

1. Establishing the context (internal, external, and risk management)
2. Risk assessment (identification, analysis, and evaluation)

3. Risk treatment (selection and implementation of options)
4. Communication and consultation throughout the process
5. Monitoring and review to ensure controls remain effective

This process-oriented approach helps organizations systematically address security risks by considering them within broader contexts and ensuring appropriate treatment based on analysis. ISO 31000 emphasizes that risk management should be integrated into all organizational processes and decision-making activities, supporting the view that security is not a separate function, but an integral part of business operations.

The National Institute of Standards and Technology (NIST) Risk Management Framework provides specific guidance for managing information security risks. The NIST framework includes seven steps:

1. Prepare to execute the RMF
2. Categorize systems and information
3. Select security controls
4. Implement controls
5. Assess control effectiveness
6. Authorize systems based on risk
7. Monitor controls on an ongoing basis

While focused specifically on information security, the NIST RMF can be integrated with ERM processes by connecting system-level risks to business impacts. The framework helps translate technical security controls into risk management activities that support business objectives.

When comparing these frameworks, several common elements emerge as seen in Table 4.1. All frameworks emphasize the importance of:

- Aligning risk management with organizational objectives
- Establishing clear risk appetite and tolerance levels
- Implementing a structured process for risk assessment
- Ensuring appropriate risk ownership and accountability
- Monitoring and reviewing risks on an ongoing basis

These common elements provide a foundation for integrating security risks into ERM processes, regardless of which specific framework an organization adopts.

These ERM frameworks enable the integration benefits we discussed in Chapter 1, where evidence shows that organizations with integrated risk approaches experience fewer breaches and more effective incident response.

Table 4.1 Comparison of risk management frameworks

Feature	*COSO ERM framework*	*ISO 31000*	*NIST risk management framework*
Primary focus	Strategic alignment of risk management with business objectives	Process for managing risk across all organizational levels	Information security risk management with compliance orientation
Key principles	• Risk aligned with strategy • Risk appetite guides decisions • Risk linked to performance • Enterprise-wide approach • Communication focus	• Risk management integrated into all organizational processes • Structured and comprehensive approach • Customized to organization • Inclusive of stakeholders • Dynamic and responsive	• Prepare for risk assessment • Categorize information systems • Select, implement, and assess security controls • Authorize systems based on risk • Monitor controls continuously
Risk definition	Effect of uncertainty on achievement of objectives	Effect of uncertainty on objectives	Function of likelihood and magnitude of harm occurring
Governance approach	Board oversight with strong emphasis on tone at the top	Integrated throughout decision-making processes	System authorization process with defined roles
Business alignment	Links risk to strategic and operational objectives	Focuses on objectives but less emphasis on strategy alignment	Technical orientation with links to business through system categorization
Best for	Organizations seeking to integrate risk management with strategic planning	Organizations needing a flexible process-based approach that works across different risk domains	Organizations with regulatory compliance requirements and technical security focus
Implementation complexity	More complex, requires significant organizational buy-in	More straightforward, adaptable to different organizational contexts	Highly detailed for technical implementation but narrower in scope

4.6.2 Applying ERM principles to security

Applying ERM principles to security requires translating security terminology into business risk language. Security professionals often describe risks in technical terms – vulnerabilities, threats, exploits – while business leaders think in terms of financial impacts, operational disruptions, and strategic consequences. Bridging this gap is essential for effective integration.

As we explored in Chapter 2's discussion of translation gaps, security risks must be reframed from technical descriptions to business impact terms when applying ERM principles. This translation becomes particularly important when documenting risks in enterprise frameworks, where technical vulnerabilities like SQL injection must be expressed as business scenarios that quantify potential financial and operational consequences.

Several common elements across ERM frameworks can be applied to security:

- Risk identification within business processes: Security risks should be identified as part of broader business process analysis, not just through technical vulnerability scanning. This helps connect security concerns to specific business activities and objectives.
- Consistent risk assessment methodology: Organizations should apply the same assessment approach across all risk domains, including security. This might involve rating risks on scales of likelihood and impact, calculating expected loss, or using other quantitative methods.
- Risk portfolio view: Security risks should be considered alongside other enterprise risks to enable appropriate prioritization. A moderate security risk might warrant more attention than a low financial risk, or vice versa, depending on the organization's risk appetite and context.
- Risk tolerance and acceptance processes: Decisions about accepting security risks should follow the same governance process as other risk acceptance decisions, with appropriate escalation paths based on the potential impact to the organization.

The widespread adoption of centralized GRC programs we explored in Chapter 1 provides the foundation for integrating security risks into ERM and achieving organizational alignment. However, organizations face several challenges when applying ERM principles to security:

- Quantification difficulties: Security risks can be difficult to quantify because of limited historical data and the evolving nature of threats. Organizations may need to rely on industry benchmarks, scenario analysis, and expert judgment to estimate potential impacts.
- Technical complexity: Security vulnerabilities often involve complex technical details that may be difficult to translate into business terms without oversimplification. Risk managers need to balance accuracy with clarity.
- Dynamic threat landscape: The rapidly changing market economics and actor incentives for security threats makes it challenging to maintain up-to-date risk assessments. ERM processes designed for more stable risk environments may need to be adapted for the dynamic security context.
- Compliance vs. risk management tension: Organizations may focus on meeting compliance requirements rather than managing actual security risks. Effective integration requires balancing compliance activities with risk-based security programs.

Despite these challenges, the benefits of applying ERM principles to security contexts are substantial. Organizations that successfully integrate security into their ERM processes can make more informed decisions about resource allocation, risk acceptance, and control implementation.

4.6.3 ERM maturity and security risk management

Organizations typically progress through several stages of maturity as they integrate security risk management into their ERM processes. Understanding these stages can help organizations assess their current state and identify opportunities for improvement. As we saw in Chapter 1, evidence increasingly shows that organizations integrating cybersecurity into broader business risk frameworks achieve better outcomes – experiencing fewer breaches and responding more effectively when incidents occur.

Stage 1: Siloed Risk Management – At this initial stage, security risks are managed separately from other enterprise risks. The security team identifies and addresses technical vulnerabilities with limited connection to business impacts. Risk reporting focuses on technical metrics like vulnerability counts or patch status rather than business risk indicators. Communication between security and business units is limited, and security investments are not clearly tied to risk reduction.

Stage 2: Coordinated Risk Management – As organizations mature, they begin to coordinate security risk management with enterprise risk processes. Security risks are documented using similar formats and terminology as other risk domains, allowing for limited comparison and prioritization. Security teams start translating technical issues into business impact terms, and some governance mechanisms emerge to coordinate risk management activities across domains.

Stage 3: Integrated Risk Management – At this advanced stage, security risks are fully integrated into ERM processes. The organization maintains a comprehensive risk portfolio that includes security alongside other risk domains. Risk assessment methodologies are consistent across domains, enabling meaningful comparison and prioritization. Security investments are evaluated based on risk reduction potential, and risk acceptance decisions consider the organization's overall risk appetite.

Stage 4: Strategic Risk Management – The most mature organizations view security risk management as a strategic function that supports business objectives. Security risks are considered during strategy development and major business decisions. The organization maintains a dynamic understanding of its risk profile and adjusts its controls in response to changing business priorities and threat landscapes. Security investments are optimized based on their contribution to enterprise risk reduction.

Integrated versus siloed approaches to security risk management have distinct characteristics:

Siloed Approach:

- Security team operates independently from enterprise risk function
- Different methodologies for assessing security vs. other risks
- Security metrics focus on technical rather than business impacts
- Security investments evaluated separately from other risk investments
- Limited executive visibility into security risks

Integrated Approach:

- Security team collaborates closely with enterprise risk function
- Consistent methodology for assessing all risks
- Security metrics linked to business impacts and objectives
- Security investments evaluated alongside other risk investments
- Regular executive reporting on security risks in business terms

To assess your organization's maturity in ERM-security integration, consider the following questions:

1. Do security risks appear in your enterprise risk register alongside other risk domains?
2. Are security risks assessed using the same methodology as other enterprise risks?
3. Does your risk acceptance process apply consistently across security and other risk domains?
4. Do security risk reports include business impact assessments?
5. Are security investments prioritized based on risk reduction potential?
6. Do business leaders understand the security risks relevant to their areas?
7. Is security risk considered during strategic planning and major business decisions?

Organizations that answer "yes" to most of these questions likely have achieved at least Stage 3 maturity, while those with few positive answers may be at earlier stages in their maturity journey.

To improve framework integration, organizations should identify key opportunities such as:

- Aligning security risk assessment terminology with enterprise risk language
- Incorporating security risks into the enterprise risk register
- Including security representation in enterprise risk committees
- Developing consistent risk quantification approaches across domains
- Creating integrated risk reporting for executive leadership
- Establishing clear escalation paths for security risks that exceed tolerance levels

By advancing through these maturity stages, organizations can better manage security risks within their ERM framework, leading to more effective risk-based decision making.

The maturity model presented here can help organizations assess their current integration level, a critical first step in the implementation roadmap we'll explore in Chapter 10.

While ERM frameworks provide the conceptual foundation for integrating security risks, organizations need practical tools to operationalize this integration. Risk registers emerge as the primary mechanism for translating framework concepts into day-to-day risk management activities, creating a structured approach for documenting and tracking security risks alongside other enterprise risks.

CFO'S PERSPECTIVE: CONNECTING SECURITY TO FINANCIAL RISK

CFO's reviewing these frameworks will want to understand how they help:

Quantify Security Investments: COSO's alignment with strategy helps justify security spending based on business value protection rather than technical features.

Integrate with Existing Financial Controls: ISO 31000's process orientation aligns with how we already manage financial risks, allowing consistent treatment of security risks alongside financial ones.

Connect to Disclosure Requirements: These frameworks help identify which security risks rise to the level of materiality requiring financial disclosures or reserves.

Make Resource Allocation Decisions: By understanding where security fits in with our overall risk landscape, I can better balance limited resources across competing priorities.

Support Business Decisions: Security risk quantification using these frameworks transforms technical requests into business cases I can evaluate using familiar financial metrics (ROI, NPV, etc.).

The key value for financial executives is that these frameworks create a common language between security and finance teams, replacing technical jargon with business impact discussions that directly connect to financial performance and risk management.

Downloadable Resource: Security-ERM Integration Maturity Assessment Framework

4.7 IMPLEMENTING RISK REGISTERS FOR SECURITY INTEGRATION

Risk registers serve as the operational bridge between security assessments and ERM processes. These structured repositories enable organizations to document security risks alongside other business risks, creating consistency in how risks are identified, assessed, and prioritized across the enterprise. When properly implemented, risk registers transform technical security findings into business risk language that executives can understand and act upon, ensuring security considerations receive appropriate attention in resource allocation decisions.

4.7.1 Understanding risk registers and their purpose

Risk registers serve as a central repository for documenting and tracking risks across an organization. They provide a structured format for recording risk information, facilitating analysis, supporting decision-making, and enabling ongoing monitoring. For security risks, a well-maintained risk register creates visibility and ensures these risks are considered alongside other enterprise risks.

Effective risk registers typically include several key components:

Risk identification: A clear description of each risk, including its causes and potential consequences. For security risks, this might include the threat source, vulnerability, and potential business impact.

Risk assessment: An evaluation of the likelihood and impact of each risk, often using consistent rating scales. This may include both inherent risk (before controls) and residual risk (after controls are applied).

Risk ownership: Identification of the individual or role responsible for managing each risk, ensuring clear accountability for risk treatment and monitoring.

Risk response: Documentation of how the organization plans to address each risk, whether through acceptance, avoidance, transfer, or mitigation. For security risks, this includes specific controls implemented to reduce risk.

Risk monitoring: Information about how each risk will be monitored over time, including Key Risk Indicators, review schedules, and escalation triggers.

Risk registers support decision-making processes in several ways. They:

- provide a comprehensive view of the organization's risk landscape, enabling leaders to understand the full range of risks they face across different domains

- facilitate prioritization by presenting risks in a consistent format, allowing decision-makers to focus on the most significant issues
- create transparency around risk management activities, ensuring that risk treatment decisions are visible to appropriate stakeholders

From the 2025 IT Risk and Compliance Benchmark Report (Hyperproof, 2025): "The majority of respondents (64%) use dedicated risk management software, and 72% of organizations use software that monitors their security controls and provides compliance posture reporting." This adoption of risk management software supports the operationalization and integration of cybersecurity risks into enterprise risk registers, ensuring that risk decisions are documented and managed consistently.

For security integration specifically, risk registers serve as a bridge between technical security assessments and ERM. They help translate technical vulnerabilities into business risks, document the business impact of security issues, and ensure security considerations are visible to enterprise risk committees and executive leadership. This relationship is shown in Figure 4.1.

A well-implemented risk register becomes the single source of truth for risk information, reducing duplication of effort and preventing risks from "falling through the cracks" between different management systems. It also creates a historical record of risk management activities, enabling organizations to learn from experience and demonstrate due diligence to regulators and other stakeholders.

Risk registers build directly on the Business Impact Analysis methodology we explored in Chapter 3, creating a documentation system that captures both technical findings and their business implications.

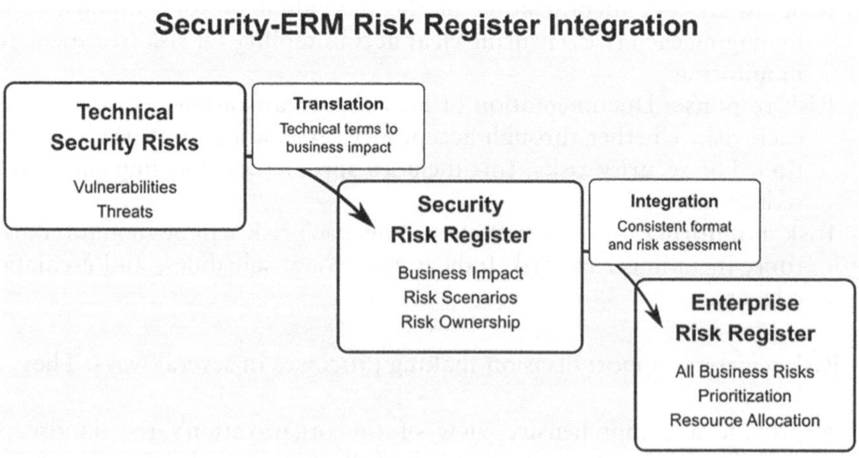

Figure 4.1 Security-ERM risk register integration.

4.7.2 Creating integrated security risk registers

Creating an integrated security risk register begins with developing security risk scenarios that connect technical vulnerabilities to business contexts. These scenarios should describe how a security event could impact business objectives, helping translate technical concerns into terms that business leaders understand.

Effective security risk scenarios include four key elements:

1. **Asset identification:** What business asset or process is at risk? This might include systems, data, intellectual property, or business operations.
2. **Threat description:** What could cause harm to the asset or process? This includes both intentional threats (like malicious attackers) and unintentional threats (like employee errors or system failures).
3. **Vulnerability or condition:** What weakness or gap might allow the threat to materialize? This could be a technical vulnerability, a process gap, or an absence of controls.
4. **Business impact:** What would be the consequence to the business if the risk materializes? This should focus on business impacts like monetary loss, operational disruption, regulatory penalties, or reputation damage.

For example, rather than simply listing "SQL injection vulnerability in customer portal" as a risk, an effective scenario might be: "External attackers could exploit SQL injection vulnerabilities in our customer portal to access sensitive customer data, potentially resulting in regulatory fines, remediation costs, and reputation damage estimated at $2-4 million."

When documenting security risks, it's important to address both threat likelihood and business impact. Likelihood assessment may consider factors such as:

- Historical data on similar events (internal or external)
- Threat intelligence about active attack patterns
- Presence and strength of existing controls
- Exposure of vulnerable systems
- Attractiveness of the target to potential attackers

Business impact assessment should consider both direct and indirect consequences:

- Direct financial costs (remediation, legal fees, regulatory fines)
- Operational impacts (downtime, productivity loss)
- Customer impacts (service disruption, privacy violations)
- Reputational damage (loss of customer trust, brand impact)
- Strategic impacts (competitive disadvantage, delayed initiatives)

Connecting security controls to risk responses is another important aspect of integrated risk registers. For each identified risk, the register should document specific controls implemented to address the risk, along with an assessment of control effectiveness. This creates transparency around how security investments contribute to risk reduction and helps identify potential gaps in control coverage.

Organizations may adopt either quantitative or qualitative approaches for security risk assessment, each with distinct advantages and challenges:

- Qualitative approaches use descriptive categories or rating scales to assess likelihood and impact. For example, risks might be rated on a scale from "very low" to "very high" based on defined criteria. Qualitative assessments are relatively straightforward to implement but may lack precision and comparability across different risk domains.
- Quantitative approaches assign numerical values to likelihood and impact, often using techniques like expected loss calculation or Monte Carlo simulation. For example, an organization might estimate the annual loss expectancy for each risk based on its probability and potential financial impact. Quantitative assessments provide more precise inputs for decision-making but require more data and analytical capabilities.

Many organizations adopt a hybrid approach, using qualitative assessments for initial risk screening and quantitative methods for high-priority risks that warrant deeper analysis. The key is ensuring consistency in how security risks are assessed compared to other enterprise risks, enabling meaningful comparison and prioritization.

4.7.3 Maintaining risk registers across the organization

Maintaining effective risk registers requires established processes for regular review and updates. Organizations need to define clear review cycles that ensure risk information remains current without creating excessive administrative burden.

Typical review cycles include:

- Quarterly reviews of high-priority risks to assess changes in likelihood, impact, or control effectiveness
- Annual comprehensive reviews of the entire risk register to validate existing entries and identify additional risks
- Event-triggered reviews when significant changes occur, such as new business initiatives, system changes, or emerging threats
- Post-incident reviews to incorporate lessons learned from security incidents or near-misses

In addition to these scheduled reviews, organizations need processes for updating risk registers when additional risks are identified or existing risks change. This includes clear procedures for risk entry, approval workflows for risk updates, and notification mechanisms to alert stakeholders when significant changes occur.

Tools and technologies can significantly enhance risk register management. These include:

- Dedicated GRC platforms that provide structured repositories for risk information, workflow automation, and reporting capabilities
- Integration with security tools to automatically update risk information based on vulnerability scans, threat intelligence, or incident data
- Dashboards and visualization tools that present risk information in formats tailored to different stakeholders
- Collaboration features that facilitate input from various stakeholders across the organization

Prioritizing risks across domains is a key challenge in integrated risk management. Organizations need methods for comparing risks from different areas using consistent criteria. Some approaches include:

- Risk scoring frameworks that apply consistent rating scales across all risk domains
- Financial impact modeling to express different risks in common monetary terms
- Multi-criteria analysis that considers various impact dimensions (financial, operational, reputational) with appropriate weightings
- Risk appetite alignment to prioritize risks based on their relationship to established tolerance levels

To illustrate these concepts, consider creating a sample integrated risk register entry:

- Risk ID: SEC-2025-034 Risk Description: Insufficient authentication controls on customer data management system could allow unauthorized access to sensitive customer information, potentially resulting in data breach affecting up to 50,000 records.
- Risk Category: Information Security
- Risk Owner: Director of Application Security Inherent Risk Assessment:
- Likelihood: Medium (3/5) – Based on threat intelligence indicating increased targeting of similar systems
- Impact: High (4/5) – Potential financial impact of $1.8-2.4 million including notification costs, regulatory fines, and remediation
- Inherent Risk Rating: High (12/25)

- Controls:
  - Multi-factor authentication implementation (in progress)
  - Access review process (implemented)
  - Data encryption (implemented)
  - User activity monitoring (planned)
- Residual Risk Assessment:
  - Likelihood: Low (2/5)
  - Impact: High (4/5)
- Residual Risk Rating: Medium (8/25)
  - Risk Response: Mitigation – Complete multi-factor authentication implementation and user activity monitoring deployment
  - Risk Acceptance: None required at current residual risk level
  - Monitoring Approach: Quarterly review of access logs and security incidents; reassessment upon completion of planned controls

To evaluate current risk documentation and identify integration gaps, organizations should consider:

- Do security risks appear in enterprise risk discussions, or are they confined to technical forums?
- Are security risks documented using the same format and terminology as other enterprise risks?
- Do security risk entries include clear business impact assessments?
- Is there a consistent approach to risk rating across security and other risk domains?
- Are there clear linkages between security controls and risk reduction?
- Do risk registers facilitate appropriate escalation of security concerns to executive leadership?

Addressing gaps in these areas can significantly improve the integration of security risks into enterprise risk processes, ensuring that security considerations are appropriately factored into business decisions.

4.7.4 Quick start guide: implementing a security risk register

Getting started with a security risk register doesn't have to be overwhelming. Follow these five steps to establish an effective foundation:

1. START WITH YOUR CROWN JEWELS
   - Identify 3–5 of your most critical business processes
   - Document the key information assets supporting these processes
   - Focus initial risk identification on these high-value targets
     Quick win: Interview business owners to identify their most significant security concerns

2. **ADOPT A SIMPLE RISK TEMPLATE**
    - Create a standard format with these essential fields:
    - Risk ID and description (in business terms)
    - Business owner and technical owner
    - Inherent risk rating (likelihood × impact)
    - Current controls and their effectiveness
    - Residual risk rating
    - Treatment plan and timeline

    Quick win: Start with a spreadsheet before investing in GRC tools
3. **ESTABLISH CLEAR RATING CRITERIA**
    - Define 3–5 levels for both likelihood and impact
    - For impact, include financial, operational, and reputational dimensions
    - Create a simple risk scoring matrix (3×3 or 5×5)

    Quick win: Use dollar ranges for financial impact to make assessments concrete (e.g., <$100K, $100K–$1M, >$1M)
4. **INTEGRATE WITH EXISTING GOVERNANCE**
    - Identify which committees will review the risk register
    - Establish regular review cycles (monthly for high risks)
    - Define clear escalation thresholds and paths

    Quick win: Add security risks as a standing agenda item to existing risk or governance committees
5. **DEMONSTRATE EARLY VALUE**
    - Translate 2–3 recent security incidents into risk register entries
    - Show how controls would have reduced likelihood or impact
    - Create a simple dashboard for executive visibility

    Quick win: Map existing security projects to specific risks to demonstrate how they reduce business risk

IMPORTANT: The goal of your initial implementation is not comprehensiveness but establishing the integration between security risks and business impacts. Start small, demonstrate value, and expand as the process matures.

Risk registers create a documentation structure for integrated risk management, but their effectiveness depends on organizational structures that support collaboration between security and business teams. The way organizations design governance models, allocate responsibilities, and foster communication determines whether risk registers become valuable management tools or administrative burdens that fail to drive meaningful risk decisions.

4.8 ORGANIZATIONAL STRUCTURES FOR INTEGRATED RISK MANAGEMENT

Integrating security into ERM requires more than frameworks and documentation – it demands organizational structures that support collaboration between security and business teams. The way an organization distributes roles, responsibilities, and decision rights can either enable or hinder effective risk management. Clear governance models, appropriate organizational design, and systematic approaches to breaking down silos create the foundation for security risks to be managed as business risks rather than technical afterthoughts.

4.8.1 Governance models for integrated risk management

Effective governance models provide the foundation for integrated risk management by establishing clear roles, responsibilities, and reporting relationships. These models ensure that security risks are properly overseen and managed within the broader enterprise risk context.

The Three Lines of Defense model as summarized in Figure 4.2, is widely used for risk governance and can be effectively applied to security risk management:

First Line (Operational Management): Business unit leaders who own and manage risks directly. For security, this includes system owners, application developers, and business process owners who implement security controls within their areas of responsibility. The first line makes day-to-day risk decisions and implements controls to mitigate identified risks.

Second Line (Risk Management and Compliance Functions): Specialist functions that provide oversight, expertise, and challenge to the first line. For security, this typically includes the information security team, who establish security policies, provide guidance on control implementation, and monitor compliance with security standards. The second line helps ensure that security risks are properly identified, assessed, and managed.

Third Line (Internal Audit): Independent assurance function that evaluates the effectiveness of risk management, control, and governance

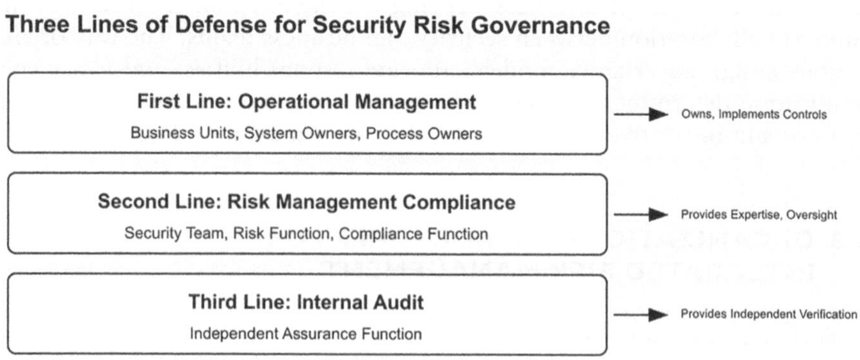

Figure 4.2 Three lines of defense for security risk governance.

processes. Internal audit reviews both first- and second-line activities, providing objective assessment of security control effectiveness and risk management practices. The third line reports directly to the board or audit committee, ensuring independent oversight.

This model clarifies who is responsible for implementing security controls (first line), who provides security expertise and oversight (second line), and who independently validates that controls are working effectively (third line). It helps prevent security from becoming an isolated function and emphasizes that security risk management is a shared responsibility across the organization.

The board and executive committees play important roles in security risk governance. Typical responsibilities include:

Board of Directors: Approves risk appetite statements including security risk tolerance, provides oversight of risk management practices, ensures adequate resources for security risk management, and reviews significant security risks that could impact strategic objectives.

Risk Committee: Reviews enterprise risk profile including security risks, ensures alignment between security risk management and enterprise risk processes, and oversees risk assessment and treatment practices.

Audit Committee: Reviews results of security audits and assessments, ensures appropriate management response to audit findings, and provides independent challenge to security risk management practices.

Executive Leadership Team: Sets tone at the top regarding security risk management, ensures appropriate resources for security programs, and makes decisions about risk acceptance for significant security issues.

In addition to these general governance bodies, many organizations establish security-specific governance structures such as:

Security Steering Committee: Cross-functional body that reviews security risks, approves security policies, and ensures alignment between security initiatives and business objectives.

Security Working Groups: Specialized teams focused on specific security domains (such as application security or third-party risk management) that develop detailed standards and provide domain-specific expertise.

Security Architecture Review Board: Reviews recent technology initiatives to ensure security requirements are addressed during design phases rather than retrofitted later.

The trend toward centralized GRC teams discussed in Chapter 1 reflects this recognition that effective risk management, including cybersecurity, requires cross-functional collaboration and automation, which are key to breaking down silos and integrating security into ERM.

Effective governance models create clear lines of communication between security teams and executive leadership, ensuring that security risks are visible at appropriate levels of the organization. They also establish mechanisms for escalating significant security issues when they exceed defined tolerance levels, ensuring timely response to emerging threats.

Chapter 8 explores how these governance models require supportive cultural elements to function effectively, addressing the human aspects that make these structures successful in practice.

4.8.2 Centralized vs. distributed risk management functions

Organizations must determine whether to centralize security risk management functions or distribute them across business units. Both approaches have advantages and challenges, and many organizations adopt a hybrid model that combines elements of each.

In a centralized model, a single security risk management function provides services across the entire organization. This function typically includes:

- Security risk assessment teams who evaluate risks across different business units
- Policy and standards development groups who establish enterprise-wide security requirements
- Security operations teams who monitor threats and incidents
- Security architecture teams who provide design guidance for new initiatives

Advantages of centralization include:

- Consistency: Security practices are applied uniformly across the organization, reducing variations in risk management approaches.
- Specialized expertise: The centralized function can develop deep expertise in security domains and deploy specialists where needed.
- Efficiency: Resources are pooled, reducing duplication of effort and potentially lowering overall costs.
- Visibility: The centralized function has enterprise-wide visibility into security risks, enabling better correlation and pattern recognition.

Challenges of centralization include:

- Disconnect from business context: Centralized teams may lack detailed understanding of specific business processes and objectives.
- Potential bottlenecks: If all security decisions must flow through the central function, delays may impact business agility.
- Resistance: Business units may view the central security function as a constraint rather than a partner.

In a distributed model, security resources are embedded within business units, with each unit responsible for managing its own security risks. This might include:

- Business unit security officers who manage security within their specific areas
- Embedded security engineers who work directly with development teams
- Local security operations capabilities tailored to specific business requirements

Advantages of distribution include:

- Business alignment: Security resources understand the specific business context and can tailor approaches accordingly.
- Responsiveness: Security teams can quickly respond to local needs without navigating central bureaucracy.
- Ownership: Business units have direct responsibility for security, encouraging better integration into business processes.

Challenges of distribution include:

- Inconsistency: Security practices may vary significantly across different parts of the organization.
- Resource constraints: Smaller business units may lack adequate security resources or expertise.
- Limited visibility: Without central coordination, enterprise-wide security issues may be difficult to identify.

Many organizations adopt matrix structures for complex security risk management. In these models, security professionals have dual reporting relationships – to both the central security function and the business units they support. This approach aims to balance consistency with business alignment.

A typical matrix structure might include:

- Central security team that establishes policies, standards, and overall direction
- Business unit security officers who report to both business leaders and the central security team
- Communities of practice that bring together security professionals from across the organization
- Shared services for common security functions like vulnerability management or security monitoring

4.8.3 Case study: Marriott International – a costly lesson in Enterprise Risk Management during M&A

4.8.3.1 Context

Marriott International stands as one of the largest hotel chains globally, operating more than 7,000 properties throughout the United States and across more than 130 countries. In September 2016, Marriott significantly expanded its global footprint by acquiring Starwood Hotels & Resorts, a move that consolidated brands including Marriott, Courtyard, Ritz-Carlton, Sheraton, Westin, W Hotels, and St. Regis under one corporate umbrella. This acquisition made Marriott the largest hotel chain in the world, accounting for approximately 1 in 15 hotel rooms worldwide.

When guests make reservations at Marriott properties, they provide substantial personal information including names, addresses, email addresses, phone numbers, and payment card information. In some instances, Marriott also collects passport information, room preferences, travel destinations, and other personal data. Both companies maintained privacy statements assuring customers that this sensitive information would be protected.

4.8.3.2 Challenge

What Marriott executives didn't know during the acquisition was that they were purchasing a company with an active, undetected security breach. The breach began in July 2014, approximately two years before Marriott's acquisition of Starwood, and remained undetected until September 2018. This meant that for nearly four years, unauthorized actors had access to Starwood's guest reservation database.

The acquisition process presented Marriott with a critical ERM challenge that was ultimately mishandled. Marriott failed to complete a detailed cybersecurity audit of Starwood's networks and technology during the acquisition process. As a result, Marriott was unable to identify ongoing cybercriminal activity within Starwood's guest reservation system – permitting the attackers to remain undetected throughout the acquisition.

The risk management failures continued after the acquisition was complete. Despite acquiring Starwood in 2016, the Starwood brands were still using legacy IT infrastructure in 2018, two years after the acquisition. Rather than adopt uniform networks and technology following the acquisition, Marriott allowed Starwood properties to move forward with their current operations – utilizing a compromised guest reservation system.

4.8.3.3 Approach

On September 8, 2018, Marriott finally discovered the breach when an internal security tool flagged a suspicious attempt to access the internal guest reservation database for Marriott's Starwood brands. The security tool was monitored by Accenture, which had been running IT and information security for Starwood before the merger and continued to do so for the legacy network afterwards.

Upon discovery, Marriott launched an investigation that revealed a Remote Access Trojan (RAT) along with MimiKatz, a tool for sniffing out username/password combinations in system memory. Together, these two tools could have given the attackers control of administrator accounts.

In September 2018 – a full two years after the acquisition – Marriott finally identified the breach due to a system security alert. Upon this discovery, Marriott reported the incident to law enforcement officials and consulted forensic specialists to launch an investigation.

However, Marriott waited more than two months to notify guests, with the public announcement coming on November 30, 2018.

4.8.3.4 Outcome

The breach had massive implications for Marriott and its customers. Marriott disclosed that the breach impacted at least 383 million guest records, including nearly 24 million passport numbers and more than 9 million credit and debit cards.

The stolen information included names, addresses, phone numbers, email addresses, passport numbers, Starwood Preferred Guest account information, dates of birth, gender, arrival and departure information, reservation dates, communication preferences, payment card numbers, payment card expiration dates, and tools needed to decrypt cardholder data.

The financial and legal repercussions were substantial:

- Marriott agreed to pay $52 million to resolve state and federal claims related to the breaches (In Re: Marriott Interntional, Inc., Customer Data Security Breach Litigation, 2019)
- Marriott incurred nearly $30 million in overall recovery expenses. This total includes costs related to investigating the cause of the breach, notifying impacted customers, providing these customers with year-long access to security monitoring software, developing an international call center related to the breach, and implementing updated cybersecurity measures to prevent future incidents.
- In July 2019, the UK's Information Commissioner's Office (ICO) levied a fine of £99 million – more than $120 million – for violating British citizens' privacy rights under the GDPR.

Between direct costs and indirect losses caused by customers shying away from the company in the future, Marriott could ultimately see billions of dollars in lost revenue because of the breach.

Legal proceedings extended for years. Multiple class action lawsuits were consolidated into multidistrict litigation in the U.S. District Court for the District of Maryland. Judge Paul W. Grimm granted certification to eight classes on May 3, 2022, spanning six states with an estimated 47.7 million exposed customer records.

The breach was also significant from a national security perspective. The FBI led the investigation of the data theft, and investigators suspected the hackers were working on behalf of the Chinese Ministry of State Security. Government sources speculate that it was part of a broader Chinese effort to acquire massive amounts of data on American government employees and intelligence officers, as Marriott is the top hotel provider for the U.S. government and military.

4.8.3.5 Lessons

The Marriott breach offers several key lessons about integrating security into ERM, particularly during mergers and acquisitions:

1. **Inadequate due diligence creates significant enterprise risk**
   The breach highlights the critical importance of cybersecurity due diligence during mergers and acquisitions. Companies involved in M&A activities should be carefully evaluated for potential cybersecurity gaps. A proper plan for rectifying or – at the very least – mitigating these exposures should be developed prior to the finalization of the M&A event.
2. **Integration delays compound security risks**
   In many cases, it can be advantageous for merged companies to adopt shared digital processes and security policies to maintain uniform defense strategies against cybercriminals. The two-year delay in integrating Starwood's systems allowed the breach to continue undetected.
3. **Enterprise Risk Management requires cross-functional governance**
   The case demonstrates how security risks can't be managed in isolation. The acquisition process typically involves finance, legal, and operations teams, but security considerations must be integrated into this broader ERM approach. The breach emphasizes that cybersecurity must be a top priority during any M&A activity, which requires governance structures that support integrated risk management.
4. **Clear risk ownership and accountability are essential**
   As the Court of Appeals noted in addressing the breach: "The evolution of the economic loss doctrine shows that the doctrine is applicable to the service industry only where the duty of the party performing the service is defined by the contract that he executes with his client. Where a duty arises outside of the contract, the economic loss doctrine does not prohibit recovery in tort for the negligent breach of that duty."

This legal principle underscores the importance of establishing clear risk ownership and accountability across organizational silos. In the Marriott case, the distributed responsibility between Marriott, Starwood, and Accenture (the IT services provider) created gaps in risk management.

5. **Security risks translate to significant business impacts**

   The significant legal and financial consequences of data security failures show why security risks must be integrated into enterprise risk registers. These are not merely technical issues but business risks with measurable impacts on the organization's financial performance, regulatory compliance, reputation, and strategic objectives.

The Marriott breach demonstrates how security failures stemming from poor risk management can generate hundreds of millions of dollars in direct costs and potentially billions in long-term business impact. By integrating security risks into ERM frameworks, organizations can better identify, assess, and mitigate these risks before they lead to costly incidents.

When designing an organizational structure for security risk management, organizations should consider:

- The organization's overall operating model (centralized, federated, or decentralized)
- The diversity of business operations and their specific security requirements
- The maturity of existing security and risk management capabilities
- Available security talent and expertise
- Regulatory requirements that may influence organizational design

The chosen structure should balance the need for enterprise-wide consistency with the flexibility to address unique business requirements.

4.8.4 Breaking down organizational silos

Organizational silos between security and business units can significantly hinder effective risk management. Breaking down these silos requires establishing communication channels, implementing joint risk assessment methodologies, and developing shared metrics and reporting structures.

Effective communication channels between security and business units include:

- Business relationship managers: Security professionals dedicated to specific business units who serve as liaisons between security and business teams. These individuals develop a deep understanding of business operations and translate security requirements into business terms.

- Regular risk review meetings: Structured forums where security and business leaders jointly review risks, discuss emerging issues, and align on risk treatment approaches. These meetings create a cadence for ongoing communication and collaboration.
- Security champions programs: Networks of security-savvy individuals embedded within business teams who advocate for security considerations and facilitate communication with the security function. These champions receive additional security training and serve as local resources for their teams.
- Executive briefings: Targeted communications to executive leadership that frame security risks in business terms, focusing on strategic implications rather than technical details. These briefings help ensure executive awareness without overwhelming leaders with technical information.

Joint risk assessment methodologies help integrate security considerations into business decision-making. Approaches include:

- Business Impact Analysis: Collaborative assessments that identify critical business processes and the potential impact of disruptions, including those caused by security incidents. These assessments help prioritize security investments based on business criticality.
- Security risk workshops: Facilitated sessions where security and business teams jointly identify and assess security risks relevant to specific business activities. These workshops leverage business expertise on potential impacts and security expertise on threats and vulnerabilities.
- Security requirements in project methodologies: Integration of security risk assessment into project approval processes, ensuring security considerations are addressed during planning rather than retrofitted later. This might include security stages in stage-gate processes or security checkpoints in agile methodologies.
- Third-party risk assessments: Collaborative evaluations of security risks associated with vendors, partners, and other third parties, considering both security and business perspectives. These assessments help ensure that third-party relationships don't introduce unacceptable security risks.

Shared metrics and reporting structures create a common language for discussing security risks. Effective approaches include:

- Business-aligned security metrics: Security measurements that relate to business objectives, such as availability of critical services, protection of sensitive data, or resilience of key processes. These metrics help business leaders understand security in terms relevant to their goals.
- Integrated risk dashboards: Reporting tools that present security risks alongside other business risks, enabling leaders to see the full risk

landscape. These dashboards typically include trend data, emerging issues, and status of risk treatment activities.
- Executive-level risk reporting: Concise summaries of security risks that focus on business implications rather than technical details. These reports highlight key risks, their potential impacts, and recommended actions in business terms.
- Shared Key Risk Indicators: Metrics that serve as early warning signs for both security and business teams, triggering collaborative responses when thresholds are exceeded. These indicators help ensure timely attention to emerging risks.

To map current organizational risk relationships, consider conducting an exercise that:

- Identifies all stakeholders involved in security risk decisions
- Documents current communication patterns and decision rights
- Highlights gaps in collaboration or awareness
- Identifies opportunities for improved integration

This mapping exercise can reveal where silos exist and guide efforts to break them down through improved communication, joint methodologies, and shared metrics.

When designing an integrated risk governance structure, organizations should consider:

- Creating clear escalation paths for security issues that exceed defined tolerance levels
- Establishing joint ownership of security risks between security and business teams
- Ensuring security representation in enterprise risk committees
- Developing integrated reporting that presents security alongside other risk domains
- Implementing cross-functional teams for addressing complex security risks

By breaking down organizational silos, organizations can ensure that security risks are managed collaboratively by security and business teams, leading to more effective risk management and better business outcomes.

Chapter 7 expands on these organizational concepts with detailed governance models, reporting relationships, and committee structures that support integrated security risk management. And Chapter 8 expands on these concepts by addressing the cultural aspects of breaking down silos, providing frameworks for building cross-functional collaboration and shared risk ownership.

Organizational structures provide the framework for collaboration, but effective risk management requires clear ownership and accountability for specific risks. Even the best governance models can fail if stakeholders remain unclear about who makes decisions, who bears responsibility for outcomes, and how performance is measured and reported across the organization.

Downloadable Resource: Cross-Functional Risk Assessment Workshop

4.9 ESTABLISHING RISK OWNERSHIP AND ACCOUNTABILITY

Without explicit ownership, security risks may go unaddressed as stakeholders assume someone else bears responsibility for managing them. Clear risk ownership models ensure that individuals with appropriate business context and decision-making authority take accountability for security risks that could impact their operations. Formal processes for risk acceptance, escalation, and performance measurement create the accountability mechanisms necessary to sustain effective security risk management over time.

4.9.1 Defining risk ownership models

Clear risk ownership is foundational to effective security risk management. Without explicit ownership, risks may go unaddressed as everyone assumes someone else is responsible. Different ownership models exist, each with distinct implications for how security risks are managed. These are models and their pros and cons are summarized in Figure 4.3.

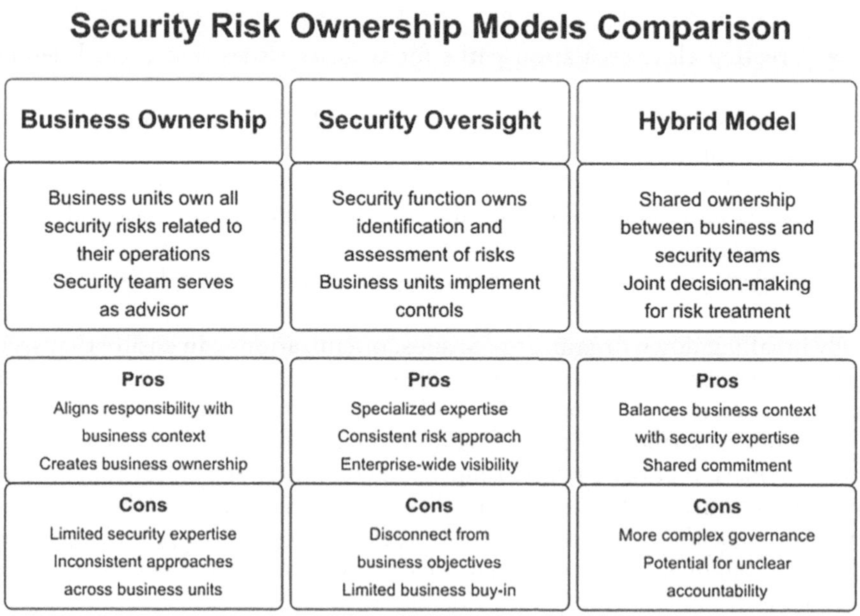

Figure 4.3 Security risk ownership models comparison.

In a business ownership model, business unit leaders own the risks associated with their operations, including security risks. They are responsible for:

- Identifying security risks that could impact their business objectives
- Determining appropriate risk responses based on business context
- Allocating resources for security controls within their areas
- Accepting residual risks that cannot be fully mitigated

Under this model, the security function serves as an advisor, providing expertise, guidance, and support to business owners as they manage their security risks. Business ownership aligns responsibility with authority, as those who make business decisions also own the associated security risks.

In a security oversight model, the security function owns the identification and assessment of security risks across the organization. They are responsible for:

- Conducting security risk assessments across business units
- Recommending appropriate security controls and mitigations
- Monitoring compliance with security requirements
- Escalating significant risks to executive leadership

Under this model, business units implement security controls based on guidance from the security function but may not directly own the underlying risks. Security oversight creates specialized expertise for risk assessment but may distance risk ownership from business decision-making.

Most organizations implement a hybrid model where ownership is shared between business and security teams:

- Business units own the business risks associated with their operations
- Security teams own the identification and assessment of security risks
- Joint decision-making occurs for risk treatment and acceptance
- Executive leadership provides the ultimate oversight of significant risks

This hybrid approach balances business context with security expertise, ensuring that both perspectives inform risk management decisions.

Clearly defined roles are essential for effective risk management. Key roles include:

- Risk Owners: Typically, business unit leaders who have ultimate accountability for managing specific risks. They make decisions about risk treatment and acceptance based on business context and risk tolerance.

- Control Owners: Individuals responsible for implementing and maintaining specific security controls. They ensure controls operate effectively and report on control performance to risk owners.
- Risk Managers: Security professionals who facilitate the risk management process. They conduct assessments, provide expertise, and support risk owners in making informed decisions.
- Executive Sponsors: Senior leaders who provide oversight into significant risks. They ensure adequate resources for risk management and make decisions about enterprise-level risk acceptance.

Accountability mechanisms ensure that risk owners fulfill their responsibilities. These mechanisms might include:

- Regular risk review meetings where owners report on risk status
- Performance metrics tied to effective risk management
- Internal audit reviews of risk ownership implementation
- Executive oversight of significant risk decisions

Escalation paths define how security risks that exceed tolerance levels are elevated to appropriate decision-makers. A typical escalation path might include:

1. Initial risk identification by business or security teams
2. Assessment and documentation in the risk register
3. Review by the risk owner and determination of response
4. Escalation to security leadership for risks exceeding defined thresholds
5. Further escalation to executive committee for enterprise-significant risks
6. Board notification for risks with potential strategic impact

Decision rights frameworks clarify who has the authority to make different types of risk decisions. For example:

- Business unit leaders may accept risks within defined tolerance levels for their areas
- The CISO may approve exceptions to security policies for limited periods
- The executive risk committee must approve acceptance of risks exceeding defined thresholds
- The board must be informed of risks with potential material impact to the organization

These frameworks ensure that risk decisions are made at appropriate levels based on potential business impact, creating consistency and accountability across the organization.

Chapter 7 expands on these ownership concepts with comprehensive decision authority frameworks that clarify who has responsibility for different types of security decisions. These ownership models also require corresponding cultural changes to succeed, a topic we'll explore in depth in Chapter 8's discussion of implementing shared risk ownership across the organization.

4.9.2 Risk acceptance and exception processes

Formal risk acceptance procedures establish a structured approach for documenting and approving security risks that cannot be fully mitigated. These documented procedures ensure that risk acceptance decisions are made consciously, with full understanding of potential consequences and appropriate approval from authorized stakeholders. An overview of this framework is seen in Figure 4.4.

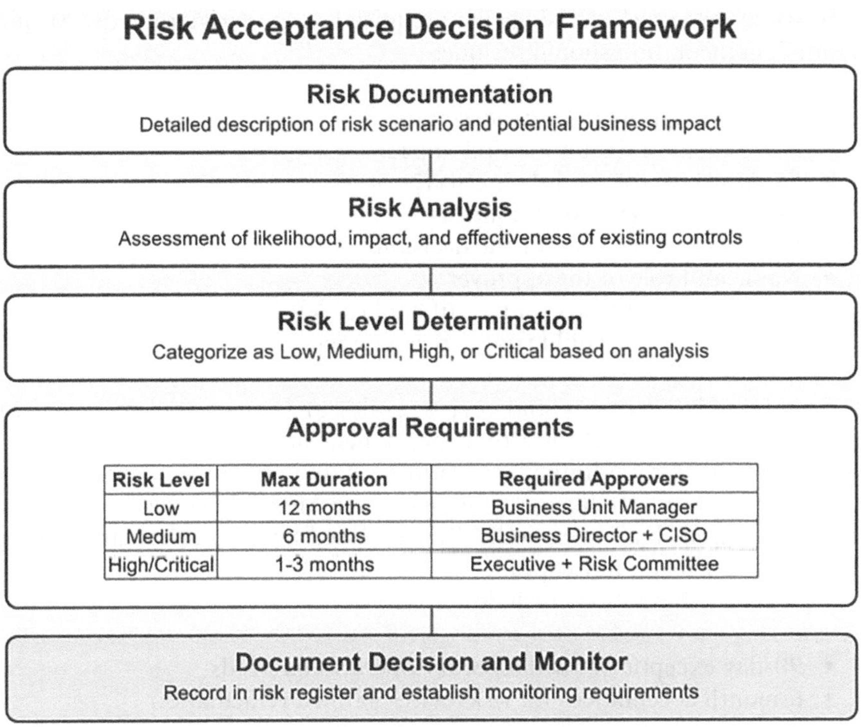

Figure 4.4 Risk acceptance decision framework.

An effective risk acceptance process typically includes:

- Risk documentation: Detailed description of the risk, including the threat scenario, vulnerable conditions, and potential business impacts. This documentation ensures decision-makers understand what they are accepting.
- Risk analysis: Assessment of likelihood and impact, often including both qualitative ratings and quantitative estimates where possible. This analysis helps decision-makers understand the magnitude of the risk.
- Control assessment: Description of existing controls and their effectiveness in mitigating the risk. This assessment clarifies what protections are already in place.
- Acceptance rationale: Business justification for accepting the risk rather than implementing additional controls. This rationale explains why acceptance is the appropriate response.
- Approval requirements: Specification of who must approve the risk acceptance based on the risk level. Higher-risk acceptances typically require more senior approval.

Documentation requirements for risk decisions should be proportionate to the level of risk. Critical risk acceptances warrant comprehensive documentation, while lower-risk decisions may require less extensive records. At minimum, documentation should include:

- Risk description and categorization
- Assessment of likelihood and impact
- Existing controls and their effectiveness
- Residual risk level after controls
- Business justification for the decision
- Name and role of the approver
- Time limit for the acceptance (if applicable)
- Conditions that would trigger reassessment

Time-bound exceptions and review cycles are essential elements of risk acceptance processes. Rather than permanent acceptance, many organizations implement time-limited exceptions with mandatory review requirements. This approach ensures that risk acceptances don't become "set and forget" decisions but are periodically reassessed based on changing business contexts and threat landscapes.

Typical time limitations include:

- 90-day exceptions for temporary operational needs
- 6-month acceptances for risks with planned remediation
- Annual review requirements for ongoing acceptances
- Automatic expiration unless explicitly renewed

Conditions that might trigger reassessment before the scheduled review include:

- Changes to the system or process affected by the risk
- New threats or vulnerabilities relevant to the risk
- Incidents or near-misses related to the risk
- Changes in regulatory requirements or business priorities

Escalation paths for unresolved risks ensure issues don't remain in limbo when agreement cannot be reached at lower levels. A typical escalation process might include:

1. Initial discussion between security team and business unit
2. Formal review by security leadership and business unit leadership
3. Escalation to cross-functional risk committee if not resolved
4. Executive decision if committee cannot reach consensus
5. Board notification for risks with potential material impact

These escalation paths prevent security risks from being ignored because of disagreements about ownership or treatment, ensuring that appropriate attention is given to significant issues.

Downloadable Resource: Risk Acceptance Decision Framework

4.9.3 Measuring and reporting on risk management performance

Measuring the performance of integrated risk management helps organizations understand whether their approach is effective and identify opportunities for improvement. Key performance indicators for integrated risk management may include:

Process metrics that measure the efficiency and completeness of risk management activities:

- Percentage of systems with completed security risk assessments
- Average time to address identified high-priority risks
- Rate of risk register updates and reviews
- Compliance with risk acceptance procedures

Outcome metrics that measure the effectiveness of risk management in preventing security incidents:

- Number and severity of security incidents
- Financial impact of security events
- Downtime or disruption caused by security issues
- Regulatory findings related to security controls

Integration metrics that measure how well security is embedded in enterprise risk processes:

- Percentage of enterprise risks with security considerations
- Security representation in enterprise risk committees
- Business unit engagement in security risk assessments
- Alignment between security and business risk priorities

Executive dashboards and reporting structures should present security risk information in business terms, focusing on the implications for organizational objectives rather than technical details. Effective dashboards typically include:

- Summary of current risk profile with trend information
- Status of high-priority risk treatment activities
- Key Risk Indicators with thresholds and alerts
- Recent and upcoming risk assessment activities
- Significant risk acceptance decisions

Different stakeholders require distinct levels of detail in risk reporting:

- Board members need strategic-level information focused on material risks
- Executive leaders need business impact information and resource implications
- Business unit leaders need risk information specific to their areas
- Operational teams need detailed information about control implementation

Organizations often face resistance to changes in risk ownership, particularly when moving from a security-owned to a business-owned model. Common sources of resistance include:

- Lack of security expertise within business units
- Concern about additional responsibilities without added resources
- Uncertainty about accountability for security incidents
- Preference for delegating "technical" issues to security teams

Addressing this resistance requires a thoughtful change management approach:

- Providing security training and support for business owners
- Gradually transitioning ownership with appropriate support
- Celebrating early successes and sharing best practices
- Ensuring executive sponsorship for the ownership model

A RACI matrix (Responsible, Accountable, Consulted, Informed) can clarify roles for key risk scenarios. For example, for a scenario involving a vulnerable customer-facing application:

- Business Application Owner: Accountable for risk decision, responsible for implementing controls
- Security Team: Responsible for risk assessment, consulted on control selection
- IT Operations: Responsible for implementing technical controls, consulted on risk assessment
- Legal/Compliance: Consulted on regulatory implications, informed of risk decisions
- Executive Leadership: Informed of high-impact risks, consulted on risk acceptance above thresholds

This matrix clarifies who makes decisions, who does the work, who provides input, and who needs to be kept informed, reducing confusion and ensuring appropriate involvement from all stakeholders.

To establish clear risk ownership for top security risks, organizations should:

- Identify their most significant security risks based on potential business impact
- Determine the appropriate business owner for each risk based on affected processes
- Document ownership in the risk register with explicit accountabilities
- Establish regular review processes to ensure owners are fulfilling responsibilities
- Provide support from security teams to help owners understand and manage their risks

Clear risk ownership ensures that security risks are managed by those with the appropriate context and authority, leading to more effective risk-based decision making.

These accountability models form the foundation for the decision authority frameworks we'll explore in Chapter 7, where we provide detailed guidance for establishing who makes different types of security risk decisions.

4.10 CONCLUSION

Integrating security into ERM represents a fundamental shift in how organizations approach security risks. Rather than treating these risks as technical issues managed in isolation, integration embeds security considerations into the organization's broader approach to managing risk across all domains.

This approach ensures security investments align with business priorities, risk acceptance decisions consider broader enterprise context, and security risks receive appropriate visibility at executive levels.

The key to successful integration lies in leveraging established ERM frameworks and adapting them to security. Organizations must develop risk registers that document security risks alongside other enterprise risks, using consistent methodologies for assessment and prioritization. Appropriate organizational structures provide the foundation for integration, clarifying roles and responsibilities while breaking down silos between security and business teams. Clear risk ownership ensures accountability for security risk management, with formal processes for risk acceptance and escalation.

Organizations commonly face resistance when integrating security into ERM. Business leaders may view security as a technical discipline rather than a business concern, while security teams may resist sharing ownership of security risks. Overcoming this resistance requires education, communication, and a clear vision of how integration benefits the entire organization. Executive sponsorship is essential, demonstrating leadership commitment to integrated risk management.

Integration is not a one-time project but an ongoing journey that evolves as the organization's risk landscape changes. Maturity models provide a roadmap for this journey, helping organizations progress from siloed approaches toward truly integrated security risk management. This progression requires sustained effort, cultural change, and continuous improvement in risk management practices.

By integrating security into ERM, organizations can make more informed decisions about security investments, risk acceptance, and control implementation. They can ensure security considerations are factored into strategic planning and business decisions, reducing the likelihood and impact of security incidents. Perhaps most importantly, they can move beyond compliance-driven approaches to true risk management that supports business objectives.

In the next chapter, we will explore how to build effective business cases for security investments, leveraging the integrated risk management approach described here to demonstrate value and secure necessary resources. By framing security investments in terms of risk reduction and business impact, security leaders can more effectively compete for limited resources and demonstrate their contribution to organizational success.

4.11 ACTION ITEMS FOR READERS

1. Assess your organization's current ERM-security integration maturity by reviewing whether security risks appear in enterprise risk discussions, use consistent terminology with other risk domains, and receive appropriate executive visibility alongside business risks.

2. Create an integrated security risk register starting with 3–5 critical business processes, documenting risks using business impact scenarios that connect technical vulnerabilities to financial, operational, and reputational consequences.
3. Conduct a stakeholder mapping exercise to identify all parties involved in security risk decisions, document current communication patterns, and highlight gaps in collaboration between security and business teams.
4. Establish clear risk ownership assignments for your top 10 security risks by identifying the appropriate business owners, documenting their accountabilities in writing, and creating escalation paths for risks exceeding defined tolerance levels.
5. Develop executive-level security risk reporting that presents security risks in business terms alongside other enterprise risks, focusing on strategic implications rather than technical details, with regular review cycles that ensure ongoing stakeholder engagement.

Chapter 5

Building the business case for security investments

Chapter in One Sentence: Successful security investment proposals translate technical requirements into business-aligned value propositions that demonstrate how security enables strategic objectives, quantify financial benefits, and position security as a competitive advantage rather than just a necessary cost.

5.1 EXECUTIVE SUMMARY

This chapter addresses the fundamental challenge security leaders face: translating technical security requirements into business language that resonates with executives who control funding decisions. The chapter establishes that moving beyond fear-based arguments represents a necessary evolution in security advocacy, as catastrophic breach stories create momentary concern but rarely drive sustainable investment. Instead, security must be repositioned as a business enabler rather than just a cost center.

The chapter outlines a structured approach to building business-aligned security investment proposals by understanding how business leaders evaluate investment opportunities. It introduces several economic models for quantifying security value, including Total Cost of Ownership (TCO), Annualized Loss Expectancy (ALE), and Risk Reduction ROI. These frameworks allow security professionals to translate abstract risks into concrete financial terms that business executives understand and can compare against other investment opportunities.

A cornerstone concept is the Security-Business Alignment Matrix, which explicitly maps security capabilities to strategic business objectives, converting technical requirements into business-focused investment proposals. This approach demonstrates how security enables and protects an organization's most important strategic priorities rather than presenting security as a standalone technical function.

The chapter also emphasizes demonstrating security's value beyond risk reduction, showing how security investments can accelerate business initiatives,

DOI: 10.1201/9781003744146-5

create competitive advantage, and improve operational efficiency. Key performance indicators such as time-to-market improvements, customer trust metrics, and compliance efficiency measurements help demonstrate this broader business value.

For competing against other business priorities, the chapter presents strategies for effective resource advocacy, including building cross-functional coalitions, timing proposals to align with business cycles, and leveraging external factors like regulatory changes. The chapter concludes with approaches for overcoming common objections to security spending, such as the "nothing bad has happened yet" challenge and the compliance-only mindset. The Anthem data breach case study provides a powerful real-world example of how inadequate security investment decisions can lead to substantial financial and reputational harm.

5.2 KEY TAKEAWAYS

- Security investment proposals must explicitly connect security capabilities to strategic business objectives, shifting from technical specifications to business outcomes
- Economic models like ALE and Risk Reduction ROI provide quantitative frameworks for comparing security investments against other business opportunities
- Building cross-functional coalitions transforms security from an isolated technical concern to a business imperative with organization-wide implications and advocacy
- Security leaders should prepare data-driven responses to common objections, focusing on business enablement rather than just risk reduction
- The most effective security investment cases balance proactive protection with demonstrable value creation

5.3 APPLICATION QUESTIONS

1. How might you reframe your current security investment proposals to highlight how they specifically enable or protect your organization's top three strategic business objectives?
2. What quantifiable metrics could you track to demonstrate your security program's value beyond risk reduction, and how would these metrics resonate with your executive leadership team?
3. Which stakeholders across your organization would benefit from your proposed security investments, and how could you engage them early in the proposal development process to build a coalition of support?

5.4 TOOLS REFERENCED IN THIS CHAPTER

All tools available at kaynemcgladrey.com/myth/

- Security-Business Alignment Matrix
- Exercise: Security-Business Alignment Worksheet
- Security Investment Financial Analysis Toolkit
- Exercise: ROI Calculator Template
- Security Value Dashboard for Executives
- Security Investment Prioritization Matrix
- Exercise: Opportunity Cost Analysis
- Executive Objection Response Toolkit

5.5 INTRODUCTION

The CFO looks across the conference table with a skeptical expression. "So, you're asking for another $1.2 million for security tools, but I still don't understand how this helps our business grow." It's a scene that plays out in boardrooms daily, where security investments struggle to gain approval when presented in technical rather than business terms.

Security leaders face a fundamental communication challenge: translating complex security needs into language that resonates with executives and boards. While security professionals understand the technical necessity of controls, decision-makers evaluate investments based on business impact. This disconnect often leads to underfunded security programs and increased organizational risk.

Moving beyond fear-based arguments represents an important maturation step in security advocacy. Stories of catastrophic breaches may create momentary concern but rarely drive sustainable investment. Instead, business-focused justifications that show tangible value are far more likely to secure ongoing support and resources.

Security must be repositioned as a business enabler rather than just a cost center. When properly aligned with strategic priorities, security investments can accelerate business initiatives, enhance customer trust, and create competitive advantage. This perspective transforms how organizations view security spending – from grudging insurance expense to strategic business investment.

This chapter builds on the integrated risk approach established previously, providing practical frameworks for connecting security efforts to enterprise objectives. By systematically aligning security investments with business goals, quantifying their value, and effectively competing for resources, security leaders can build compelling business cases that resonate with decision-makers.

In the following sections, we'll explore frameworks and methods for business-aligned security investment proposals, approaches for quantifying security value, techniques for demonstrating benefits beyond risk reduction, strategies for competing against business alternatives, and methods for overcoming common objections. By mastering these business-focused approaches, security leaders can transform their advocacy efforts and drive more effective security investments.

5.6 FOUNDATIONS OF BUSINESS-ALIGNED SECURITY INVESTMENT PROPOSALS

Securing funding for security initiatives requires understanding how business leaders evaluate investment opportunities and aligning security proposals accordingly. This foundation helps security professionals to speak the language of business and position security investments within the broader context of organizational strategy.

5.6.1 Understanding the business investment mindset

Business leaders approach capital allocation through a disciplined framework designed to maximize returns while managing risks. They evaluate investments based on their potential to drive revenue, reduce costs, improve efficiency, or achieve strategic objectives. Every investment proposal, including security initiatives, competes within this framework.

Executives typically evaluate competing investment proposals through standardized financial metrics. Return on Investment (ROI) measures the financial return relative to cost. Payback period quantifies how quickly an investment will recover its initial expense. Net Present Value (NPV) calculates the current worth of future cash flows, while opportunity cost acknowledges what the organization gives up by choosing one investment over alternatives.

These criteria create unique challenges for security investments. Unlike revenue-generating initiatives with clear financial returns, security investments primarily prevent negative outcomes. Their benefits often appear as costs avoided rather than revenue gained. Additionally, security investments frequently address low-probability, high-impact events whose timing is unpredictable.

Some senior leaders, particularly those from financial backgrounds, may view security only through a cost lens rather than as a strategic necessity. This perspective can result in underinvestment that leaves organizations vulnerable. Conversely, technically oriented executives might approve security investments based on features rather than business value, potentially leading to sophisticated solutions that don't address the organization's most pressing business risks.

In this environment, security professionals must adapt traditional business metrics to security needs while educating leaders on security's unique value proposition. This requires translating technical requirements into business terms and demonstrating how security investments support broader organizational objectives.

This investment mindset helps explain the executives' dilemma we explored in Chapter 2, where competing priorities and translation gaps often prevent security investments from receiving appropriate attention.

5.6.2 Aligning security investments with business objectives

Successful security investment proposals explicitly connect security capabilities to business goals. This alignment demonstrates how security enables and protects the organization's most important strategic priorities. Rather than presenting security as a standalone technical function, this approach positions it as an integrated component of business success. This framework can be seen in Figure 5.1.

Several techniques can help map security investments to strategic objectives. Start by identifying the organization's publicly stated goals and priorities – these appear in annual reports, investor presentations, and strategic plans. Then, analyze how specific security capabilities support these objectives. For example, if international expansion is a corporate priority, demonstrate how security investments in regional compliance capabilities directly enable market entry.

The PwC research (PwC, 2024) cited in Chapter 1 reinforces that top-performing organizations approach security as a strategic enabler rather than a separate technical function. By treating security as integral to business success, these organizations achieve superior outcomes across both security and business metrics.

Risk appetite and risk tolerance play crucial roles in investment decisions. These guardrails, established by leadership, define acceptable risk levels and guide appropriate control investments. Security leaders should frame

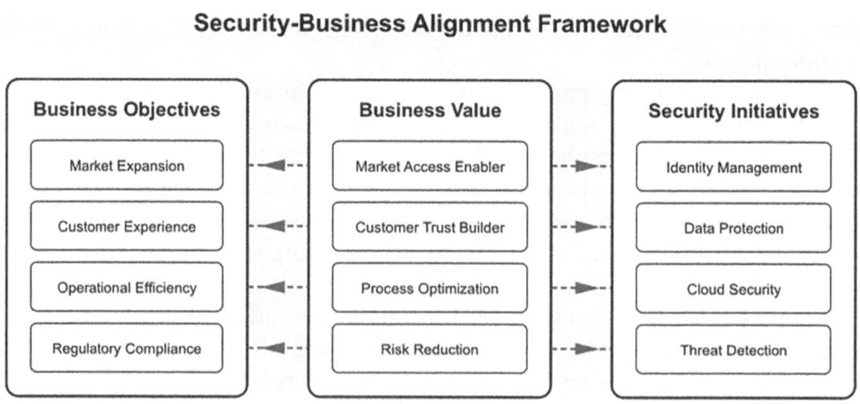

Figure 5.1 Security-business alignment framework.

investment proposals within these defined parameters, showing how proposed solutions help maintain risk within acceptable thresholds.

Downloadable Resource: Security-Business Alignment Matrix

5.6.3 Framework for structuring security investment proposals

A comprehensive framework for security investment proposals ensures all business-critical elements are addressed while technical details remain appropriately contextual. This structured approach helps security leaders communicate effectively with business stakeholders and increase proposal success rates.

Effective security investment proposals contain several essential components. The executive summary provides a concise overview of the investment request, business rationale, and expected outcomes. The business context section establishes relevance by connecting the proposal to organizational objectives, industry trends, and regulatory requirements. Options analysis presents alternatives with their respective costs, benefits, and risks. The implementation approach outlines execution strategy, timelines, and success metrics.

Balancing technical details with business implications requires careful consideration of audience needs. While technical details provide the context for implementation, they should never overshadow business outcomes. Technical descriptions should be concise, focused on capabilities rather than features, and explicitly connected to business results.

Proposals must be tailored for different stakeholder audiences. Board presentations should emphasize strategic alignment, risk governance, and long-term value. Executive committee proposals should focus on annual objectives, budget impacts, and cross-functional benefits. Line-of-business leaders need to understand specific operational impacts, implementation requirements, and how security enables their objectives.

When developing security investment proposals, consider the following principles:

- Lead with business outcomes, not technical features
- Quantify benefits wherever possible
- Acknowledge and address implementation challenges
- Present a range of options with different risk/benefit profiles
- Include both immediate and long-term value consideration

Understanding how business leaders evaluate investments provides the foundation for effective security proposals, but this knowledge becomes actionable only when security professionals can translate their initiatives into the financial language that executives use daily. Converting abstract security benefits into concrete financial terms requires systematic approaches that enable direct comparison with other business investments competing for the same resources.

5.6.3.1 Exercise: security-business alignment worksheet

To apply these concepts, complete this alignment exercise for your next security investment:

1. List your organization's top 3–5 strategic objectives for the current fiscal year
2. For each objective, identify how your security investment supports or enables that goal
3. Quantify the business impact if the objective is not achieved due to security issues
4. Develop a one-paragraph value statement connecting your security investment to each objective
5. Create three versions of your proposal summary tailored to: board members, executive committee, and line-of-business leaders

By systematically aligning security investments with business objectives and structuring proposals to address stakeholder concerns, security leaders can significantly improve their success rate in securing necessary resources while demonstrating their business acumen to leadership.

5.7 QUANTIFYING SECURITY INVESTMENT VALUE

Translating security value into financial terms provides a common language that business leaders understand. By quantifying security investment benefits, security professionals can present compelling business cases that stand up to financial scrutiny and comparison with other investment opportunities.

FINANCIAL CONCEPTS FOR SECURITY INVESTMENTS

Core financial metrics

Return on Investment (ROI) – The percentage return on an investment relative to its cost. A 50% ROI means you gain half the value of your investment back (e.g., spending $100,000 to save/earn $150,000).

Payback Period – The time required to recover the initial cost of an investment. A shorter payback period (e.g., 18 months vs. 36 months) generally indicates a more attractive investment.

Net Present Value (NPV) – The current value of all future cash flows generated by an investment, minus the initial investment amount. Positive NPV indicates a financially beneficial investment.

Opportunity Cost – The value of what you give up by choosing one option over another. For example, the opportunity cost of a security investment might be the expected return from a business project that couldn't be funded.

SECURITY ECONOMIC MODELS

Total Cost of Ownership (TCO) – The complete cost of a security solution across its lifecycle, including:

- *Initial purchase price*
- *Implementation and integration costs*
- *Ongoing maintenance and support*
- *Staff training and time*
- *Future upgrades or replacement*

Single Loss Expectancy (SLE) – The expected financial impact of a single security incident. For example, a data breach might have an SLE of $2 million.

Annual Rate of Occurrence (ARO) – The estimated frequency of a specific security incident occurring per year. An ARO of 0.1 means a 10% chance of occurrence annually.

Annualized Loss Expectancy (ALE) – The expected yearly financial loss from a security risk, calculated as:

$$ALE = SLE \times ARO$$

Example: If a breach costs $2M (SLE) with a 10% annual probability (ARO), the ALE is $200,000.

Risk Reduction ROI – The Return on Security Investments measured by the reduced financial risk exposure:

Risk Reduction ROI = (Risk Reduction Value ÷ Investment Cost) × 100%

Example: A $500,000 investment that reduces ALE by $150,000 annually provides a 30% annual Risk Reduction ROI.

RISK VALUATION APPROACHES

Quantitative Risk Analysis – Uses specific numerical values and probabilities to calculate precise risk estimates, enabling direct comparison with other investments.

Qualitative Risk Analysis – Uses relative values (high/medium/low) based on expert judgment to assess risks when precise numbers aren't available.

Risk Exposure – The potential financial impact of identified risks, calculated by multiplying threat likelihood by potential impact.

Monte Carlo Simulation – A mathematical technique that runs thousands of calculations with randomly varied inputs to predict the range and probability of possible outcomes for investments with uncertainty.

5.7.1 Economic models for security investments

Several economic models provide frameworks for evaluating security investments; a comparison can been seen in Figure 5.2. TCO represents the comprehensive cost of a security solution, including acquisition, implementation, operation, maintenance, and eventual replacement. TCO analysis often reveals that purchase price represents only 20–30% of lifetime costs, with significant implications for budget planning and vendor selection.

ALE quantifies potential annual losses from security incidents by multiplying the single loss expectancy (SLE) by the Annual Rate of Occurrence (ARO). For example, if a data breach costs $2 million (SLE) and has a 10% annual probability (ARO), the ALE equals $200,000. This calculation helps determine whether security investments are cost-effective compared to potential losses.

According to IBM Security's Cost of a Data Breach Report 2023 (IBM, 2023), in 2023,

> the average cost of a data breach rose to USD 4.45 million, marking a 2.3% increase from the previous year's figure of USD 4.35 million. Over a longer period, this represents a 15.3% rise from the 2020 average cost of USD 3.86 million, highlighting a consistent upward trend in data breach expenses.

These rising costs highlight the increasing financial impact of security incidents and provide concrete figures for ALE calculations.

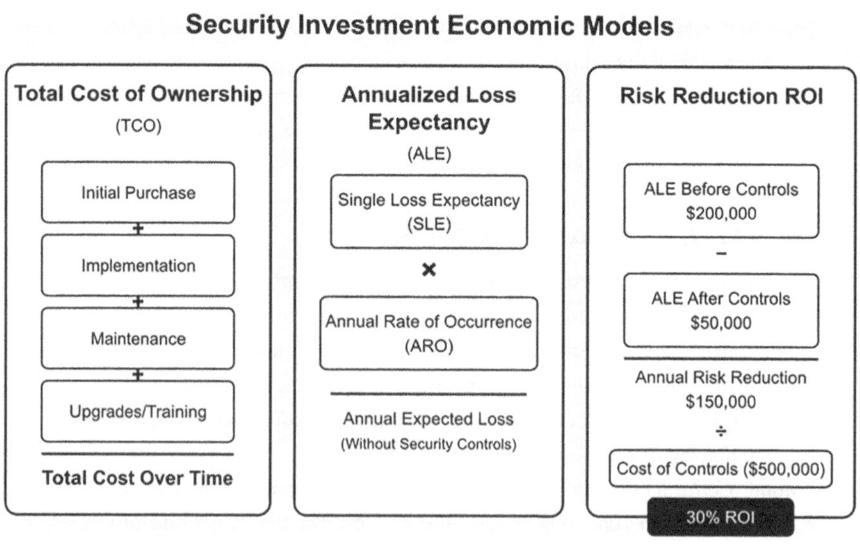

Figure 5.2 Security investment economic model.

Risk Reduction ROI measures the Return on Security Investments by dividing risk reduction (calculated as the difference between pre-investment and post-investment ALE) by investment cost. For example, if a $500,000 security investment reduces ALE from $200,000 to $50,000, the annual risk reduction equals $150,000, yielding a 30% ROI. This metric enables direct comparison with other business investments.

Quantitative approaches to valuation use precise financial calculations based on historical data and detailed risk analysis. These methods produce specific numbers that can be directly compared with other investments. Qualitative approaches rely more on expert judgment and relative risk rankings. While less precise, qualitative methods can be implemented more quickly and require less historical data. Many organizations use a hybrid approach, applying quantitative methods to their most significant risks while evaluating others qualitatively.

Building on the risk exposure calculations introduced in Chapter 3, organizations can adapt this methodology specifically for investment prioritization by emphasizing the financial dimension of potential impacts. This framework allows security leaders to prioritize investments based on financial exposure rather than technical severity alone.

These economic models build directly on the impact quantification techniques introduced in Chapter 3, providing financial frameworks for evaluating security investments. Chapter 9 builds on these economic models with business metrics that demonstrate security's contribution to revenue generation, customer retention, and operational efficiency.

5.7.2 Risk-based prioritization of security investments

A risk register provides the foundation for risk-based investment prioritization by documenting identified risks, their likelihood, potential impact, and current controls. This systematic inventory of risks enables organizations to direct investments toward their most significant exposures rather than the most recent security incident or the most technically interesting solution.

Several techniques help compare and rank security risks based on business impact. Risk heat maps, as seen in Figure 5.3, visually represent risks according to likelihood and impact, highlighting those requiring immediate attention. Business impact assessments quantify how security events affect critical processes, providing a clearer picture of operational and financial consequences. Risk velocity and persistence analysis examines how quickly risks might materialize and how long their effects might last, providing additional prioritization criteria.

Determining optimal investment levels across different risk categories requires balancing protection across the threat landscape. Some organizations allocate security investments proportionally to risk exposure, ensuring resources address the most significant business risks. Others establish baseline protection levels for all assets, then concentrate additional investments on

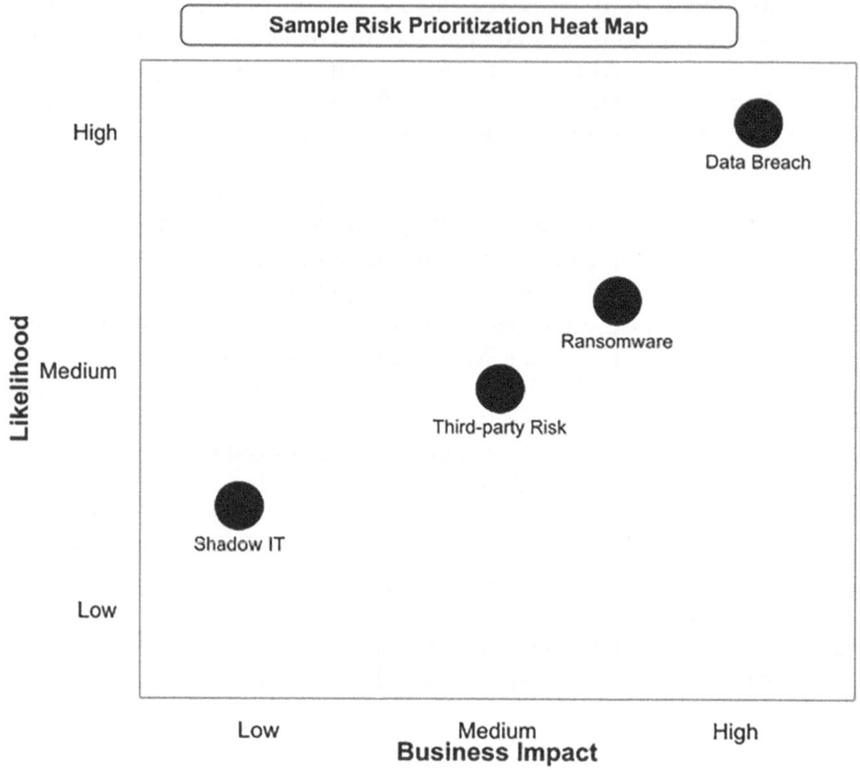

Figure 5.3 Sample risk prioritization heat map.

their crown jewels. Still others prioritize based on compliance requirements, particularly in highly regulated industries.

Organizations must also balance proactive and reactive security spending. Proactive investments in security architecture, secure development, and threat intelligence help prevent incidents, but their value can be difficult to show. Reactive investments in detection and response capabilities address events that occur despite preventive measures. While a balanced approach is typically advisable, organizations with limited resources might need to emphasize one strategy based on their specific risk profile and business constraints.

Risk-based prioritization ultimately enables security leaders to demonstrate that they are directing limited resources toward the organization's most significant business risks. This approach transforms security investment decisions from technical preferences into business-focused resource allocation aligned with the organization's risk appetite. This prioritization approach builds on the Business Impact Analysis methodology from Chapter 3, using quantified business impacts to guide investment decisions.

🔗 *Downloadable Resource: Security Investment Financial Analysis Toolkit*

5.7.3 Building and using the business case financial model

Creating effective financial models for security investments requires a structured approach. Begin by identifying all costs, including software, hardware, professional services, internal labor, and ongoing maintenance. Next, quantify benefits, considering both risk reduction (calculated through ALE) and business enablement value. Then, calculate financial metrics like ROI, NPV, and payback period. Finally, document assumptions and limitations to provide necessary context for decision-makers.

Security investments generate both direct and indirect benefits. Direct benefits include reduced incident costs, lower insurance premiums, and operational efficiencies. For example, automating vulnerability management might reduce labor costs by $200,000 annually. Indirect benefits include improved customer trust, competitive differentiation, and enhanced business agility. While harder to quantify, these benefits often represent significant long-term value.

Financial projections inherently contain uncertainty. Security professionals can address this challenge through several approaches. Sensitivity analysis examines how changing key variables affects outcomes, identifying which assumptions have the greatest impact on results. Monte Carlo simulation runs thousands of calculations with randomly varied inputs to determine the range and probability of possible outcomes. Three-point estimation uses optimistic, pessimistic, and most likely scenarios to establish confidence intervals.

Scenario planning explores how different future conditions might affect security investment returns. For example, how would the value proposition change under increased regulatory requirements, accelerated digital transformation, or significant changes in threat activity? This approach helps leaders understand how security investments perform under various business conditions, building confidence in their long-term value.

While quantifying security's risk reduction value provides a solid foundation for investment justification, organizations that limit their security business cases to loss prevention may significantly understate their proposals' true worth. Security investments often generate substantial business benefits that extend far beyond incident prevention, creating opportunities for revenue generation, operational improvements, and competitive advantage that can strengthen investment cases considerably.

Downloadable Exercise: ROI Calculator Template

5.8 DEMONSTRATING VALUE BEYOND RISK REDUCTION

While risk reduction remains a core security function, demonstrating security's broader business contributions significantly strengthens investment cases. By positioning security as a business enabler that creates competitive advantage and operational benefits, security leaders can secure stronger support from business partners.

5.8.1 Security as a business enabler

Security investments can accelerate business initiatives by removing barriers and creating foundations for innovation. For example, strong identity management capabilities allow organizations to safely offer new digital services to customers without increasing fraud risk. Cloud security frameworks allow rapid deployment of new business applications while maintaining consistent protection. These capabilities transform security from a perceived business inhibitor into a catalyst for growth.

Numerous opportunities exist where security creates competitive advantage. Strong data protection practices differentiate organizations in privacy-conscious markets. Robust supply chain security enables partnerships with security-sensitive customers and vendors. Industry-leading security capabilities can create market differentiation, particularly in sectors where trust is paramount. By identifying these opportunities, security leaders can position investments as business growth enablers rather than compliance costs.

Security capability development directly supports digital transformation by securing new technologies and business models. As the PwC 2024 Global Digital Trust Insights report notes, leading organizations have positioned themselves for greater productivity and faster growth are those that have streamlined their security solutions, making risk management easier and more effective. (PwC, 2024) This security-enabled confidence accelerates innovation adoption and creates first-mover advantages.

The "opportunity ROI" of security investments measures how security enables business initiatives that would otherwise be too risky to pursue. For example, a financial institution might quantify how its fraud prevention investments enable entry into new markets, calculating the revenue generated from these opportunities as part of the security ROI. This approach demonstrates how security creates business value beyond risk reduction.

Chapter 9 expands on this concept with comprehensive frameworks for identifying, measuring, and communicating how security enables business objectives beyond risk reduction.

5.8.2 Key performance indicators for security business value

Several metrics help link security investments to business outcomes. Time-to-market measurements demonstrate how security enables faster deployment of new products and services. Revenue protection metrics quantify business continuity improvements. Market expansion indicators track new opportunities accelerated or facilitated partially by security capabilities. These

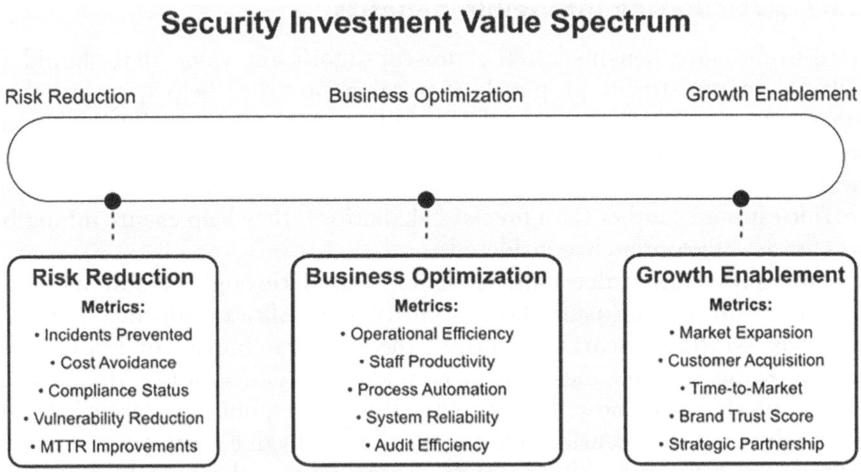

Figure 5.4 Security investment value spectrum.

business-aligned metrics demonstrate security's contribution to organizational objectives and are shown in Figure 5.4.

Operational efficiency metrics highlight how security investments improve business processes. Time savings from automated security workflows reduce operational costs. Mean time to detect (MTTD) and mean time to respond (MTTR) improvements minimize business disruption during incidents. Resource utilization metrics show how security investments optimize existing business technologies. These efficiencies translate into financial benefits beyond risk reduction.

Customer trust represents a significant measurable benefit of security investments, with these metrics detailed comprehensively in Chapter 9. Customer retention rates can be correlated with security capabilities, particularly following publicized incidents. New customer acquisition metrics may reveal how security features influence purchase decisions. These connections show how security directly contributes to revenue performance.

Compliance capabilities also enable market access opportunities, with frameworks for leveraging compliance for growth detailed in Chapter 9. These metrics highlight security's role in business growth and operational freedom.

Ongoing measurement and reporting require establishing baselines before implementation and tracking improvement over time. Integration with existing business metrics ensures security measurements align with organizational reporting. Regular executive updates maintain awareness of security's business contributions. This continuous demonstration of value sustains support for security investments between funding cycles.

Downloadable Resource: Security Value Dashboard for Executives

5.8.3 Articulating intangible benefits

Hard-to-measure benefits often represent significant value that should be included in investment proposals. Several approaches help quantify these benefits. Proxy metrics use measurable indicators to represent intangible values. Benchmark comparisons leverage industry data to estimate value. Survey methods capture stakeholder perceptions of value. While these approaches provide estimates rather than precise calculations, they help ensure intangible benefits are appropriately considered.

Brand protection value can be demonstrated through several methods. Customer surveys measure how security capabilities influence purchase decisions. Market research quantifies the financial impact of brand damage following security incidents at competitor organizations. Media sentiment analysis tracks how security practices affect public perception. These approaches connect security investments to brand value protection.

Improved decision-making capabilities represent another valuable but intangible benefit. Better risk visibility enables more confident business decisions. Enhanced security analytics improve operational insights. Threat intelligence capabilities provide competitive awareness. Organizations can illustrate these benefits through case examples of how security information improved business decisions.

Security investments also support corporate social responsibility objectives. Data privacy protections show ethical business practices. Supply chain security requirements ensure ethical treatment extends to partners. Environmental considerations in security infrastructure decisions support sustainability goals. These connections position security as supporting broader organizational values beyond risk management.

While intangible benefits may be harder to quantify precisely, excluding them from business cases significantly understates security's value contribution. By developing consistent and defensible approaches to articulate these benefits, security leaders can present a more complete picture of security's business impact.

Demonstrating comprehensive security value through both risk reduction and business enablement creates compelling investment proposals, yet even the most well-crafted business cases must compete against other organizational priorities in resource allocation decisions. Understanding this competitive environment and developing targeted advocacy strategies can significantly improve security leaders' success rates in securing necessary funding.

5.9 COMPETING FOR RESOURCES AGAINST BUSINESS ALTERNATIVES

Security investments inevitably compete against other business priorities for limited resources. Understanding the resource allocation process and developing effective advocacy strategies helps security leaders secure necessary funding in today's competitive environment.

5.9.1 Understanding the business resource allocation process

Organizations make trade-off decisions through structured processes designed to optimize resource allocation. Most employ multi-criteria decision analysis, weighing factors like financial return, strategic alignment, risk reduction, and operational necessity. Understanding these criteria helps security leaders position their proposals effectively. Some organizations use formal scoring models, while others rely more heavily on executive judgment, but all must balance competing demands against limited resources.

The annual planning and budgeting cycle provides the primary framework for resource allocation in most organizations. This process typically begins with strategic planning that establishes priorities, continues with departmental budget development, and concludes with executive review and approval. Understanding this cycle helps security leaders time their proposals appropriately and align them with broader organizational priorities. Missing key planning milestones often results in deferred funding regardless of the proposal's merit.

Capital expenditure (capex) and operating expense (opex) considerations significantly impact funding decisions. Capital investments typically undergo more rigorous financial analysis but may be easier to fund during growth periods. Operating expenses directly impact profitability metrics and face greater scrutiny during cost-control periods. Security leaders should understand their organization's financial structure and preferences when developing investment proposals.

Timing plays a crucial role in resource allocation. Mid-year requests often face higher hurdles than proposals incorporated into the annual budget. Requests following security incidents typically receive more favorable consideration than preventive proposals. End-of-year surplus funds may create opportunities for accelerated investments. Strategic security leaders develop multi-year roadmaps while remaining flexible enough to capitalize on timing opportunities.

According to the 2024 Security Budget Benchmark Summary Report from IANS and Artico Search (IANS Research and Artico Search, 2024), "Anecdotally, many CISOs think their budgets should be larger. Despite this, it is notable that only 28% expressed outright dissatisfaction with their budget, while 52% indicated being somewhat or very satisfied." This finding suggests that effective alignment of security spending with organizational risk awareness and leadership engagement leads to greater perceived resource adequacy.

🔗 *Downloadable Resource: Security Investment Prioritization Matrix*

5.9.2 Strategies for effective resource advocacy

Building coalitions of support across business functions significantly strengthens security investment proposals. Identify stakeholders who benefit from the proposed investment and engage them early in the development process. Document how the investment supports their objectives and secure their advocacy during approval discussions. Cross-functional support demonstrates business alignment and reduces the perception of security as an isolated technical function.

Timing proposals to align with business cycles and priorities increases success probability. Coordinate major security investments with relevant business initiatives rather than presenting them as standalone projects. Align with digital transformation efforts, customer experience improvements, or operational efficiency programs. This integration positions security investments as enabling business objectives rather than competing against them.

External factors can significantly influence investment decisions. Regulatory changes create compliance mandates that may receive priority funding. Recent security incidents at peer organizations elevate awareness and willingness to invest. Industry trends and analyst recommendations provide external validation for proposed investments. Strategic security leaders monitor these factors and leverage them appropriately in investment proposals.

Presenting security investments as part of broader business initiatives improves reception. Rather than requesting a "security budget," frame investments as enabling specific business outcomes. For example, position identity management improvements as enabling customer experience enhancements. Embed security costs within business project budgets where appropriate. This approach shifts the perception from "security spending" to "business investment with security components."

5.9.3 Comparative analysis techniques

Several methods help directly compare security investments against other business investments. Cost-effectiveness analysis measures the expense required to achieve specific risk reduction outcomes, enabling comparison across different control types. Security ROI calculations quantify financial returns from risk reduction and business enablement, allowing direct comparison with other investment ROIs. Using consistent metrics across different investment types ensures fair comparison. Financial metrics like NPV and ROI provide common evaluation criteria. Risk reduction measurements quantify security's specific contribution. Business enablement metrics demonstrate security's role in achieving strategic objectives. This consistent measurement framework helps security investments compete on level ground with other business investments.

Security investments typically balance short-term and long-term value considerations. Short-term investments may deliver immediate operational benefits but require ongoing updates or work. Long-term architectural investments often have higher initial costs but provide sustainable value over time. Organizations need both types of investments, and security leaders should present a balanced portfolio rather than focusing exclusively on either horizon.

Investment portfolios that balance risk and opportunity optimize overall security value. Just as financial portfolios diversify across investment types, security portfolios should balance investments in prevention, detection, response, and recovery capabilities. They should also distribute resources across different risk categories based on the organization's risk profile. This balanced approach ensures comprehensive protection while maximizing Return on Security Investment.

Strategic resource advocacy and coalition building provide important advantages in competitive funding environments, but security leaders frequently encounter predictable objections that can derail otherwise sound investment proposals. Preparing effective responses to these common challenges allows security professionals to maintain momentum in funding discussions and address stakeholder concerns with business-focused counterarguments.

5.9.3.1 Exercise: opportunity cost analysis

Evaluate the true opportunity cost of security investments using this framework:

1. For your proposed security investment:
   - List all direct costs (purchase, implementation, maintenance)
   - Identify resources required (staff time, management attention, technical infrastructure)
   - Document business impacts during implementation
2. For each alternative use of these resources:
   - Quantify expected financial return
   - Identify strategic objectives supported
   - Document risks created or perpetuated
3. For the "do nothing" security alternative:
   - Calculate expected loss exposure (ALE)
   - Identify compliance gaps created
   - Document strategic initiatives potentially blocked
4. Comparative analysis:
   - Create a side-by-side comparison of financial impacts
   - Evaluate alignment with strategic priorities
   - Assess risk/return profiles of each alternative

This comprehensive analysis helps demonstrate that security investments represent optimal resource use compared to alternatives, including the "do nothing" option that appears to preserve resources but creates significant risk exposure.

5.10 OVERCOMING COMMON OBJECTIONS TO SECURITY INVESTMENTS

Security leaders regularly encounter predictable objections to their investment proposals. By anticipating these challenges and developing effective counterarguments, they can increase their success rate in securing necessary resources. Common objections, sample reframing strategies, and business-focused responses are shown in Figure 5.5.

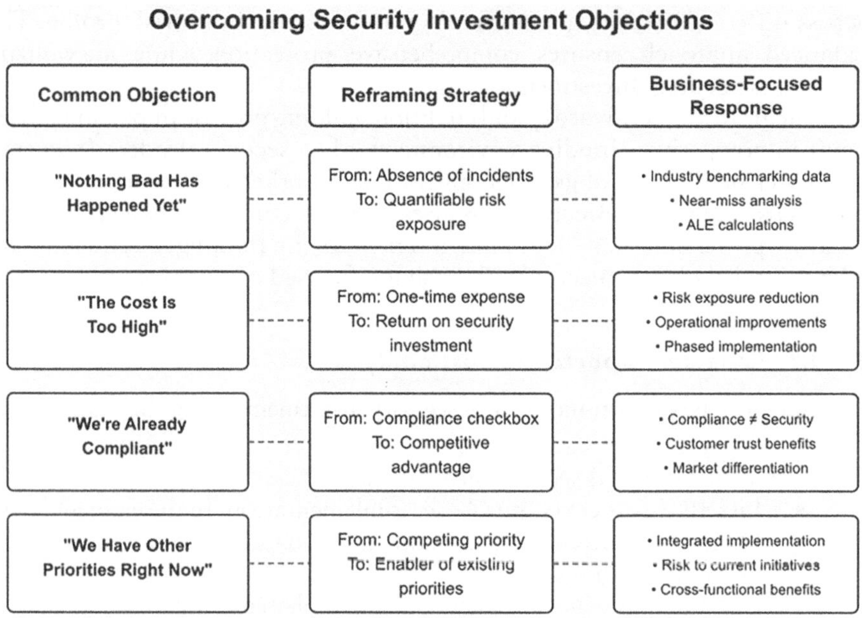

Figure 5.5 Overcoming security investment objections.

5.10.1 Addressing the "nothing bad has happened yet" challenge

The absence of visible security incidents often creates complacency that undermines investment cases. Several strategies can help illustrate risk without relying on fear tactics. Industry benchmarking shows how organizations of comparable size and industry experience security incidents. Risk quantification translates abstract threats into concrete financial exposure. Gap analysis identifies specific vulnerabilities in current protection. These approaches replace vague warnings with specific business risks.

Near-miss events and industry examples provide powerful illustrations without resorting to scare tactics. Organizations typically experience numerous "almost breaches" that were prevented by existing controls or good fortune. Documenting these near misses demonstrates actual threat activity targeting the organization. Similarly, incidents at peer organizations with similar risk profiles demonstrate realistic possibilities without implying inevitability.

Making abstract risks concrete requires translating technical vulnerabilities into business scenarios. Rather than discussing technical details, describe how vulnerabilities would affect business operations. For example, instead of focusing on unpatched systems, explain how exploiting those vulnerabilities would impact production, customer service, or financial reporting. These business scenarios make risks more accessible to non-technical stakeholders.

Security faces a fundamental visibility challenge: when it works perfectly, it appears unnecessary. Balancing this invisibility problem with business results requires showing value beyond incident prevention. Document operational improvements created by security investments. Highlight customer trust enhancements. Demonstrate how security capabilities accelerate business initiatives. These positive contributions complement risk reduction arguments.

As the IBM breach cost data (IBM, 2023) discussed in Section 2.1 demonstrates, waiting to address vulnerabilities increases potential impact. This upward trend in breach costs helps counter the 'nothing bad has happened yet' objection by showing that incident costs continue to rise, making proactive investments more cost-effective than reactive responses.

5.10.2 Countering the compliance-only mindset

Many organizations view security primarily through a compliance lens, investing only enough to satisfy regulatory requirements. This mindset creates significant business risk exposure requiring security leaders to distinguish between compliance requirements and comprehensive risk management. While compliance establishes minimum standards, it rarely addresses an organization's specific risk profile. Security leaders should map compliance controls to business risks, identifying gaps where significant risks remain despite technical compliance. This mindset represents the 'compliance trap' we discussed in Chapter 1, where organizations focus on meeting regulatory requirements rather than addressing their actual risk exposure.

The business value gap between compliance and security can be substantial. Compliant organizations still experience breaches with significant financial impact. According to numerous studies, most breached organizations were compliant with relevant standards at the time of the breach. This disconnect highlights that compliance represents a minimum baseline, rather than optimal protection. Security leaders should quantify residual risks that remain after achieving compliance to demonstrate this gap.

Organizations should view compliance as a foundation rather than a ceiling for security investments. Compliance requirements provide a starting point that ensures minimum acceptable practices. Risk-based security builds upon this foundation to address the organization's specific threat profile and business objectives. This layered approach ensures both regulatory compliance and appropriate business protection.

Reframing compliance spending as a strategic investment helps overcome the compliance-only mindset. Connect compliance requirements to broader business objectives like customer trust and market access. Demonstrate how exceeding minimum requirements creates competitive advantages. Show how integrated security and compliance programs reduce overall costs compared to separate compliance-only efforts. This approach transforms compliance from a cost of doing business into a strategic business advantage.

5.10.3 The Anthem data breach case study

5.10.3.1 Context

In 2015, Anthem Inc., one of the nation's largest health insurance companies, made headlines for all the wrong reasons. The healthcare giant that employs more than 37,000 people and serves millions of Americans through brands like Blue Cross and Blue Shield, Anthem Insurance Company, and many others, experienced a massive data breach that would ultimately change how the industry viewed security investments.

Before the breach, Anthem maintained a database containing personal information of its members, including names, addresses, dates of birth, Social Security numbers, health identification numbers, and employment information. This valuable data represented both a business asset and a serious liability if compromised. Like many organizations, Anthem made business decisions about which security controls to implement and which to forego based on their assessment of priorities, requirements, and resources.

5.10.3.2 Challenge

The fundamental challenge Anthem faced was not unique in healthcare or any industry: determining what level of security investment would appropriately protect sensitive data while balancing other business priorities. This difficulty was compounded by the fact that, under federal law (specifically HIPAA), health insurance companies were not required to encrypt user data stored in their databases.

In December 2014, Anthem employees noticed suspicious database queries being made against their systems. These unauthorized activities continued throughout December and into January 2015. By January 29, 2015, investigators confirmed that unknown attackers had gained access to Anthem's servers, compromising approximately 80 million records containing highly sensitive personal information.

Post-breach analysis revealed a stark reality: while Anthem had implemented various security measures, they had chosen not to encrypt the personal data stored in their databases. As Anthem spokesperson Kristin Binns told *The Wall Street Journal*, "We use other measures, including elevated user credentials, to limit access to the data when it is residing in a database." The company only encrypted personal data when it was moving in or out of the database.

This business decision – to forego database encryption – became the focal point of scrutiny. While initially described as a "sophisticated attack" in Anthem's public statements, security experts later questioned this characterization, pointing instead to what many considered a basic security failure.

5.10.3.3 Approach

Anthem's approach to the breach aftermath demonstrated both strengths and weaknesses in their security investment strategy. After confirming the breach, the company promptly notified the FBI – a response that an FBI spokesperson praised, calling it a model for other companies and organizations facing similar circumstances.

The company took several important steps:

1. They established individual notification for current and former members whose information had been compromised
2. They partnered with AllClear ID to provide 24 months of credit monitoring and identity theft repair services
3. They engaged Mandiant, a leading cybersecurity firm, to investigate the breach and review security protocols
4. They limited communications with members to written form to help members distinguish legitimate communications from phishing attempts

However, perhaps the most telling aspect of Anthem's approach came after the settlement, when they agreed to:

- Nearly triple their annual spending on cybersecurity for three years
- Implement specific cybersecurity controls and reforms recommended by plaintiffs' cybersecurity experts
- Fix core vulnerability issues in their database warehouse
- Retain an outside expert to conduct annual cybersecurity reviews

These post-breach security investments highlighted the gap between pre-breach security spending decisions and what was ultimately deemed necessary to protect the business and its customers.

5.10.3.4 Outcome

The financial and reputational consequences for Anthem were substantial. On August 15, 2018, Judge Lucy H. Koh in the U.S. District Court for the Northern District of California granted final approval to a $115 million settlement (In Re Anthem, Inc. Data Breach Litigation, 2018) – the largest data breach settlement in U.S. history at that time.

The settlement provided:

- Credit protection services for affected individuals
- Reimbursement for customers who incurred costs related to the breach
- Up to $38 million in attorneys' fees

Additionally, in a parallel action, the Office for Civil Rights (OCR) investigated the breach and found potential HIPAA violations. Anthem agreed to pay a $16 million settlement to resolve these potential violations, which was the largest HIPAA settlement at that time.

Beyond these direct financial impacts, Anthem faced:

- Costs associated with investigating the breach
- Reputational damage in an industry where trust is paramount
- Customer acquisition and retention challenges
- Operational disruption during investigations
- Significantly increased security spending requirements going forward

The legal proceedings also revealed that while Anthem's security program had been deemed "reasonable" by a consortium of state insurance commissioners, this assessment proved inadequate against both the real-world threat and the subsequent legal scrutiny.

5.10.3.5 Lessons

The Anthem case offers several valuable lessons for security leaders seeking to build business cases for security investments:

1. **Cost-benefit analysis must include realistic breach scenarios**
   A proper business case for encryption would have compared the implementation cost against the potential financial impact of a breach. The \$115 million settlement plus \$16 million in HIPAA penalties far exceeded what enterprise-wide encryption would have cost. This case demonstrates how security investments should be evaluated not merely as technical solutions to vulnerabilities, but as business controls that limit financial exposure.
2. **Compliance does not equal adequate security**
   Anthem's security met the legal requirements under HIPAA, which did not mandate encryption of stored data. However, this compliance-focused approach failed to protect them from significant financial and reputational damage. Business cases for security must go beyond regulatory checkboxes to address actual business risk.
3. **Security decisions require business risk translation**
   The decision not to encrypt database contents was likely presented in technical terms rather than as a business risk decision with potential financial consequences. Security leaders must translate technical vulnerabilities into business risks with specific financial impact models to enable informed executive decisions.
4. **Post-breach spending reveals prevention blind spots**
   Anthem's agreement to triple cybersecurity spending post-breach demonstrates how breach events often reveal the true business value of security controls. Security leaders can use public breach settlements like Anthem's to create compelling "prevention value" business cases by highlighting the gap between pre-breach and post-breach security investment in similar organizations.

5. **Settlements establish industry benchmarks**
   The Anthem settlement set a benchmark that organizations of comparable size and industry can use in risk calculations. Security professionals can leverage these precedents when building business cases by showing how investment decisions may be judged against industry standards after an incident occurs.

For security leaders seeking to build effective business cases, the Anthem breach offers this final lesson: security investment decisions are ultimately business decisions with business consequences. When presented properly, with clear financial implications and risk reduction metrics, security investments can be evaluated on the same terms as any other business investment – by their ROI and their ability to protect the business from substantial financial harm.

5.11 CONCLUSION

Building effective business cases for security investments requires a fundamental shift from technical to business-focused communication. The frameworks and techniques presented in this chapter provide a practical roadmap for this transformation, enabling security leaders to secure necessary resources while demonstrating their business acumen.

The foundation of successful security investment proposals lies in aligning security capabilities with business objectives. By identifying how security enables and protects strategic priorities, security leaders transform their proposals from technical requirements into business investments. This alignment demonstrates that security is not just a cost center but a business enabler that creates competitive advantage.

Quantifying security investment value provides the financial justification that business leaders require. Economic models like TCO, ALE, and Risk Reduction ROI translate security benefits into financial terms that facilitate direct comparison with other business investments. This quantification shifts security discussions from subjective risk assessments to objective business analysis.

Demonstrating security's value beyond risk reduction significantly strengthens investment cases. By identifying how security accelerates business initiatives, improves operational efficiency, enhances customer trust, and enables market access, security leaders can position investments as creating business value rather than simply preventing losses.

Competing effectively for resources requires understanding organizational decision processes and developing targeted advocacy strategies. By building cross-functional support, timing proposals strategically, and leveraging external factors, security leaders can improve their success rate in securing necessary funding.

Overcoming common objections represents a critical skill for security leaders. By anticipating challenges like the "nothing bad has happened yet" argument and the compliance-only mindset, security professionals can develop effective counterarguments that maintain focus on business value rather than technical details.

The next chapter will build on these concepts by exploring how to measure security investment outcomes. This measurement closes the loop on security investment justification, demonstrating realized value and creating the foundation for future investment proposals. By consistently measuring and communicating security's business contribution, security leaders reinforce their role as strategic business partners rather than technical specialists.

Security investments, when properly positioned and justified, represent valuable business assets rather than necessary evils. By applying the business-focused approaches described in this chapter, security leaders can secure the resources they need while demonstrating their contribution to organizational success.

5.12 ACTION ITEMS FOR READERS

1. Identify your organization's top three strategic business objectives from recent annual reports, investor presentations, or strategic plans, then map how specific security capabilities could directly enable or protect each objective.
2. Conduct a financial analysis of your current security risks by calculating ALE for your three highest-impact potential security incidents, using historical industry data and your organization's specific operational context.
3. Create a standardized security investment proposal template that includes executive summary, business context, options analysis, and financial projections, ensuring each section addresses business outcomes rather than technical features.
4. Develop relationships with key stakeholders across finance, operations, and business units by scheduling meetings to understand their current priorities and identifying opportunities where security investments could accelerate their initiatives.
5. Establish baseline measurements for at least three business-aligned security metrics (such as time-to-market for new services, customer trust indicators, or operational efficiency gains) that will demonstrate security's contribution to business value beyond risk reduction.

Downloadable Resource: Executive Objection Response Toolkit

Chapter 6

Metrics that matter

Measuring security in business terms

Chapter in One Sentence: Security leaders must transform their measurement approach from technical metrics to business-aligned indicators that demonstrate how security activities protect revenue, reduce costs, enable operations, and create competitive advantage.

6.1 EXECUTIVE SUMMARY

This chapter addresses a critical disconnect in security measurement: traditional technical security metrics fail to resonate with business leaders, creating significant challenges in securing resources and executive support. When security leaders cannot articulate how their activities contribute to business objectives, security initiatives are viewed as cost centers rather than strategic investments.

The chapter provides a comprehensive framework for developing, implementing, and communicating security metrics that matter to business stakeholders. It begins by identifying why technical metrics like vulnerability counts and patching rates fall short – they focus on activities rather than outcomes, lack connection to business objectives, and fail to answer executives' primary question: "What does this mean for our business?"

A hierarchical approach to security measurement is presented, from operational metrics for daily management to board-level metrics for governance and oversight. Business-relevant security metrics are categorized into financial impact (such as cost avoidance and Return on Security Investment (ROSI)), risk management (including risk reduction rates), operational resilience, compliance and governance, and reputation. This structured approach ensures security metrics align with enterprise objectives while serving different organizational needs.

The chapter details how to translate technical security activities into business language, demonstrating security's contribution to revenue protection, cost reduction, competitive advantage, and operational efficiency. Rather than reporting that "multi-factor authentication has been implemented across 95% of applications," security leaders should communicate that "We've reduced the risk of unauthorized access to customer data and financial systems by 60%, protecting $50 million in annual revenue."

DOI: 10.1201/9781003744146-6

Stakeholder-specific reporting is examined, with guidance for tailoring metrics to boards, C-suite executives, business unit leaders, and regulators. Visualization and communication techniques transform security data into actionable insights, with principles for executive dashboard development and advanced visualization methods.

Throughout, the chapter emphasizes the need for security metrics to drive decisions and actions rather than merely providing information. By measuring and communicating security performance in business terms, security leaders can elevate their strategic influence, secure appropriate resources, and position security as an enabler of business success rather than a technical obligation.

6.2 KEY TAKEAWAYS

- Technical security metrics that fail to connect with business priorities are ignored in executive decision-making; effective metrics must demonstrate security's contribution to business outcomes
- Security metrics exist in a hierarchy serving different needs: operational metrics for practitioners, tactical metrics for program management, strategic metrics for executives, and board-level metrics for governance
- Translating security activities into business outcomes (revenue protection, cost reduction, competitive advantage) positions security as a strategic partner rather than a compliance function
- Security communication must be tailored to specific stakeholders, with visualization techniques that highlight business impact and support decision-making

6.3 APPLICATION QUESTIONS

1. Which of your current security metrics directly connect to your organization's top business objectives, and which metrics could be eliminated or refined to better demonstrate business value?
2. How might you translate your most important technical security achievements into business outcomes that would resonate with your CEO, CFO, and board members?
3. What visualization techniques could you implement to make security performance more immediately understandable to non-technical executives in your organization?

6.4 TOOLS REFERENCED IN THIS CHAPTER

All tools available at kaynemcgladrey.com/myth/

- Exercise: Audit Your Current Metrics
- Security Metrics Audit Tool

- Business-Aligned Security Metrics Selection Framework
- Exercise: Designing Your Metrics Framework
- Security Investment ROI Calculator
- Security-Business Value Mapping Workshop
- Exercise: Developing Stakeholder-Specific Reports
- Exercise: Dashboard Design Workshop
- Security Communication Playbook

6.5 INTRODUCTION

Building on the communication challenges outlined in Chapter 3, this chapter addresses a specific manifestation of the security-business disconnect: the measurement problem. While Chapter 3 focused on translating individual risks, here we examine how to measure and communicate security's overall business value systematically.

When security leaders cannot articulate how their activities contribute to business objectives, security initiatives are viewed as cost centers rather than strategic investments. In a boardroom where every dollar is scrutinized, security programs that cannot demonstrate business value are at risk of underfunding.

Broadly speaking, there appears to be a fundamental shift occurring in how security demonstrates value. Forward-thinking security leaders now recognize that measuring success through technical achievements alone is insufficient. Instead, they are learning to express security outcomes in terms of business impact, risk reduction, and contribution to strategic goals.

Business leaders need security metrics that align with their understanding of business performance. Rather than technical jargon about threat vectors and zero-day vulnerabilities, they require clear insights into how security affects revenue, customer trust, operational efficiency, and competitive advantage.

This chapter provides a framework for developing, implementing, and communicating security metrics that matter to business stakeholders. By translating security performance into business terms, security leaders can elevate their strategic influence, secure appropriate resources, and demonstrate security's contribution to enterprise success. Whether you're a CISO seeking to communicate more effectively with your board or a CFO trying to evaluate security investments, the approaches outlined here will help bridge the gap between security operations and business outcomes.

6.6 THE PROBLEM WITH TRADITIONAL SECURITY METRICS

Traditional security measurement approaches appear to create a significant barrier between security teams and business executives. While security professionals may find value in technical metrics like vulnerability counts and patching rates, these measurements often fail to answer the fundamental business question: "What does this mean for our organization's success?" This disconnect suggests that conventional security metrics may be measuring activities rather than outcomes, leaving executives unable to make informed decisions about security investments and risk management priorities.

6.6.1 Why technical metrics fail to resonate

Technical security metrics often create a language barrier between security and business executives. While security professionals may find significance in the number of vulnerabilities patched or alerts triaged, business leaders struggle to connect these metrics to what matters to them: business performance, customer satisfaction, and shareholder value.

Traditional metrics tend to focus on activities rather than outcomes. Reporting that "98% of critical vulnerabilities were patched within 30 days" highlights an activity but fails to answer the executive's question: "Did this make us more secure, and how did it impact our business objectives?" Activity-based metrics provide little insight into whether security efforts are effectively reducing business risk.

Most technical metrics also lack connection to business objectives and strategic goals. When the board discusses market expansion, competitive positioning, and customer acquisition, security metrics about firewall blocks and intrusion attempts seem disconnected from these priorities. This misalignment relegates security to a technical function rather than a strategic enabler.

Perhaps most problematic is the tendency to measure what's easy rather than what's important. Technical systems generate abundant data, making it simple to report on detection counts, scan results, and system logs. Measuring security's business contribution requires more thoughtful analysis, but provides significantly more value to decision-makers.

These metrics problems relate to the translation gap discussed in Chapter 2, where technical language fails to resonate with business stakeholders and drive appropriate action.

6.6.2 Common pitfalls in security measurement

Many security programs fall into the trap of measuring compliance instead of security effectiveness. While achieving regulatory compliance is necessary, meeting minimum regulatory requirements does not necessarily make an organization secure. Compliance metrics might indicate adherence to a standard but rarely reflect actual security posture or business risk exposure.

Overreliance on operational metrics represents another common pitfall. Patching rates, vulnerability counts, and security event statistics dominate many security dashboards. These metrics serve operational needs but fail to

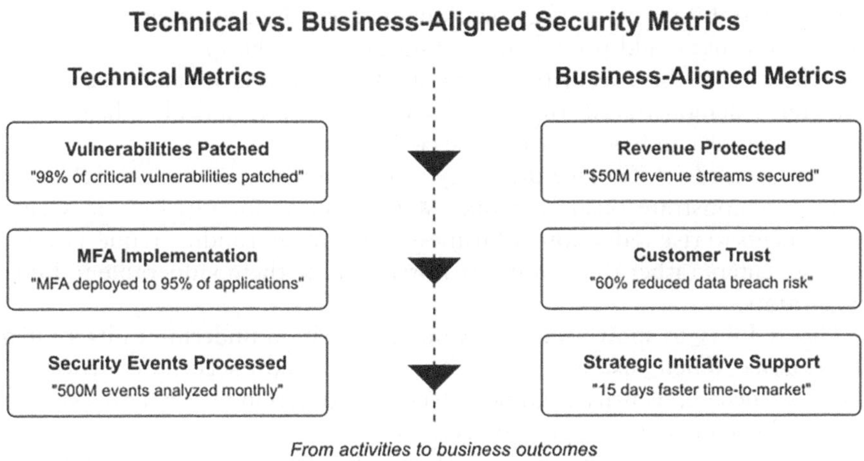

Figure 6.1 Technical vs. business-aligned security metrics.

address the executive's primary concern: "What is our risk exposure, and are we investing appropriately to protect our business assets?"

Security programs often fail to contextualize metrics within business risk. When presenting vulnerability statistics, for example, security teams may not connect these findings to potential business impacts, such as service disruption, revenue loss, or reputational damage. A sample of these are seen in Figure 6.1. Without this context, executives cannot make informed risk management decisions.

Many organizations suffer from "metrics for metrics' sake" syndrome, collecting and reporting data because it's available rather than because it's meaningful. This approach leads to information overload and obscures insights that would inform business decisions.

6.6.3 The business impact of poor measurement

Misalignment of security investments with business priorities is a direct consequence of poor measurement. When security teams cannot articulate how their activities support business objectives, investments may be directed toward addressing technical vulnerabilities rather than the most significant business risks.

According to the 2024 Security Budget Benchmark Summary Report (IANS Research and Artico Search, 2024), a majority of CISOs rely on high-level metrics such as "budget as percentage of IT spend" (67%) and "budget as percentage of annual revenue" (52%) to guide their budget and staffing decisions. More detailed measures like "security budget per employee" (43%) and "security headcount per employee" (32%) are less frequently used. This suggests that while broad financial benchmarks are favored for their simplicity and comparability, many organizations may not be leveraging more granular metrics that could provide deeper insights into the specific demands and complexities of their security programs. As the Target breach case study in Chapter 3 demonstrated, the inability to translate technical indicators into business terms can have catastrophic consequences.

Security leaders also face difficulty justifying resource requests when they cannot demonstrate business value. Without clear metrics linking security investments to risk reduction or business enablement, funding requests appear as cost centers rather than value creators, making them vulnerable to budget constraints.

The inability to show security's value proposition undermines its strategic positioning. When business executives cannot see how security contributes to business success, security becomes a technical function rather than a strategic partner in achieving enterprise objectives.

Over time, poor measurement leads to a loss of stakeholder confidence in the security program. If security investments cannot be tied to business outcomes, executives may question whether security resources are being allocated effectively, potentially leading to reduced support and funding.

6.6.3.1 Exercise: Audit your current metrics

To begin addressing these challenges, conduct an assessment of your existing security metrics and their business relevance:

1. List all security metrics currently reported to executives and the board
2. For each metric, identify whether it measures an activity, outcome, or impact
3. Map each metric to specific business objectives it supports (if any)
4. Rate each metric's effectiveness in communicating business value (low, medium, high)
5. Identify which metrics executives reference or ask questions about
6. Document any requests from business leaders for specific security information

This exercise will likely reveal significant gaps in your current measurement approach. Many organizations discover that their metrics heavily favor technical activities with minimal connection to business priorities. These gaps represent opportunities to develop more business-aligned security measurements.

When evaluating metrics' alignment with business objectives, consider both explicit connections (such as metrics directly tied to corporate goals) and implicit relationships (such as how security activities indirectly support business initiatives). This analysis provides the foundation for developing more business-relevant security metrics.

🔗 *Downloadable Resource: Security Metrics Audit Tool*

6.7 FRAMEWORK FOR BUSINESS-RELEVANT SECURITY METRICS

Effective security measurement requires a structured framework that aligns with business priorities and stakeholder responsibilities. Organizations can develop more meaningful metrics by establishing clear principles for measurement, organizing metrics into a hierarchy that serves different organizational levels, and categorizing security indicators according to their business contribution. This approach suggests that security metrics can demonstrate tangible value when they connect directly to financial impact, risk reduction, operational performance, and strategic enablement.

6.7.1 Principles of effective security measurement

Effective security metrics must align with enterprise objectives and strategy. Before defining any security measurement, security leaders should understand the organization's strategic priorities, customer promises, and competitive positioning. This alignment ensures that security metrics reflect security's contribution to what matters most to the business.

CFO PERSPECTIVE: WHY SECURITY MEASUREMENT PRINCIPLES MATTER

As a financial executive, you're accustomed to GAAP principles ensuring consistent, comparable financial reporting. Security measurement principles serve a similar purpose – they ensure security investments and risks can be evaluated using consistent business criteria.

Think of these principles as creating the "generally accepted security metrics" for your organization. Just as you wouldn't accept revenue projections without understanding the underlying assumptions, these principles ensure security metrics are built on solid business foundations rather than technical activities that may not reduce real risk.

Key question to ask: "Does this security metric help me make better investment decisions, or is it just measuring technical activity?"

6.7.2 The security metrics hierarchy

Security metrics exist within a hierarchy shown in Figure 6.2, that serves different organizational needs and stakeholders. Understanding this hierarchy helps ensure that metrics are appropriately targeted to their intended audience.

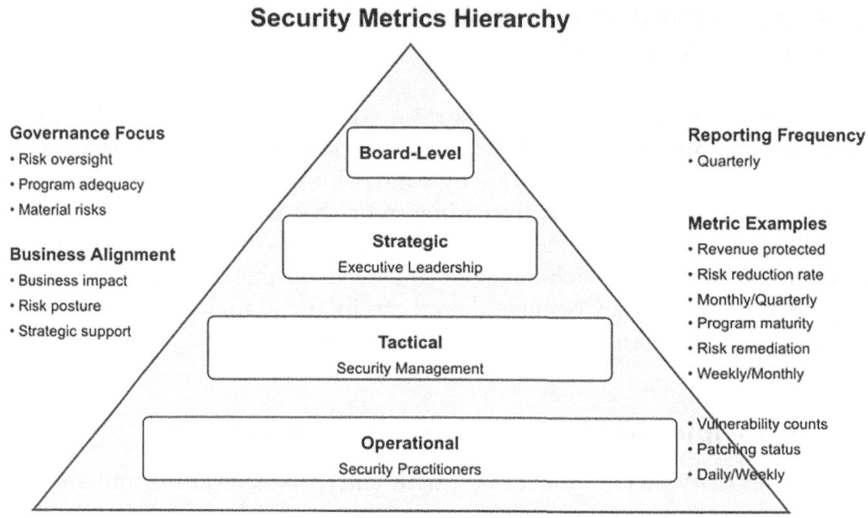

Figure 6.2 Security metrics hierarchy.

At the foundation are operational metrics focusing on day-to-day security activities. These include vulnerability management statistics, incident response metrics, and security control effectiveness measures. While these metrics may not resonate with executives, they provide essential information for security practitioners to manage daily operations effectively.

Tactical metrics measure program effectiveness and trends over time. These include security program maturity assessments, risk remediation progress, and security awareness effectiveness. Middle management and security leadership use these metrics to evaluate program performance and make tactical adjustments.

Strategic metrics address business impact and risk management at an enterprise level. These metrics translate security performance into business terms, such as reduced business risk exposure, security's contribution to customer trust, and the protection of revenue-generating systems. Strategic metrics speak directly to what executives care about most.

At the highest level, board-level metrics focus on governance and oversight responsibilities. These metrics provide board members with the information they need to fulfill their fiduciary duties, including overall risk posture, compliance with regulatory requirements, and security program adequacy relative to industry standards.

Each level in this hierarchy serves a specific purpose, and effective security measurement programs include metrics at all levels. However, when communicating with executives and board members, strategic and board-level metrics should predominate.

Downloadable Resource: Business-Aligned Security Metrics Selection Framework

6.7.3 Categories of business-relevant security metrics

Business-relevant security metrics organize into five essential categories as shown in Figure 6.3, that comprehensively demonstrate security's contribution to enterprise success. Each category addresses specific stakeholder concerns while supporting integrated business decision-making.

6.7.3.1 *Financial impact metrics*

Financial impact metrics translate security performance into monetary terms that resonate with business leaders. These metrics directly support investment decisions and demonstrate security's contribution to the bottom line.

Cost avoidance represents the most straightforward financial metric, calculating losses prevented through security controls. This includes prevented breach costs, avoided regulatory fines, and reduced fraud losses. For example, if industry data shows the average cost of a ransomware incident is $4.5M and your security controls prevent two likely incidents annually, that's $9M in cost avoidance.

Return on Security Investment (ROSI) adapts traditional ROI calculations for security contexts. The formula accounts for risk reduction value, cost

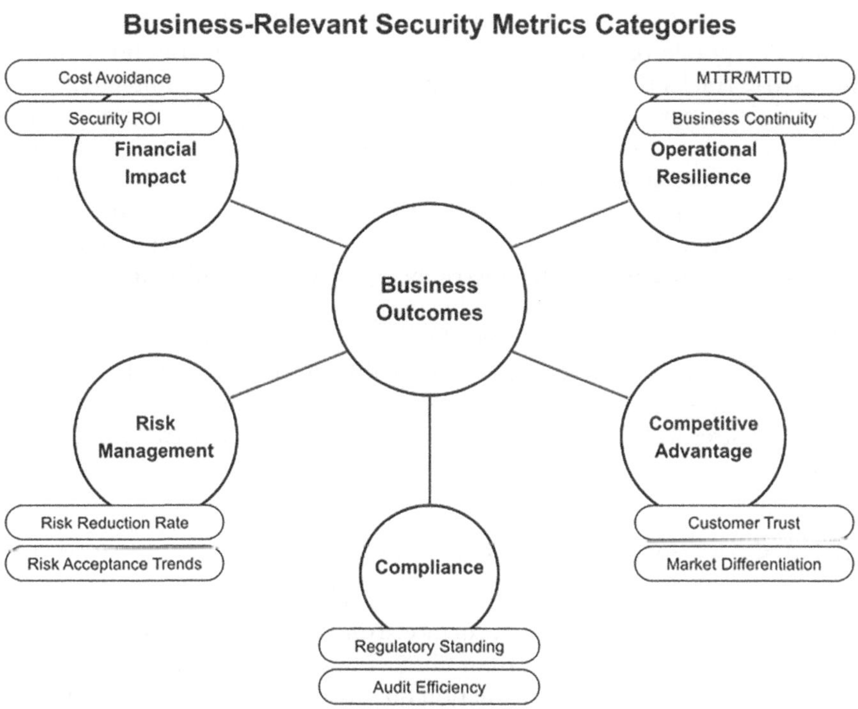

Figure 6.3 Business-relevant security metrics categories.

savings from efficiency improvements, and business enablement benefits. A well-designed identity management system might show 200% ROSI through reduced helpdesk costs, faster employee onboarding, and prevented unauthorized access incidents.

Revenue protection metrics quantify how security safeguards income streams. This includes measuring uptime of revenue-generating systems, calculating customer retention related to security confidence, and assessing security's role in winning new business. For example, tracking how an organization's security certifications shortened sales cycles by 15%, directly contributing to $12M in additional annual revenue.

According to the 2024 Cyber Claims Analysis Report (Coalition, 2024), in 2023, overall cyber claims frequency increased by 13% year over year, and claims severity rose by 10% to an average loss amount of $100,000, highlighting the importance of tracking financial metrics that reflect actual business impact.

6.7.3.2 Risk management metrics

Risk management metrics demonstrate how effectively the security program reduces enterprise risk exposure. These metrics shift the focus from technical vulnerabilities to business risk reduction.

Risk reduction velocity measures how quickly identified risks are brought within acceptable thresholds. Rather than counting vulnerabilities patched, this metric tracks the percentage of material business risks mitigated within target timeframes. Executive teams can understand "90% of high business risks addressed within SLA" better than "10,000 vulnerabilities patched."

Risk exposure trending shows whether overall security risk is increasing or decreasing relative to business growth. As organizations expand digitally, raw risk often increases – but effective security programs keep risk exposure ratios stable or declining. This metric helps executives understand if security investments are keeping pace with business expansion.

Mean Time to Remediate (MTTR) for business-critical risks provides insight into organizational agility. This differs from technical MTTR by focusing exclusively on risks that could materially impact business operations. A shorter MTTR for critical business systems demonstrates operational resilience.

6.7.3.3 Operational excellence metrics

Operational excellence metrics measure security's contribution to business efficiency and continuity. These demonstrate that security, when properly implemented, enhances rather than hinders business operations.

Security-related downtime reduction quantifies how security improvements enhance availability. Modern security architecture often improves system resilience – for example, zero-trust implementations that include redundancy and failover capabilities. Tracking availability improvements directly tied to security initiatives shows positive operational impact.

Process automation effectiveness measures how security technologies reduce manual effort across the organization. Single sign-on implementations, automated access reviews, and security orchestration platforms can dramatically reduce the time spent on routine security tasks. One healthcare organization documented 10,000 hours annually saved through identity management automation.

According to the 2024 Global Digital Trust Insights (PwC, 2024), 47% of executive leaders involved in their company's growth initiatives identified privacy and security as one of the most important technologies for achieving high enterprise revenue growth in the next three years, demonstrating the connection between operational security excellence and business growth.

Business continuity readiness assesses the organization's ability to maintain operations despite security incidents. This includes measuring recovery time objectives (RTO) achievement rates, successful disaster recovery test results, and incident response effectiveness. These metrics relate to operational resilience – a key executive concern.

6.7.3.4 *Strategic enablement metrics*

Strategic enablement metrics demonstrate security's role in facilitating business innovation and competitive advantage. These forward-looking metrics position security as a business accelerator.

Time-to-market acceleration measures how security practices speed up rather than slow down business initiatives. Pre-approved security patterns, automated security testing, and embedded security expertise can reduce project timelines. One technology company tracks how their "secure by design" framework reduced average product launch time by 20%.

Innovation project support rates indicate security's contribution to digital transformation. This metric tracks the percentage of innovation initiatives successfully supported by security without compromising risk management. High support rates demonstrate that security enables rather than blocks business evolution.

Competitive differentiation metrics assess how security capabilities influence market position. This includes win/loss analysis where security was a factor, customer trust scores compared to competitors, and security's influence on partnership opportunities. Many B2B companies find that superior security directly correlates with higher win rates.

6.7.3.5 *Compliance and governance metrics*

While compliance alone doesn't equal security, governance metrics remain important for demonstrating due diligence and regulatory adherence. These metrics should emphasize effectiveness over checkbox completion.

Regulatory compliance efficiency tracks not just compliance status, but the resources required to maintain it. Mature security programs often achieve multiple compliance frameworks with minimal incremental effort. This efficiency metric demonstrates good security governance without excessive cost.

Control effectiveness ratings move beyond control existence to measure actual risk reduction. Rather than reporting "100% of required controls implemented," this metric assesses how well controls reduce genuine business risk. This approach satisfies both regulatory requirements and business risk management needs.

Third-party risk management metrics have become increasingly important as supply chains digitize. Tracking vendor security assessment results, time to onboard secure vendors, and supply chain incident impacts demonstrates proactive governance that protects business relationships.

These five categories provide a comprehensive framework for measuring security's business value. By organizing metrics within these categories, security leaders can ensure they address all aspects of business concern while maintaining clear connections between security activities and business outcomes. The key is selecting specific metrics within each category that align with your organization's particular business priorities and risk appetite.

These business-relevant metrics provide the measurement framework needed to support the investment valuation techniques discussed in Chapter 5, enabling security leaders to demonstrate a ROSI. Chapter 9 applies these metrics within broader frameworks for demonstrating security's positive business contribution beyond risk reduction.

With a framework for business-relevant metrics established, the practical challenge becomes translating specific security activities into language that resonates with business stakeholders. This translation process requires both methodological rigor and clear communication strategies to bridge the gap between technical implementation and business value.

Downloadable Exercise: Designing Your Metrics Framework

6.8 LINKING SECURITY ACTIVITIES TO BUSINESS OUTCOMES

The translation of technical security activities into business language represents a fundamental shift in how security teams communicate their value. Rather than reporting on implementation percentages or technical achievements, security leaders can express their contributions in terms of revenue protection, cost avoidance, and business enablement. This translation process requires robust data collection methods and validation techniques to ensure that security metrics provide credible evidence of business value and risk reduction.

6.8.1 Translating technical activities into business language

The translation principles from Chapter 3's BIA methodology apply directly to security metrics. Rather than developing new translation approaches, security leaders can adapt the BIA framework to convert technical security activities into business language. For example, "We've reduced the risk of unauthorized access to customer data and financial systems by 60%, protecting $50 million in annual revenue." This translation connects security controls directly to business value protection.

Expressing security effectiveness in terms of business enablement positions security as a strategic partner rather than a barrier. For example, rather than describing cloud security assessment procedures, highlight how "Our secure cloud implementation framework has accelerated product launches by an average of 15 days while maintaining appropriate protection of customer data." This framing demonstrates security's contribution to business agility and time-to-market advantages.

Quantifying the business value of security investments transforms perceived costs into strategic investments. This may include calculating prevented losses, efficiency improvements, or competitive advantages gained through security capabilities. Even rough estimates of business value provide more meaningful context than technical metrics alone. Additional examples are shown in Figure 6.4.

Security's contribution to strategic initiatives should be explicitly measured and communicated. Whether supporting digital transformation, geographic expansion, or new product development, security metrics should demonstrate how security activities enable these initiatives to succeed while managing associated risks.

This translation approach builds on the reframing techniques we introduced in Chapter 2, where we examined how to convert technical security issues into business language. Chapter 9 builds on this translation approach with a comprehensive matrix that maps security capabilities to business objectives across multiple dimensions.

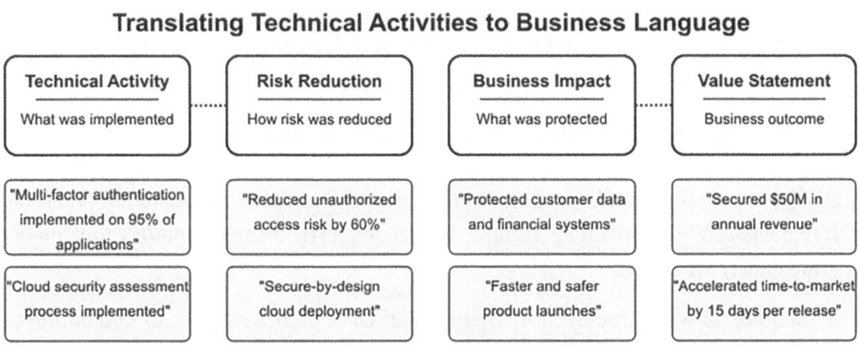

Figure 6.4 Translating technical activities to business language.

Downloadable Resource: Security Investment ROI Calculator
Downloadable Resource: Security-Business Value Mapping Workshop

6.8.2 Methods for gathering and validating metric data

Effective security measurement requires robust data collection approaches and tools. Organizations should identify authoritative data sources for each metric, establish automated collection processes where possible, and implement manual collection procedures where automation is not workable. The data collection strategy should balance comprehensiveness with efficiency to ensure sustainable measurement over time.

Data quality controls are essential for maintaining credible security metrics. These include:

- Source validation: Verifying that data comes from authoritative, reliable sources
- Consistency checks: Ensuring measurements use consistent methodologies over time
- Cross-validation: Comparing related data points to identify discrepancies
- Anomaly detection: Flagging unusual patterns for investigation before reporting
- Documentation: Maintaining clear records of data sources and calculation methods

CFO PERSPECTIVE: DATA QUALITY IN SECURITY METRICS

The data quality controls described here mirror the internal controls you expect in financial reporting. Just as you require supporting documentation for material journal entries, security metrics need similar validation to be trustworthy for decision-making.

Consider security data validation as equivalent to:

Source validation = Ensuring legitimate supporting documents

Consistency checks = Matching intercompany transactions

Cross – validation = Reconciling subsidiary ledgers to general ledger

Anomaly detection = Variance analysis on financial statements

Without these controls, security metrics are as unreliable as unaudited financial statements. When evaluating security budget requests, insist on metrics that meet these quality standards.

Red flag to watch for: Security metrics that can't be traced back to authoritative data sources or that change calculation methods between reporting periods.

Frequency considerations affect both data collection and reporting cycles. Real-time monitoring supports operational security management, while weekly, monthly, or quarterly reporting aligns with business review cycles. The appropriate frequency depends on the nature of the metric, stakeholder needs, and the volatility of the measured activity.

Validation techniques ensure the accuracy and reliability of security metrics. These may include independent verification, stakeholder feedback, and periodic audits. For particularly important metrics, consider implementing peer review processes where multiple stakeholders validate the measurement methodology and results before presentation to executives.

6.8.3 Case study: LabMD, Inc. v. FTC (2018)

6.8.3.1 Context

LabMD was a Georgia-based medical laboratory that conducted cancer detection testing services for physicians. As a healthcare provider handling sensitive patient information, the company was subject to data security regulations including those under the Health Insurance Portability and Accountability Act (HIPAA). Like many organizations in the healthcare sector, LabMD maintained a data security program designed to protect the confidential patient information it processed, which included names, birthdates, Social Security numbers, and medical test results.

The company's business operations required managing and transferring sensitive patient data among healthcare providers, insurance companies, and internal systems. This data flow was essential to its core business function of providing diagnostic test results to physicians. As a relatively small operation with limited resources, LabMD faced the common challenge of balancing security requirements with operational needs.

6.8.3.2 Challenge

In 2008, LabMD discovered that a file containing the personal information of approximately 9,300 patients had been exposed on a peer-to-peer file-sharing network. The exposure occurred when an employee, against company policy, installed LimeWire (a popular file-sharing application) on a company computer used for billing. This installation inadvertently made a 1,718-page spreadsheet containing patient information accessible to millions of users on the Gnutella network.

The exposure was first identified not by LabMD's internal security controls, but by Tiversa, a security company that specialized in monitoring peer-to-peer networks. After discovering the file, Tiversa contacted LabMD and attempted to sell remediation services. When LabMD declined these services, the patient information file eventually made its way to the Federal Trade Commission (FTC).

Following a lengthy investigation, the FTC filed an administrative complaint against LabMD in 2013, alleging that the company had engaged in "unfair acts or practices" by failing to provide "reasonable and appropriate" security for personal information. This launched what would become a pivotal legal battle centered on a fundamental question: What constitutes "reasonable" security, and how should it be measured?

The FTC's complaint did not allege specific security failures with clear metrics or standards. Instead, it broadly claimed that LabMD:

- Failed to develop and maintain a comprehensive information security program
- Did not use readily available measures to identify risks
- Failed to train employees adequately
- Did not require appropriate authentication measures
- Did not maintain and update operating systems
- Failed to employ readily available measures to prevent unauthorized access

The challenge for LabMD extended beyond the original security incident – they now faced a regulatory action based on undefined standards of "reasonableness" without specific metrics to determine compliance.

6.8.3.3 Approach

LabMD took several immediate steps to address the specific security issue by removing the file-sharing software from the affected computer and securing the exposed file. However, the company chose to challenge the FTC's authority and approach rather than accept a consent decree with ongoing compliance requirements.

The case proceeded through multiple stages:

1. Initially, an Administrative Law Judge (ALJ) dismissed the FTC's complaint in 2015, ruling that the agency failed to prove that LabMD's data security practices caused or were likely to cause substantial injury to consumers.
2. The FTC Commission reversed this decision in 2016, finding that LabMD's security practices were indeed "unfair" under Section 5 of the FTC Act. The Commission issued a final order requiring LabMD to implement a "comprehensive information security program that is reasonably designed to protect the security, confidentiality, and integrity of personal information."
3. LabMD appealed to the U.S. Court of Appeals for the Eleventh Circuit, challenging both the FTC's authority and the enforceability of its order.

Throughout this process, LabMD's approach focused on highlighting the absence of specific, measurable security standards in the FTC's case against them. The company argued that the FTC's allegations were based on an undefined standard of "reasonableness" rather than specific security requirements that could be objectively measured and implemented.

6.8.3.4 Outcome

In June 2018, the Eleventh Circuit ruled in LabMD's favor (LabMD, Inc. v. Federal Trade Commission, 2019) finding that the FTC's cease and desist order was unenforceable. Importantly, the court did not rule on whether the FTC had the authority to regulate data security practices. Instead, it focused on the lack of specificity in the order itself.

The court's decision highlighted several key issues directly relevant to security metrics:

1. The order contained no prohibitions of specific acts or practices. Instead, it commanded "a complete overhaul of LabMD's data-security program" without specifying how this should be accomplished.
2. The requirement to implement a "reasonably designed" security program lacked any measurable standard to determine compliance.
3. Enforcement would be impossible because neither the company nor a court could objectively determine what would constitute a "reasonably designed" program.

The court illustrated this problem by describing a hypothetical enforcement scenario: If the FTC alleged that LabMD failed to implement a specific security measure (call it "x"), and LabMD's expert testified that "x" was not necessary for a reasonable security program while the FTC's expert disagreed, how would a court determine which expert was correct? Without specific metrics in the order, this would be impossible.

The court stated: "The practical effect of repeatedly modifying the injunction at show cause hearings is that the district court is put in the position of managing LabMD's business in accordance with the Commission's wishes. It would be as if the Commission was LabMD's chief executive officer and the court was its operating officer."

By the time of this ruling, LabMD had effectively ceased operations, though it still existed as a company and continued to secure its computers and patient data.

6.8.3.5 Lessons

The LabMD case offers several valuable lessons about security metrics that align directly with this chapter's focus on measuring security in business terms:

1. Vague standards are unenforceable and unmeasurable. Without specific, measurable security requirements, organizations cannot determine compliance, regulators cannot enforce standards, and courts cannot

adjudicate disputes. Security metrics must be precise enough to determine when they have been met.
2. "Reasonable" is not a metric. Terms like "reasonable" and "appropriate" are subjective qualifiers, not quantifiable measures. Effective security metrics must specify what is being measured and what threshold constitutes success.
3. Security programs need operational definitions. As the court noted, without specific guidance on what constitutes compliance, security requirements become moving targets subject to changing interpretations. Organizations need clearly defined metrics that enable consistent evaluation.
4. Business impact requires measurable standards. Without clear metrics, organizations cannot effectively budget for, implement, or measure the success of security programs. This creates business uncertainty and potential regulatory risk.
5. Metrics enable governance and compliance. The case demonstrates that both regulated entities and regulators benefit from clearly defined, measurable security standards that can be objectively evaluated.

For security leaders like CISOs and CFOs, the LabMD case underscores the business necessity of developing concrete security metrics that:

- Define specific security controls and practices required
- Establish clear thresholds for compliance
- Enable objective measurement of security posture
- Facilitate meaningful reporting to business stakeholders
- Support defensible security investment decisions

As Judge Tjoflat wrote in the Eleventh Circuit's opinion, "it commands LabMD to overhaul and replace its data-security program to meet an indeterminable standard of reasonableness. This command is unenforceable. Its unenforceability is made clear if we imagine what would take place if the Commission sought the order's enforcement." This question encapsulates why vague security standards without specific metrics create significant business risk – they leave organizations unable to determine compliance, measure progress, or demonstrate value.

The most enduring lesson from the LabMD case is that security must be measured in concrete, business-relevant terms rather than abstract concepts of "reasonableness." Only then can organizations effectively manage security risks, communicate with business leaders, and meet regulatory requirements in a demonstrable way.

The LabMD case has important implications for the regulatory and compliance aspects of security governance that we'll explore further in Chapter 7, where we discuss legal drivers for integrated security governance.

Once security teams can effectively translate their activities into business terms, the next consideration involves tailoring these communications to meet the specific needs and responsibilities of different organizational stakeholders. Each audience brings distinct perspectives and information requirements that influence how security metrics should be presented and discussed.

6.9 STAKEHOLDER-SPECIFIC METRICS AND REPORTING

Different stakeholders across the organization require distinct types of security information to fulfill their specific responsibilities and make appropriate decisions. Board members, executives, business unit leaders, and regulators each bring unique perspectives and information needs to security discussions. Effective security reporting appears to require customization of metrics, frequency, and format to match stakeholder responsibilities while maintaining consistency in underlying measurement approaches.

6.9.1 Tailoring metrics to different audiences

Effective security communication requires tailoring metrics to the specific concerns and responsibilities of different stakeholders. One-size-fits-all reporting fails to address the unique information needs of various audiences.

For the Board of Directors, security metrics should focus on governance, risk management, and compliance responsibilities. Board members need assurance that the organization's risk exposure aligns with its risk appetite, that security investments are appropriate relative to the threat landscape, and that the organization meets its legal and regulatory obligations. Effective board metrics include aggregated risk posture, security program adequacy compared to peers, and significant security risk trends that could impact corporate strategy.

C-Suite executives require metrics addressing strategic alignment, resource allocation, and competitive positioning. These leaders need to understand how security supports business objectives, whether security resources are optimally distributed, and how security capabilities compare to industry peers and competitors. Metrics for this audience might include security investment efficiency, security program maturity compared to industry benchmarks, and security's contribution to strategic business initiatives.

Business Unit Leaders focus on operational impact, enablement, and productivity concerns. These stakeholders need insights into how security affects their specific operations, how security requirements influence their projects and initiatives, and what security risks are specifically relevant to their business functions. Effective metrics include security's impact on time-to-market, security-related process friction, and business unit-specific risk assessment results.

Regulators require evidence of compliance, due diligence, and reasonable security practices. These stakeholders need assurance that the organization is meeting specific regulatory requirements, implementing appropriate safeguards for sensitive information, and exercising due care in its security program. Metrics for regulators typically include compliance status, control effectiveness assessments, and documentation of the organization's risk-based approach to security.

These board-level metrics support the governance structures discussed in Chapter 7, where we explore the board's evolving role in security risk oversight.

6.9.2 Frequency and format considerations

The timing and presentation of security metrics can significantly impact their effectiveness. Security leaders must balance the need for timely information with the risk of creating information overload.

Real-time monitoring versus periodic reporting requires careful consideration. While security operations teams need continuous visibility into security events and anomalies, executives typically benefit from consolidated reporting at regular intervals aligned with business review cycles. Reserve real-time reporting for exceptional circumstances that require immediate executive attention.

The choice between push and pull information delivery affects stakeholder engagement. Push delivery (proactively providing reports on a scheduled basis) ensures consistent visibility but risks information overload. Pull delivery (making information available for stakeholders to access as needed) respects stakeholders' time but may cause inconsistent awareness. Many organizations adopt a hybrid approach, pushing summary reports while making detailed information available on-demand.

Standardized reports provide consistency while ad hoc analysis addresses emerging concerns. Regular reporting should follow standardized formats to facilitate trend analysis and ensure comprehensive coverage. However, security leaders should maintain the capacity for targeted analysis addressing specific executive questions or emerging risk concerns outside the standard reporting cycle.

Balancing detail with clarity and actionability represents an ongoing challenge. Technical details provide the necessary context for security professionals but can obscure key insights for executives. Effective security reporting leads with business implications before providing supporting technical details, allowing stakeholders to engage at their preferred level of depth.

Understanding stakeholder-specific needs establishes the foundation for developing presentation approaches that maximize the impact of security communications. The effectiveness of security metrics often depends as much on how information is visualized and communicated as on the underlying measurement methodology itself.

Downloadable Exercise: Developing Stakeholder-Specific Reports

6.10 VISUALIZATION AND COMMUNICATION TECHNIQUES

The presentation and visualization of security information can significantly influence stakeholder understanding and decision-making effectiveness. Clear communication principles, well-designed executive dashboards, and advanced visualization techniques may transform complex security data into actionable business insights. These approaches suggest that how security information is presented can be as important as what information is shared, particularly when communicating with non-technical business leaders.

6.10.1 Principles of effective security communication

The communication principles established in Chapter 3 for risk documentation apply equally to metrics presentation. Building on those foundations, metrics-specific communication requires additional considerations. Each security metric should be presented within the context of related business objectives, industry trends, or historical performance. This contextual framing helps stakeholders understand why the information matters and what actions it might warrant.

Consistency in format and terminology builds understanding over time. Security communications should maintain consistent definitions, calculation methodologies, and visual formats across reporting periods. This consistency allows stakeholders to focus on changes in the metrics rather than deciphering new presentation formats or terminology with each report.

A storytelling approach drives understanding and action more effectively than raw data. Rather than presenting a collection of metrics, effective security communication weaves these data points into a coherent narrative that explains what happened, why it matters, and what should be done as a result. This narrative structure makes security information more memorable and actionable for business leaders.

6.10.2 Dashboard development for executive audiences

Executive security dashboards consolidate key security metrics into a visual format that facilitates quick understanding and decision-making. Effective security dashboards balance comprehensiveness with usability, providing sufficient detail without overwhelming the audience.

Key components of effective security dashboards include:

- Executive summary highlighting critical insights and required actions
- Key performance indicators showing current status against targets
- Trend indicators demonstrating performance changes over time
- Risk exposure assessment showing overall security posture

- Exception reporting highlighting areas requiring attention
- Forward-looking indicators predicting future risk developments

Dashboards should be customized for different stakeholders based on their specific responsibilities and interests. While maintaining a consistent overall structure, dashboard content should emphasize metrics most relevant to each audience. For example, a CFO's dashboard might highlight financial risk exposures and security investment effectiveness, while a COO's dashboard would focus on operational resilience and security program efficiency. An example of a dashboard for a security executive is shown in Figure 6.5.

Various tools and technologies support dashboard implementation, from sophisticated security information platforms to simple spreadsheet-based visualizations. The appropriate technology depends on data volume, update frequency, and integration requirements. For many organizations, starting with simpler visualization tools allows for refinement of metrics and formats before investing in more complex dashboard technologies.

These visualization approaches complement the communication strategies introduced in Chapter 2, providing powerful tools for translating complex security concepts into business-relevant insights. Chapter 9 extends these dashboard concepts with specific approaches for executive communications that position security as a business investment rather than an expense.

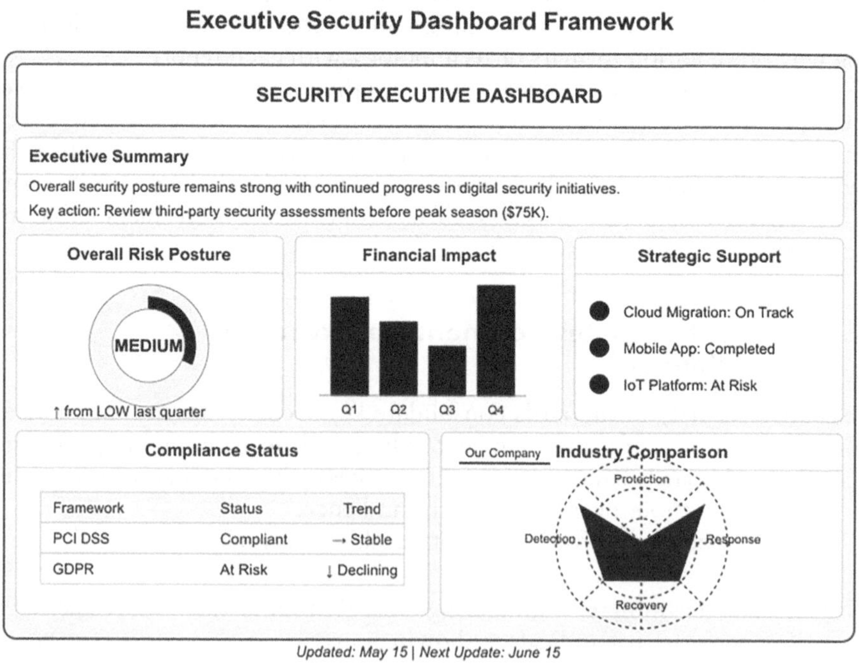

Figure 6.5 Executive security dashboard framework.

6.10.3 Advanced visualization techniques

Heat maps provide an intuitive visualization of risk prioritization, using color intensity to indicate risk levels across different categories. This technique is particularly effective for showing the distribution of risk across business units, systems, or threat categories. Heat maps allow executives to identify high-risk areas requiring attention without wading through detailed risk registers.

CFO PERSPECTIVE: SECURITY VISUALIZATIONS THAT DRIVE FINANCIAL DECISIONS

These visualization techniques translate complex security data into formats familiar from financial analysis:

Heat maps for risk = Like credit risk matrices showing probability vs. severity

Trend analysis = Like revenue forecasting, but for security incidents and costs

Comparative benchmarking = Industry peer analysis for security spending efficiency

Scenario modeling = Sensitivity analysis showing security ROI under different threat conditions

The goal isn't to become a security expert, but to see security information presented in ways that support capital allocation decisions. Request visualizations that answer: "What's our security ROI compared to other investments?" and "How does our security risk compare to other enterprise risks?"

What to request: Ask for security dashboards that look more like financial dashboards – showing variances, trends, and comparative performance rather than technical statistics.

Trend analysis and forecasting visualizations help stakeholders understand how security metrics change over time and what future developments may occur. Line charts showing metric trajectories, forecasting models predicting future values, and variance indicators highlighting deviations from expected trends all provide valuable temporal context for security metrics.

Comparative benchmarking visualizations place an organization's security performance in context relative to industry peers, best practices, or historical baselines. Radar charts comparing multiple security dimensions, percentile rankings showing relative position among peers, and gap analysis visuals highlighting deviation from targets all help executives understand whether security performance is adequate.

According to the 2024 Global Digital Trust Insights (PwC, 2024), top-performing organizations – identified as the top 5% or "stewards of digital trust" – report that 96% consistently communicate cyber strategy and practices in a way that helps earn the trust of customers and business partners, compared to just 30% overall, underscoring the importance of translating technical security information into business-relevant insights for leadership.

This statistic demonstrates that effective communication and visualization of security information in business terms is a hallmark of high-performing organizations and is important for building trust and executive support.

Scenario modeling and simulation visualizations illustrate potential outcomes based on different risk conditions or security investments. Decision trees showing alternative risk response paths, impact scenarios demonstrating potential business consequences, and investment optimization models comparing security control options all help executives understand the implications of security decisions before they are made.

Downloadable Exercise: Dashboard Design Workshop

6.11 CONCLUSION

Security metrics must transform from technical measures to business indicators if security leaders hope to secure appropriate resources and strategic influence. This fundamental shift requires security professionals to think differently about what they measure and how they communicate performance to business stakeholders.

Effective measurement requires alignment with enterprise objectives and stakeholder needs. Security metrics that fail to connect with business priorities will be ignored or discounted in executive decision-making. By contrast, metrics that demonstrate security's contribution to revenue protection, cost avoidance, competitive advantage, and operational resilience position security as a strategic business function rather than a technical specialty.

The framework presented in this chapter provides a structured approach to developing business-relevant metrics. By categorizing metrics according to the security metrics hierarchy, considering different stakeholder perspectives, and implementing robust data collection and validation processes, security leaders can create measurement systems that drive better business decisions.

Regular evaluation and refinement of metrics ensure continued relevance and value. As business priorities shift, technology landscapes change, and threat environments become increasingly complex, security metrics must evolve accordingly. Establishing a process for periodically reviewing and updating security metrics ensures that measurement continues to inform effective decision-making.

The next chapter will explore how these metrics support governance structures for ongoing security program management. With business-relevant metrics in place, security leaders can implement governance frameworks that align security investments with enterprise risk appetite, ensure appropriate oversight of security activities, and maintain accountability for security performance.

Metrics that matter form the foundation of demonstrating security's business value. By translating technical security performance into business terms, security leaders can elevate their strategic influence, secure appropriate resources, and position security as an enabler of business success rather than a cost center. In today's business environment, this business alignment is no longer optional – it is essential for security program effectiveness and organizational resilience.

6.12 ACTION ITEMS FOR READERS

1. Audit your current security metrics portfolio by categorizing each metric as either activity-based (patching rates, vulnerability counts) or outcome-based (business risk reduction, revenue protection), then identify which metrics fail to demonstrate clear business value and should be replaced or enhanced.
2. Develop baseline business-aligned metrics by selecting 2-3 metrics from each of the five categories (Financial Impact, Risk Management, Operational Excellence, Strategic Enablement, and Compliance & Governance) that directly connect to your organization's strategic priorities and can be measured with existing data sources.
3. Conduct stakeholder interviews with your board members, C-suite executives, and business unit leaders to understand their specific information needs, decision-making processes, and preferred communication formats, then map these requirements to appropriate metric categories and reporting frequencies.
4. Create stakeholder-specific security dashboards that translate your technical security performance into business language, ensuring each dashboard emphasizes metrics most relevant to that audience's responsibilities and includes contextual information that explains why the metrics matter for business success.
5. Establish a quarterly metrics review process to evaluate metric effectiveness, validate data accuracy, and refine measurements based on changing business priorities, stakeholder feedback, and the ability of current metrics to drive appropriate security investment decisions.

Downloadable Resource: Security Communication Playbook

Chapter 7

Governance models for integrated security and risk

Chapter in One Sentence: Effective security governance integrates technical expertise with business objectives through clear decision rights, appropriate committee structures, and tailored implementation models that enable managing security as a true business risk rather than an isolated technical specialty.

7.1 EXECUTIVE SUMMARY

This chapter addresses the critical need to bridge the gap between technical security expertise and business decision-making through integrated governance models. Historically, security governance operated in isolation from broader business risk management, leading to misaligned priorities, inefficient resource allocation, and security investments that failed to address key business risks. As digital transformation expands attack surfaces and security breaches increasingly impact business operations, integrating security governance with business risk management has become essential.

The chapter provides practical frameworks for establishing governance structures that balance security requirements with business objectives. It examines decision authority models that clarify who makes different types of security risk decisions, from board-level oversight to operational implementation. Decision rights should be assigned based on risk impact, with appropriate thresholds guiding escalation paths. The board's role has changed significantly in recent years, with 82% of board members reporting increased involvement in cybersecurity oversight compared to two years ago.

Various governance structures are explored, including board committees, executive risk committees (now present in 58% of organizations), and CISO reporting relationships. The chapter analyzes centralized, federated, and hybrid implementation models, highlighting how each approach balances consistency with business alignment. Centralized models offer standardization but may create business disconnects, while federated models improve

DOI: 10.1201/9781003744146-7

business alignment but challenge enterprise-wide consistency. Most organizations benefit from hybrid approaches that combine centralized policies with distributed implementation.

Organizations typically evolve through predictable maturity stages, from initial ad hoc approaches to optimized governance. Successful implementation requires addressing resistance from both security leaders concerned about preserving expertise and business executives who may view security as merely a technical specialty. The chapter concludes that effective governance creates structures where security is managed as a true business risk, supporting informed decisions about security investments, risk acceptance, and control implementation.

7.2 KEY TAKEAWAYS

- Effective security governance requires balancing technical expertise with business alignment through transparent, accountable, and proportional approaches that connect security decisions to business outcomes
- Decision authority should be assigned based on potential business impact, with clear frameworks specifying who makes different types of security risk decisions under various circumstances
- The board's oversight role has expanded significantly, requiring formal committee structures, regular security reporting, and clear risk appetite statements that guide management decisions
- No single governance model works for all organizations; most benefit from hybrid approaches that combine centralized policies with flexibility in implementation based on business context
- Sustainable governance requires ongoing adaptation through regular reviews, succession planning, and strong connections to organizational security culture

7.3 APPLICATION QUESTIONS

1. How might your organization's existing security governance structures be enhanced to better align security decisions with business objectives while maintaining appropriate technical oversight?
2. Where do security risk decisions currently happen in your organization, and are these decisions being made at the appropriate level based on potential business impact?
3. What specific steps could you take to overcome resistance from both security leaders and business executives to create more integrated governance models?

7.4 TOOLS REFERENCED IN THIS CHAPTER

All tools available at kaynemcgladrey.com/myth/

- Decision Authority Matrix for Security Risks
- Risk Appetite Statement Development Framework
- Exercise: Decision Rights Mapping
- Exercise: Governance Structure Assessment
- Exercise: Governance Implementation Planning
- Security Governance Maturity Assessment
- Exercise: Resistance Mapping and Mitigation

7.5 INTRODUCTION

Security risk governance has historically operated in isolation from broader business risk management practices, creating significant challenges for organizations. Technical teams often make security decisions without an adequate business context, while business leaders may approve initiatives without understanding their security implications. As discussed throughout this book, this disconnect has led to misaligned priorities, inefficient resource allocation, and security investments that fail to address the most important business risks.

Modern organizations require integrated approaches that connect security decisions directly to business outcomes. This integration has become particularly urgent as digital transformation initiatives accelerate, expanding the attack surface and increasing potential business impacts from security incidents. When security governance operates separately from business governance, organizations struggle to make risk-informed decisions that balance security requirements with business objectives.

This chapter bridges the gap between security expertise and business decision-making by providing practical frameworks for integrated governance. Rather than treating security as a technical specialty disconnected from business concerns, these models position security as a fundamental business risk that requires coordinated oversight and management. This approach ensures that security investments align with business priorities and that business decisions incorporate appropriate security considerations.

The governance models introduced here promote sustainable integration by establishing clear decision rights, committee structures, and reporting relationships. These elements work together to create a cohesive system that supports informed decision-making at all levels of the organization. Unlike purely technical governance approaches, these models explicitly connect security decisions to the business context, risk appetite, and strategic objectives.

Boards, executives, and security leaders must collaborate effectively for proper security risk oversight. Each group brings an important perspective – boards provide strategic direction and risk oversight, executives balance competing priorities across business functions, and security leaders contribute technical expertise and threat awareness. The models presented in this chapter clarify how these stakeholders can work together to manage security risks while supporting business objectives.

Understanding these governance models sets the stage for managing security as a true business risk rather than a technical specialty. Organizations that implement effective integrated governance can make better-informed decisions about security investments, respond more effectively to emerging threats, and maintain appropriate security oversight without creating unnecessary friction. This chapter provides practical guidance for establishing governance structures that support these outcomes across organizations of different sizes, industries, and maturity levels.

7.6 FOUNDATIONS OF INTEGRATED SECURITY GOVERNANCE

Security governance has traditionally operated as an isolated function, creating disconnects between technical security decisions and business priorities. Organizations that maintain these silos often struggle with misaligned investments, inefficient resource allocation, and security measures that fail to address material business risks. This section examines the drivers pushing organizations toward integrated approaches and establishes the core principles that support sustainable integration between security expertise and business objectives.

7.6.1 The evolution from siloed to integrated governance

Historically, security governance has operated separately from broader business risk management processes. As mentioned in chapter one, this separation emerged naturally as security functions developed as technical specialties requiring specific expertise. Security teams typically reported through IT organizations and maintained their own governance processes focused on technical controls, standards compliance, and vulnerability management. Meanwhile, business risk governance addressed financial, operational, and strategic risks through separate structures and reporting lines.

Several important drivers have pushed organizations toward more integrated approaches in recent years. Boards are paying increased attention to security risks following high-profile breaches with significant business impacts. The 2017 Equifax breach, which affected 147 million consumers and resulted in a $575 million settlement, exemplifies the type of incident that has elevated security to board-level concern. Regulatory requirements have also expanded, with regulations like the SEC's 2023 cybersecurity disclosure rules mandating more formal security oversight.

The growing business impact of security incidents has further highlighted the need for integration. When Colonial Pipeline shut down operations following a ransomware attack in 2021, the business impact extended far beyond IT systems to affect fuel availability across the eastern United States. Such incidents demonstrate that security risks now represent material business risks requiring coordinated governance.

Integrating security governance with business risk management provides several important benefits. Decision quality improves when security and business perspectives are considered together, leading to more balanced risk management approaches. Resource allocation becomes more effective as security investments align with business priorities rather than technical preferences. Risk visibility improves at all levels of the organization, ensuring that senior leaders understand security risks in a business context.

Research supports this trend toward integration. According to the 2025 IT Risk and Compliance Benchmark Report (Hyperproof, 2025), "91% of organizations have a centralized governance, risk, and compliance (GRC) program that operates across business units and geographies." This statistic demonstrates the widespread adoption of centralized GRC programs, which are foundational for supporting integrated security risk management and effective reporting relationships across the enterprise.

Organizations that maintain siloed governance structures may struggle with several common problems. Security teams often struggle to get business buy-in for important security initiatives because they cannot effectively articulate business value. Business leaders may make decisions without understanding security implications, leading to increased risk exposure. Resource allocation becomes inefficient when security investments are not prioritized based on business impact. These challenges highlight the importance of moving toward more integrated governance models.

This governance evolution directly addresses the historical separation discussed in Chapter 1, providing structural solutions to the organizational silos that have traditionally separated security from business risk management.

7.6.2 Core principles of effective security governance

Effective security governance relies on several core principles that support sustainable integration with business risk management. These principles provide a foundation for designing governance structures that balance security expertise with business objectives.

Transparency forms the first essential principle. Security risks must be visible to business decision-makers in terms they can understand and act upon. Rather than obscuring risks behind technical jargon or complexity, effective governance makes security risks clear to all stakeholders. This transparency includes communicating risk levels, control effectiveness, and potential business impacts in business language.

Accountability represents another fundamental principle. Integrated governance requires clear ownership of both risks and control effectiveness. This accountability should extend to both security and business leaders – security teams are accountable for identifying risks and recommending controls, while business leaders are accountable for risk acceptance decisions and ensuring adequate resources for risk management. Without clear accountability, security risks may fall through organizational cracks or be improperly managed.

Proportionality ensures that governance approaches match the organization's size and risk profile. Small organizations with limited resources need lightweight governance that addresses key risks without creating unnecessary overhead. Large enterprises with complex risk landscapes may require more formal governance structures with dedicated committees and detailed decision frameworks. Governance that is disproportionate to organizational needs creates either inadequate risk management or excessive bureaucracy.

Business alignment connects security decisions directly to strategic objectives. Rather than making security decisions based solely on technical factors, aligned governance considers how security supports or constrains business goals. This alignment includes connecting security investment decisions to business priorities, adapting security requirements to different business contexts, and ensuring that security governance operates at a speed compatible with business needs.

When effectively applied, these core principles create security governance that supports rather than hinders business objectives. Security becomes a business enabler rather than just a cost center or compliance function. Business leaders gain confidence that security decisions reflect business priorities, while security teams gain the organizational support needed to address important risks. Most importantly, integrated governance based on these principles helps organizations manage security as a true business risk rather than a technical specialty.

7.6.3 Regulatory and legal drivers of security governance

Regulatory requirements and legal precedents have become increasingly important drivers of security governance structures. Organizations must navigate a complex landscape of regulations that mandate specific governance practices for security risk management.

The SEC is a particularly important regulator for public companies in the United States. Its 2023 cybersecurity rules require disclosure of board oversight practices for cybersecurity risks, creating direct pressure for more formal governance structures. These rules require companies to "describe the board's oversight of risks from cybersecurity threats," including which board committees are responsible for cybersecurity risk oversight and how the board is informed about these risks.

Other regulations impose similar requirements across different industries and geographies. The EU's General Data Protection Regulation (GDPR) requires organizations to implement appropriate security measures based on risk, implying the need for risk-based security governance.

Industry-specific regulations like HIPAA in healthcare and the New York Department of Financial Services (NYDFS) Cybersecurity Regulation in financial services mandate specific governance practices for security risk management.

Legal precedents are also establishing board duties for security oversight. The Delaware Court of Chancery's opinion in the Marriott case (Firemen's Ret. Sys. of St. Louis v. Sorenson, 2021) recognized cybersecurity as a "mission-critical" risk requiring board oversight. This opinion established that boards have a fiduciary duty to monitor "mission-critical" corporate risks, including cybersecurity risks, and may face liability for failing to establish reporting systems for these risks.

The Marriott case has implications for governance structures. The court highlighted the importance of regular board-level reporting on security risks and the need for directors to address red flags indicating potential control deficiencies. This decision suggests that boards should establish formal oversight structures for security risks, receive regular reporting on these risks, and actively address identified issues.

These regulatory and legal drivers are pushing organizations toward more formal, documented governance structures for security risk management. Organizations that fail to establish appropriate governance may face regulatory penalties, shareholder lawsuits, and potential director liability. However, compliance-focused governance that does not adequately consider business context may create unnecessary friction without effectively managing the most important risks.

7.6.4 Common governance challenges

Organizations implementing integrated security governance often encounter several common challenges that can undermine effectiveness. Understanding these challenges helps organizations design governance structures that avoid typical pitfalls.

Authority conflicts between security and business units often arise when governance roles are unclear. Security teams may believe they have authority to mandate controls across the organization, while business units may expect full autonomy in risk acceptance decisions. These conflicts can lead to adversarial relationships, with security teams labeled as "business blockers" and business units viewed as "security risks." Effective governance clarifies decision rights and establishes collaborative processes for resolving conflicts.

Decision paralysis can result from unclear approval processes for security-related decisions. When multiple stakeholders must approve decisions without clear criteria or timeframes, important security initiatives may stall indefinitely. Similarly, business initiatives may be delayed when security review processes lack clear scope and timelines. This paralysis often occurs when governance structures do not specify decision authority or establish efficient approval workflows.

Over-governance leads to operational friction that can harm business agility. When security governance requires extensive documentation, multiple approvals, and lengthy review cycles for routine decisions, business teams may see security as an impediment rather than a partner. This friction often drives business units to bypass governance entirely, increasing risk. Effective governance balances oversight with operational efficiency, reserving more rigorous processes for higher-risk decisions.

Under-governance results in inadequate risk management when important decisions lack appropriate oversight. This may occur when governance structures do not extend to all business units or when risk acceptance occurs without proper evaluation. Under-governance often emerges when organizations implement governance structures without adequate resources or accountability mechanisms. The result is governance that exists on paper but does not meaningfully influence decision-making.

Organizations may also struggle to maintain effectiveness in governance as they evolve. Governance structures that work well for small organizations may become ineffective as the organization grows. Similarly, governance designed for stable business environments may break down during periods of rapid change. Effective governance includes mechanisms for periodic review and adaptation to changing organizational needs.

With these foundational principles established, organizations need practical frameworks for implementing integrated governance. The starting point for any governance model lies in clarifying who has the authority to make different types of security decisions and under what circumstances.

7.7 DECISION AUTHORITY FRAMEWORKS

Clear decision authority represents the foundation of effective security governance, yet many organizations struggle with ambiguous approval processes and unclear risk ownership. When security decisions lack defined authority structures, organizations may experience either decision paralysis or authority conflicts that undermine both security effectiveness and business agility. This section provides frameworks for assigning decision rights based on business impact while balancing technical expertise with business accountability.

7.7.1 Determining decision rights for security risks

Organizations need clear frameworks for determining who has the authority to make different types of security risk decisions. These frameworks should balance expertise, accountability, and impact considerations to ensure that decisions are made at the appropriate level.

Decision models for security risks range along a spectrum, from highly centralized to broadly distributed. Centralized models concentrate decision authority in specialized security functions or committees, ensuring consistency but potentially creating bottlenecks. Distributed models push decision authority to business units, improving responsiveness but potentially sacrificing consistency. Most organizations benefit from a balanced approach that centralizes certain decisions while distributing others based on clear criteria.

Organizations should assign decision authority based on the potential business impact of the risk. Low-impact risks that affect only a single system or department may be managed through distributed decision authority, with business unit leaders making risk acceptance decisions. Medium-impact risks that could affect multiple departments typically require collaborative decision-making involving both security and business stakeholders. High-impact risks with potential enterprise-wide effects generally warrant centralized decision authority, often at the executive or board level.

A matrix approach using responsibility assignment models provides clarity for complex security governance. The RACI model (Responsible, Accountable, Consulted, Informed) helps organizations document decision rights across different risk scenarios and stakeholder groups. These matrices specify who must perform the work (Responsible), who has ultimate accountability (Accountable), who provides input (Consulted), and who receives communication about decisions (Informed). A sample RACI chart can be seen in Figure 7.1. Such matrices help prevent both decision gaps and authority conflicts.

Security Risk Decision Authority Matrix

	Board	CEO	CISO	Business Unit	Security Team
Strategic Decisions					
Security Strategy	A	R	R	C	C
Risk Appetite	A	R	R	C	C
Operational Decisions					
Security Policies	I	I	A/R	C	R
Risk Acceptance		I	C	A/R	R
Incident Response					
Critical Incidents	I	I	A	I	R

R Responsible **A** Accountable **C** Consulted **I** Informed

* Based on RACI responsibility assignment model. Only one role should be Accountable for each decision type.

Figure 7.1 Security risk decision authority matrix.

Decision thresholds based on risk appetite and business impact help organizations determine where decision authority should reside. For example, an organization might establish thresholds specifying that risks potentially exceeding $500,000 in impact require executive approval, while those potentially exceeding $5 million require board notification. These thresholds ensure that decision authority aligns with potential business impact, supporting the principle of proportionality.

Research confirms the importance of clear decision rights for security risks. According to the 2025 IT Risk and Compliance Benchmark Report from Hyperproof (Hyperproof, 2025), over 80% of organizations have designated owners for distinct risks. Assigning ownership for specific risks, including cybersecurity, is essential for accountability and effective decision-making within integrated governance frameworks. Organizations without clear risk ownership often struggle with both accountability gaps and authority conflicts.

Effective decision rights frameworks balance several competing considerations. Technical decisions requiring security expertise should generally involve security leaders, while business risk acceptance decisions should involve business leaders accountable for the affected operations. Collaborative decisions involving multiple stakeholders require clear processes for resolving disagreements. Decision timeframes should match the urgency of the risk, with expedited processes for time-sensitive decisions.

These decision frameworks build upon the risk ownership models introduced in Chapter 4, providing detailed guidance for determining who the has authority to make different types of security risk decisions. Implementing these decision frameworks successfully requires addressing the organizational and cultural barriers discussed in Chapter 10, where we provide strategies for overcoming resistance.

🔗 *Downloadable Resource: Decision Authority Matrix for Security Risks*

7.7.2 The board's role in security risk governance

The Board of Directors plays an increasingly important role in security risk governance, providing oversight that connects security risks to enterprise strategy and risk appetite. This role has changed significantly as security risks have become material business risks with the potential to affect shareholder value.

Determining appropriate board involvement requires balancing oversight with management delegation. Boards should generally avoid involvement in operational security decisions, which properly belong to management. Instead, boards should focus on oversight activities: approving security strategy and risk appetite, monitoring security risk trends, ensuring adequate resources for security risk management, and holding management accountable for control effectiveness. This oversight role helps ensure that security risks are managed according to shareholder interests without creating unnecessary governance

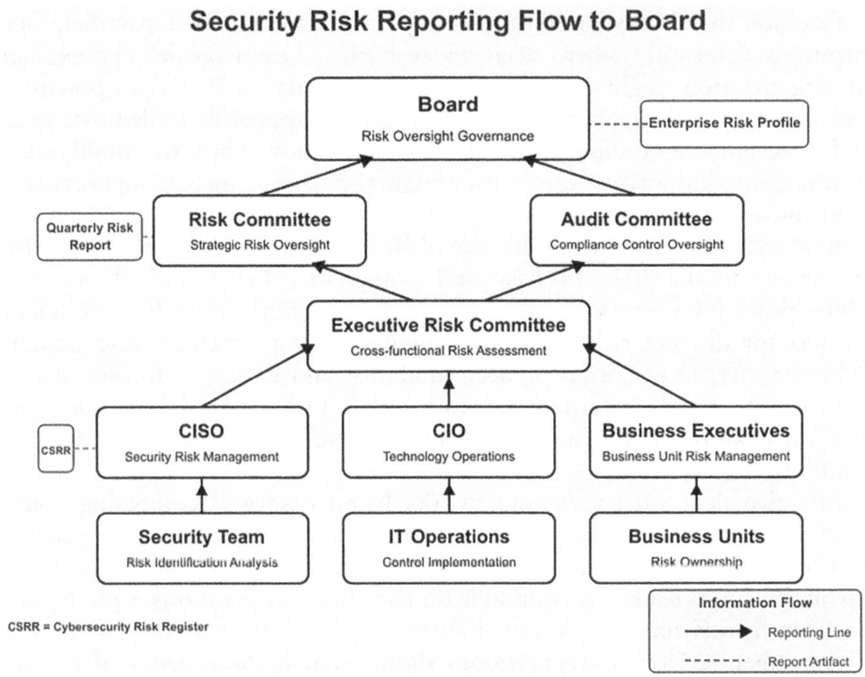

Figure 7.2 Security risk reporting flow to board.

friction. A sample information flow diagram based on typical observed processes is shown in Figure 7.2.

Committee structures support effective board governance by providing focused attention to security risks. Some organizations establish dedicated technology or cybersecurity risk committees that focus specifically on security oversight. Others integrate security oversight into existing audit or risk committees with broader mandates. The appropriate committee structure depends on the organization's size, industry, and risk profile. Regardless of structure, committee charters should clearly define security oversight responsibilities, meeting frequency, and reporting requirements.

Boards require specific information to fulfill their security oversight role effectively. This information typically includes Key Risk Indicators showing security risk trends, significant security incidents and response effectiveness, major compliance gaps or regulatory issues, and strategic security initiatives with associated resource requirements. This information should be presented in clear business language, focusing on risk exposure and business impact rather than technical details. Regular reporting cadences (typically quarterly) should be supplemented by ad hoc reporting for significant events or changing risk conditions.

Setting and monitoring risk appetite statements provides an important mechanism for board-level security governance. These statements define the organization's tolerance for security risk in business terms, providing guidance for management decisions. For example, a board might approve a risk appetite statement specifying that "the organization will not accept risks that could result in unauthorized access to customer financial data, even if the probability is low." Management then uses these statements to guide security investment decisions and risk acceptance practices.

Research reports confirm the increasing importance of board involvement in security oversight. According to PwC's 2024 Global Digital Trust Insights, "82% of board members say they are more involved in cyber risk management than they were two years ago, reflecting a growing recognition of cybersecurity as a board-level issue." This highlights the increasing involvement of boards in cybersecurity oversight, underscoring the importance of board-level governance models for integrated risk management.

To support effective board oversight, organizations need clear escalation paths for significant security risks. These paths should specify which risks require board attention, how risks should be communicated to the board, and what response is expected. Without these paths, important risks may remain invisible to the board or receive attention only after significant incidents occur.

The board's role directly influences how security investments align with business objectives, as discussed in Chapter 5, ensuring that security resources support strategic priorities.

🔗 *Downloadable Resource: Risk Appetite Statement Development Framework*

7.7.3 Executive-level decision authority

Executive leaders play a crucial role in security governance, bridging the gap between board-level oversight and operational security management. Their authority encompasses both setting security direction and making key risk decisions.

CIO and CISO authority boundaries require careful definition to prevent both gaps and conflicts. The CISO typically has the authority to establish security standards, approve exceptions to these standards, and implement security controls within approved budgets. The CIO often has broader authority over technology investments and operations but should collaborate with the CISO on security implications. These boundaries should be documented in formal role descriptions and governance charters to prevent confusion or conflict. Organizations should also establish clear escalation triggers that specify when security risks require escalation from the CISO to the CIO, CEO, or board.

Business executives have important roles in security risk acceptance decisions affecting their areas of responsibility. When security risks impact specific business functions, the executives responsible for those functions should participate in risk acceptance decisions. This participation ensures that risk decisions incorporate business context and that executives understand the security implications of their operations. The governance framework should specify which risks require business executive approval and what criteria should guide these decisions.

Collaborative decision models provide effective mechanisms for addressing cross-functional security impacts. These models bring together security leaders and business executives to evaluate risks and make decisions that balance security requirements with business needs. For example, a security governance committee comprising both security and business executives might review significant security risks, major policy exceptions, and important security initiatives. This collaborative approach helps prevent both security decisions that impede business operations and business decisions that create unacceptable security risks.

The balance between security expertise and business judgment presents an ongoing challenge for executive-level governance. Security leaders bring specialized knowledge about threats and controls, while business executives bring understanding of operations and strategic priorities. Neither perspective alone provides an adequate basis for security decisions. Effective governance creates forums where these perspectives can be shared and balanced, leading to decisions that appropriately address both security and business requirements.

Organizations should establish clear documentation requirements for executive-level security decisions. These requirements should specify what information must be presented to support decision-making, how risk acceptance decisions should be documented, and how long such decisions remain valid before requiring review. This documentation creates accountability for both security and business executives while providing an audit trail for regulatory compliance.

7.7.4 Operational decision frameworks

Day-to-day security decisions require efficient frameworks that maintain appropriate governance without creating operational bottlenecks. These frameworks should specify who can make different types of security decisions at the operational level and what processes apply to each decision type.

Operational security decisions encompass a wide range of activities, from routine access approvals to security architecture changes. Organizations should categorize these decisions based on potential risk impact and required expertise, then define appropriate approval processes for each category. For example, routine access requests might require only manager approval, while changes to security architecture might require security architect review and CISO approval. This categorization helps ensure that governance overhead matches risk impact.

Delegation models help maintain governance without creating bottlenecks for routine decisions. These models push decision authority to the lowest appropriate level while maintaining accountability through clear documentation and periodic review. For example, a CISO might delegate authority for specific security exceptions to security managers, who can approve exceptions within defined parameters without requiring CISO review. This delegation improves operational efficiency while ensuring that exceptions remain visible to security leadership.

Documentation requirements should vary based on the significance of the decision. High-impact decisions typically require formal documentation including risk assessment, mitigation measures, approval signatures, and review dates. Low-impact decisions may require only minimal documentation to support audit and compliance requirements. These varying requirements help balance governance needs with operational efficiency, ensuring appropriate oversight without unnecessary overhead.

Security champions within business units can support operational governance by providing security expertise closer to business operations. These champions typically maintain their primary business roles but receive additional security training and serve as liaisons between business and security teams. They can help identify security implications of business initiatives, facilitate security reviews, and support implementation of security controls. This distributed expertise helps integrate security considerations into business operations without requiring constant involvement from central security teams.

Clear decision rights require supporting organizational structures to function effectively. Decision frameworks without appropriate committee structures and reporting relationships may leave important decisions without proper oversight or stakeholder input.

7.7.4.1 Exercise: decision rights mapping

Organizations can use the following exercise to map security decision types to appropriate roles:

- Identify key security decision categories (e.g., policy exceptions, new technology approval)
- Document which roles are Responsible, Accountable, Consulted, and Informed for each decision type
- Define approval thresholds and escalation triggers based on risk impact
- Review the resulting matrix for gaps and conflicts
- Validate the matrix with key stakeholders before implementation

This exercise helps organizations identify and address decision authority gaps and conflicts before they cause operational problems or governance failures.

7.8 GOVERNANCE STRUCTURES AND REPORTING RELATIONSHIPS

Organizational structures determine how security governance functions in practice, influencing everything from board oversight to operational decision-making. The choice between dedicated security committees, integrated audit oversight, and various CISO reporting relationships can significantly affect governance effectiveness and business alignment. This section examines structural options that support integrated governance while addressing the specific needs of different organizational contexts.

7.8.1 Board-level committee structures

Board committees provide focused oversight of security risks, ensuring that these risks receive appropriate attention without consuming excessive time in full board meetings. Organizations must determine whether security oversight should occur through dedicated risk committees or as a part of integrated audit committee responsibilities.

Dedicated risk committees offer several potential advantages for security governance. They allow for more detailed security discussions, can include directors with specific security expertise, and provide clear accountability for security oversight. However, these committees may also create silos if they operate separately from other risk oversight activities. Organizations considering dedicated security or technology risk committees should ensure integration with broader risk governance through clear reporting relationships and information sharing.

Integrated audit committees handle security oversight alongside other risk and compliance responsibilities. This approach helps connect security risks to other enterprise risks and leverages existing committee structures. However, it may provide less dedicated time for security discussions and require committee members to understand a broader range of risk topics. Organizations using this approach should ensure that security receives adequate agenda time and that committee members have sufficient security knowledge to provide effective oversight.

Charter elements for security oversight should clearly define committee responsibilities regardless of structure. These elements typically include oversight scope (which security risks the committee oversees), information requirements (what security reporting the committee receives), meeting frequency (how often security appears on the agenda), and escalation criteria (which security matters require committee attention). These charter elements ensure that security oversight responsibilities are clearly defined and consistently executed.

Committee membership considerations include expertise, independence, and diversity. While not all committee members need deep security expertise, the committee should include at least one member with relevant security or technology experience. Independence ensures that committee members can provide objective oversight without conflicts of interest. Diversity brings different perspectives to security oversight, potentially identifying risks or opportunities that might otherwise be overlooked.

Information flows between management and board committees require careful design. These flows should provide committees with sufficient information for oversight without overwhelming members with operational details. Typical information includes Key Risk Indicators, significant incidents, major compliance issues, and strategic security initiatives. This information should be presented in business language, focusing on risk exposure and business impact rather than technical details.

Chapter 10 examines how these governance structures manifest in successfully integrated organizations, providing evidence of their effectiveness in practice.

7.8.2 Case study: Firemen's Retirement System of St. Louis v. Sorenson (Marriott)

7.8.2.1 Context

In September 2018, Marriott International discovered a massive data breach affecting the Starwood guest reservation database, which it had acquired two years earlier. The cyberattack had begun in 2014 when certain systems of Starwood Hotels and Resorts Worldwide, Inc. were infected with malware. Unbeknownst to Marriott's Board of Directors, the attack was ongoing in September 2016 when Marriott closed on its acquisition of Starwood. By November 2018, investigators determined that the breach had exposed the personal information of up to 500 million guests, including names, passport numbers, birth dates, email addresses, payment card details, and loyalty program account information.

The discovery prompted the Firemen's Retirement System of St. Louis to file a derivative lawsuit against Marriott executives and directors in the Delaware Court of Chancery, alleging breaches of the fiduciary duty of loyalty under Caremark. The plaintiff claimed that the defendants failed to properly oversee cybersecurity risks, particularly in relation to the Starwood acquisition.

7.8.2.2 Challenge

The case highlighted three fundamental challenges in cybersecurity governance:

First, the integration of cybersecurity due diligence in mergers and acquisitions. The complaint alleged that the directors breached their fiduciary

> duties by failing to "undertake cybersecurity and technology due diligence" during the Acquisition. Despite identifying cybersecurity as a top risk, the board allegedly did not focus sufficient attention on Starwood's cybersecurity posture before completing the $13 billion deal.

Second, the implementation of appropriate reporting systems and controls for ongoing cybersecurity oversight. After the acquisition closed, the board learned that Starwood's brand standards did not mandate Payment Card Industry (PCI) compliance, tokenization, or point-to-point encryption – important security controls for protecting customer data. The plaintiff alleged that the board failed to act swiftly enough to address these deficiencies.

Third, the timing and manner of breach disclosure. The plaintiff claimed the board "concealed the data security incident until November 30, 2018," despite first learning of malware on Starwood's systems in September 2018. This raised questions about appropriate governance for security incident response and disclosure.

7.8.2.3 Approach

The court's analysis revealed Marriott's cybersecurity governance approach:

> Marriott's Board consistently ranked cybersecurity as a primary risk. Cybersecurity was viewed as the second biggest risk facing Marriott for fiscal year 2017. This demonstrated the board's recognition of cybersecurity's importance to the business.

The Board and Audit Committee were routinely apprised of cybersecurity issues after the Acquisition. They received annual reports on the Company's Enterprise Risk Assessment that specifically evaluated cyber risks. This established formal reporting channels for cybersecurity matters.

After identifying deficiencies in Starwood's systems, the company engaged PricewaterhouseCoopers (PwC) to conduct a "Starwood Security Program Assessment." Based on PwC's recommendations, management developed and presented to the board an implementation plan to address the identified issues, including efforts to implement tokenization across Starwood's data systems.

When malware was detected in September 2018, the CEO promptly notified the board the next day. Throughout the investigation, "the Board and Audit Committee receiv[ed] regular updates from management and privileged briefings from Marriott's General Counsel." This demonstrated their active engagement in security incident response.

7.8.2.4 Outcome

The Delaware Court of Chancery granted a motion to dismiss the purported derivative action under Rule 23.1 (Firemen's Ret. Sys. of St. Louis v. Sorenson,

2021) because the stockholder plaintiff failed to allege particularized facts that any member of the Board faced a substantial likelihood of liability for non-exculpated claims.

In its assessment, the court recognized that "[t]he corporate harms presented by non-compliance with cybersecurity safeguards increasingly call upon directors to ensure that companies have appropriate oversight systems in place." However, it found that Marriott's board had implemented reasonable systems:

> The court found that the Board had not "utterly failed" to implement oversight systems because the Board and Audit Committee were routinely apprised of cybersecurity issues, received annual reports on cyber risks, engaged outside consultants to audit Marriott's cybersecurity practices, and were promptly notified when vulnerabilities were detected.

Regarding potential "red flags," the court determined that none "were deliberately disregarded." Instead, when issues were presented to the board, Marriott management told the Board that it was addressing or would address the issues.

In the final paragraphs of her decision, Vice Chancellor Will acknowledged the momentousness of the data breach at issue, but squarely placed any blame for the breach on the hacker, stating that "Marriott was the victim of an illegal act rather than the perpetrator."

7.8.2.5 Lessons

This case provides several important lessons for establishing effective security governance models:

- Formalize cybersecurity oversight structures: The court emphasized that boards must "ensure that companies have appropriate oversight systems in place" for cybersecurity risks. This includes regular board-level reporting, committee responsibilities, and clear escalation paths.
- Establish documented reporting cadence: The Board and Audit Committee's routine updates on cybersecurity risks and mitigation, including annual reports evaluating cyber risks specifically, were key factors in demonstrating appropriate oversight. Regular reporting schedules help ensure timely awareness of security matters.
- Engage outside expertise: Marriott's engagement of outside consultants to improve and auditors to audit corporate cybersecurity practices demonstrated appropriate governance. Independent assessment provides valuable perspective on security programs.

- Document issue remediation plans: When deficiencies were identified, management developed and communicated plans to address them, including "Intended Actions" to implement recommendations. These documented plans demonstrated the board's good faith effort to address security issues.
- Develop clear incident response protocols: The board received "regular updates" during the breach investigation, showing active involvement in security incidents. Clear governance for security incidents enables boards to fulfill their oversight duties during crises.

While the court recognized that "corporate governance must evolve to address" the growing risks posed by cybersecurity threats, it emphasized that having appropriate oversight systems in place is what matters – not necessarily the prevention of every breach. A good governance model focuses on process rather than perfect outcomes.

As Vice Chancellor Will noted, there is a critical difference between "a flawed effort and a deliberate failure to act." For boards, establishing formal governance structures for cybersecurity oversight is not just a best practice but potentially a legal necessity to fulfill fiduciary duties in today's threat landscape.

7.8.3 Executive risk committees

Executive risk committees provide a forum for security and business leaders to collaborate on risk management, bridging the gap between technical security concerns and business objectives. These committees typically include representatives from security, IT, legal, compliance, and key business functions, ensuring diverse perspectives on security risks.

Composition models for executive security committees vary based on organizational structure and risk profile. In centralized models, a single enterprise risk committee may address security alongside other risk types. In federated models, business unit risk committees may handle security risks within their respective domains, reporting to an enterprise committee. Hybrid models combine elements of both approaches, with specialized committees handling specific risk types while reporting to an overarching risk committee. The appropriate model depends on the organization's size, complexity, and risk landscape.

Charter and scope considerations for executive risk committees should clearly define their authority and responsibilities. Charters typically specify committee purpose, membership criteria, meeting frequency, decision authority, and reporting obligations. Scope definitions outline which security risks the committee oversees and which decisions require committee approval. These elements ensure the committee operates with clear boundaries and expectations, preventing both gaps and conflicts in security governance.

Meeting cadence and agenda management significantly influence committee effectiveness. Most executive security committees meet monthly or quarterly, with additional meetings as needed for urgent issues. Effective agendas balance standing topics (like Key Risk Indicators and project updates) with deep dives into specific risk areas. Time management is critical – agendas should allocate sufficient time for meaningful discussion while respecting executives' limited availability. Many committees use consent agendas for routine approvals, reserving discussion time for strategic issues and significant risks.

Executive committees must balance operational review with strategic direction. While committees need awareness of operational security metrics, they should focus primarily on strategic issues: aligning security investments with business priorities, addressing risk trends, and ensuring adequate resources for security programs. This strategic focus helps prevent committees from becoming mired in operational details that properly belong to management.

Evidence confirms the prevalence of cross-functional risk committees. According to the 2025 IT Risk and Compliance Benchmark Report (Hyperproof, 2025), "Over half (58%) of all respondents recognize that IT risk management requires integrated efforts across roles and teams." The presence of cross-functional committees supports the breakdown of organizational silos and enables more holistic, integrated approaches to security risk governance.

Executive risk committees typically maintain formal relationships with both board committees and operational security teams. They receive detailed security information from operational teams, synthesize this information to identify key risks and trends, and provide summary reporting to board committees. This middle layer helps ensure that board committees receive appropriately filtered information while maintaining visibility into important security risks.

7.8.4 CISO reporting relationships

The CISO's reporting relationship significantly influences security governance effectiveness by affecting the CISO's authority, independence, and access to key decision-makers. Organizations should carefully consider reporting options based on their specific risk profile and organizational structure.

Reporting to the CIO represents the most common CISO reporting model. This arrangement facilitates coordination between security and IT operations, potentially improving implementation of security controls. However, it may create conflicts when security requirements constrain IT objectives or when the CISO must escalate concerns about IT practices. CISOs reporting to CIOs may also have limited visibility with business executives and board members, potentially reducing security influence on business decisions.

Reporting to the Chief Risk Officer (CRO) positions security as an enterprise risk discipline rather than a technical specialty. This arrangement connects security governance to broader risk governance, potentially improving integration. CISOs reporting to CROs typically have greater independence from IT constraints and better access to risk committees. However, they may face challenges coordinating with IT operations and may have less technical influence than CISOs reporting through technology organizations.

Reporting to the CEO elevates security to a C-suite function, providing the CISO with direct access to the top executive and typically stronger connections to the board. This arrangement signals the organization's commitment to security as a strategic priority and gives the CISO greater authority in security decisions. However, CEOs have limited bandwidth for security oversight, potentially leaving CISOs with insufficient guidance. This model may also create coordination challenges with other C-suite functions.

Reporting to Legal or Compliance has become more common as security has become increasingly regulated. This arrangement typically provides strong alignment with compliance requirements and legal risk management. CISOs reporting to Legal often have clear processes for security incident response involving legal considerations. However, this model may overemphasize compliance at the expense of strategic risk management and may reduce coordination with technology functions.

Dual reporting approaches can help balance operational and governance needs. For example, a CISO might report administratively to the CIO while maintaining a dotted-line relationship to the CRO or CEO for risk governance. These dual relationships help the CISO maintain both technical integration and risk governance connections. However, they can create role confusion if reporting expectations are not clearly defined.

CISO reporting relationships often evolve as organizations mature. Early stage security programs typically place the CISO within IT to establish foundational controls and processes. As security programs mature, many organizations elevate the CISO to report to the CRO, CEO, or Legal function, reflecting security's broader enterprise risk implications. This evolution should match the organization's security maturity and risk profile rather than following a prescribed path.

7.8.5 Cross-functional governance bodies

Cross-functional governance bodies help break down silos between security and business units, ensuring that security governance incorporates diverse perspectives. These bodies operate at various levels throughout the organization, connecting security governance to business operations. These cross-functional bodies help break down the organizational silos discussed in Chapter 4, creating forums where security and business stakeholders can collaborate on risk management.

Security working groups and steering committees typically focus on specific security domains or initiatives. For example, an identity management steering committee might include representatives from IT, security, HR, and key business units to guide identity policies and technologies. These focused groups ensure that security initiatives incorporate requirements from all affected stakeholders, improving both security effectiveness and business acceptance.

Effective feedback loops between technical and business functions help security governance adapt to changing business needs. Cross-functional bodies provide forums where business units can communicate operational requirements and challenges, while security teams can explain risk implications and control options. These exchanges help security teams develop more business-aligned approaches while helping business units understand security requirements in context.

Aligning security governance with Enterprise Risk Management structures ensures consistent risk management across the organization. This alignment typically occurs through shared committee membership, coordinated risk assessment methods, and integrated risk reporting. For example, the CISO might participate in the enterprise risk committee, security risks might be assessed using the same criteria as other risk types, and security reporting might follow the same format as other risk reporting. This consistency helps senior leaders understand security in the context of other enterprise risks.

Business unit representatives play important roles in security governance by providing operational context for security decisions. These representatives help security teams understand business processes, priorities, and constraints, leading to more effective and sustainable security approaches. They also serve as security advocates within their business units, helping communicate and implement security requirements. Organizations should carefully select these representatives based on both business knowledge and security interest.

Chapter 8 explores the cultural factors necessary for these cross-functional bodies to succeed, addressing how to build collaboration and shared ownership.

Governance structures must be implemented through models that match organizational context and capabilities. The choice between centralized, federated, or hybrid approaches shapes how these structures function in practice and determines their ultimate effectiveness.

7.8.5.1 Exercise: governance structure assessment

Organizations can assess their current governance effectiveness using the following steps:

1. Document existing governance bodies, their charters, and membership
2. Map information flows between governance bodies
3. Evaluate whether decisions occur at appropriate levels with proper stakeholder involvement
4. Identify potential gaps and redundancies in governance coverage

5. Gather feedback from both security and business stakeholders on governance effectiveness
6. Develop an improvement plan addressing identified issues

This assessment helps organizations identify structural gaps and redundancies in their security governance, providing a foundation for targeted improvements.

7.9 IMPLEMENTATION MODELS FOR INTEGRATED GOVERNANCE

Organizations must choose governance models that match their specific size, complexity, and culture while balancing consistency with business flexibility. Whether pursuing centralized, federated, or hybrid approaches, implementation decisions shape how effectively governance supports both security objectives and business operations. This section explores different models and provides guidance for selecting approaches that align with organizational maturity and business requirements. An overview of the three models can be seen in Figure 7.3.

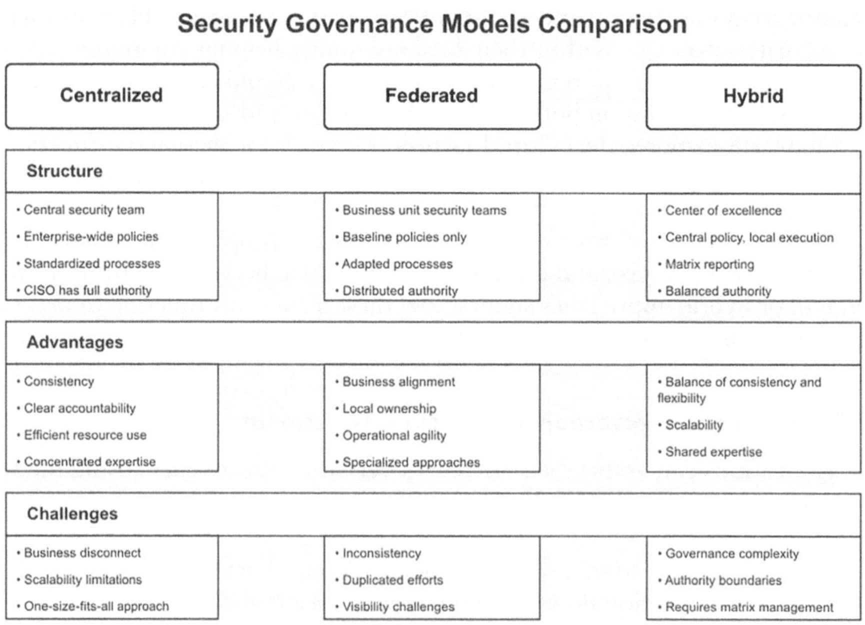

Figure 7.3 Security governance models comparison.

7.9.1 Centralized governance models

Centralized security governance concentrates authority and responsibility in a central security function that establishes policies, standards, and controls for the entire organization. This function typically reports to a senior executive (such as the CIO, CRO, or CEO) and maintains enterprise-wide authority for security decisions.

The structure of centralized governance typically includes several key elements. A central security team develops and maintains security policies, standards, and controls applicable across the organization. A security governance committee with enterprise-wide authority makes key security decisions and approves exceptions to security policies. Standardized processes ensure consistent security governance across all business units. Centralized monitoring provides visibility into security compliance and risk levels throughout the organization.

Centralized models offer several important advantages. Consistency represents a primary benefit – security policies and controls apply uniformly across the organization, reducing variation in security practices. Efficiency improves through standardized processes and technologies that reduce duplication of effort. Accountability is clear, with the CISO or security governance committee holding responsibility for security decisions. Specialized expertise can be concentrated in the central security function, improving decision quality for complex security issues.

However, centralized models also present significant disadvantages. Potential disconnect from business units can occur when central security teams have a limited understanding of business operations and constraints. Scalability challenges arise as organizations grow, potentially creating bottlenecks for security decisions. Responsiveness may suffer when business units must wait for central security approvals. One-size-fits-all approaches may impose unnecessary controls on low-risk areas while inadequately addressing unique requirements in high-risk areas.

Organizations can maintain business alignment in centralized models through several practices. Business representation on security governance committees ensures that business perspectives inform security decisions. Regular business impact assessments help security teams understand how controls affect business operations. Feedback mechanisms allow business units to raise concerns about security requirements. Differentiated controls based on risk profiles help ensure that security measures match business risk levels rather than applying uniformly across the organization.

Centralized models work best for organizations with relatively homogeneous business operations, limited geographic distribution, strong central authority structures, and cultures that value consistency and standardization. These models may struggle in highly diverse organizations where business units have significantly different operations, risk profiles, and security requirements.

7.9.2 Federated governance models

Federated security governance distributes authority and responsibility across business units while maintaining central coordination and oversight. This model balances local control with enterprise standards, allowing business units to adapt security practices to their specific needs within a common framework.

The structure of federated governance typically includes several key components. A central security function establishes baseline policies and standards that apply across the organization. Business unit security teams implement and maintain security controls within their respective units. Security governance committees exist at both enterprise and business unit levels, with clear delineation of decision authority. Coordinating mechanisms ensure consistency and information sharing across business units.

Federated models offer several important advantages. Business unit alignment improves because security decisions incorporate local business context and requirements. Scalability increases as decision authority distributes across the organization, reducing bottlenecks. Local ownership often improves security adoption as business units take responsibility for their security practices. Specialized security approaches can address unique requirements in different business areas instead of forcing standardization where it doesn't fit.

However, federated models also present significant challenges. Consistency becomes more difficult to maintain as business units adapt security practices to their local needs. Visibility may decrease as security information distributes across multiple teams and systems. Resource efficiency may suffer from duplication of security functions across business units. Governance gaps can emerge when responsibility boundaries between central and local security teams are unclear.

Organizations can maintain enterprise-wide standards in federated models through several mechanisms. Mandatory baseline requirements establish minimum security standards that apply across all business units. Centralized monitoring ensures visibility into security practices and compliance levels throughout the organization. Governance committees with enterprise-wide scope provide forums for coordinating security approaches across business units. Regular security assessments verify that business unit security practices meet organizational requirements.

Federated models work best for organizations with diverse business operations, broad geographic distribution, decentralized authority structures, and cultures that value business unit autonomy. These models may struggle in highly regulated environments requiring strict consistency in security practices or in organizations with limited security resources and expertise.

7.9.3 Hybrid approaches to security governance

Hybrid security governance combines elements of both centralized and federated models, seeking to capture the advantages of each while mitigating their respective disadvantages. These approaches balance consistency with flexibility, central oversight with local ownership.

Combining centralized policy with distributed implementation represents a common hybrid approach. In this model, central security teams establish enterprise-wide policies and standards, while business units implement controls within their local environments. Central teams focus on what security outcomes must be achieved, while business units determine how to achieve these outcomes in their specific contexts. This approach maintains policy consistency while allowing implementation flexibility.

Center of excellence models establish a central security team that provides expertise, guidance, and shared services to business units. This central team develops security standards, evaluates security technologies, and provides specialized security services. Business units maintain responsibility for security within their operations but leverage the center of excellence for expertise and support. This model helps organizations maintain security expertise while distributing implementation responsibility.

Matrix structures balance functional and business unit reporting by establishing dual reporting lines for security personnel. For example, security professionals embedded in business units might report administratively to business leaders while maintaining functional reporting to the CISO. This structure helps ensure that security professionals understand business context while remaining connected to enterprise security direction and expertise.

Organizations should tailor hybrid models to their specific size, complexity, and maturity. Small organizations with limited resources might centralize most security functions while embedding security champions in business units. Large enterprises might establish business unit security teams that follow central policies while adapting implementation to local needs. Global organizations might adopt regional security models that balance local requirements with global standards.

Hybrid models require careful attention to governance boundaries to prevent confusion about decision authority. Organizations should clearly document which decisions belong to central security teams, which belong to business units, and which require collaborative approaches. This documentation should include decision criteria, approval processes, and escalation paths for resolving disagreements.

7.9.4 Maturity model

Organizations typically evolve their security governance through predictable maturity stages, from initial ad hoc approaches to optimized governance that balances security and business needs. These can be seen in Figure 7.4. Understanding these stages helps organizations assess their current maturity and plan appropriate improvements.

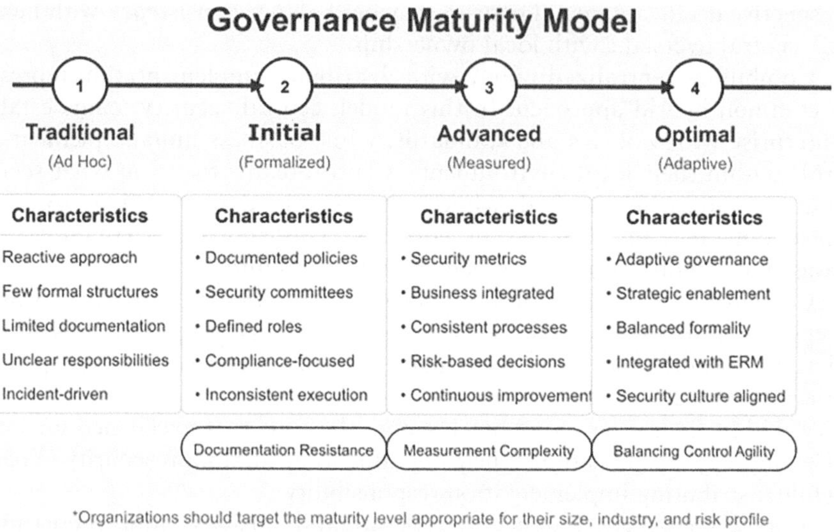

Figure 7.4 Governance maturity model.

At the traditional (ad hoc) stage, security governance occurs reactively with few formal structures or processes. Security decisions happen inconsistently, often in response to incidents or compliance requirements. Documentation is limited, roles are unclear, and governance effectiveness depends heavily on individual initiative. Organizations at this stage typically focus on establishing basic security policies and clarifying security responsibilities.

The initial stage establishes formal governance structures and processes. Security committees form with documented charters and membership. Policies and standards define security requirements and decision processes. Roles and responsibilities become clearer, though execution may remain inconsistent. Organizations at this stage focus on documenting governance processes and establishing regular security reporting.

The advanced stage implements consistent governance processes with regular measurement and improvement. Security metrics track governance effectiveness, committees operate according to established charters, and decisions follow documented processes. Business units actively participate in security governance, and security considerations integrate into business decisions. Organizations at this stage focus on improving governance efficiency and business alignment.

The optimal stage balances security governance with business agility through adaptive approaches. Governance scales efficiently with organizational changes, processes adjust based on risk levels, and continuous improvement occurs through regular governance reviews. Security governance integrates seamlessly with other governance domains, and security decisions align naturally with business objectives. Organizations at this stage focus on fine-tuning governance to maximize both security effectiveness and business support.

Common transition challenges emerge as organizations move between maturity levels. Moving from ad hoc to traditional governance often faces resistance to formalization and documentation. Transitioning from traditional to advanced governance typically encounters challenges with measurement and consistency. Evolution from advanced to optimal governance may struggle with balancing formality and flexibility. Organizations should expect these challenges and develop change management approaches to address them.

Target state considerations should reflect the organization's specific context rather than automatically targeting the highest maturity level. Small organizations with limited risk exposure may function effectively at lower maturity levels. Organizations in highly regulated industries may need higher maturity to meet compliance requirements. Target states should balance governance benefits with implementation costs and organizational readiness.

This maturity progression provides the foundation for the implementation roadmaps we'll explore in Chapter 10, which offers tailored guidance based on an organization's current integration level.

Even well-designed governance models may fail without adequate attention to implementation challenges and stakeholder concerns. Successfully implementing integrated governance requires addressing the natural resistance that emerges when changing established roles and decision processes.

7.9.4.1 Exercise: governance implementation planning

Organizations can plan governance implementation or improvement using the following steps:

- Assess current governance maturity using the maturity model
- Define target state based on organizational needs and constraints
- Identify key stakeholders affected by governance changes
- Analyze potential sources of resistance and develop mitigation strategies
- Develop an implementation roadmap with phased improvements
- Establish success metrics to track implementation progress

This planning process helps organizations develop realistic governance improvement plans that address both technical and organizational factors.

Downloadable Resource: Security Governance Maturity Assessment

7.10 SECTION 5: OVERCOMING RESISTANCE TO INTEGRATED GOVERNANCE

Implementing integrated governance typically encounters resistance from both security leaders concerned about maintaining expertise and business executives questioning the value of security participation. This resistance often reflects legitimate professional concerns rather than simple opposition to change. This section addresses specific stakeholder concerns and provides change management strategies that build support while preserving the benefits of both security expertise and business alignment.

7.10.1 Addressing security leader concerns

Security leaders often express concerns about integrated governance models, perceiving potential threats to their authority, independence, or effectiveness. Addressing these concerns directly helps organizations implement more effective governance while preserving security expertise.

As discussed in Chapter 1, concerns about preserving security expertise represent a primary objection to integration. In governance implementation, organizations can address this concern through specific structural mechanisms: establishing clear boundaries between technical security decisions (where security expertise should prevail) and risk acceptance decisions (where business context matters). Documentation of these boundaries in governance charters helps security leaders maintain appropriate authority while supporting business integration.

Maintaining independence while supporting business alignment presents another common concern. Security leaders often believe their effectiveness depends on the ability to make objective security assessments without business pressure. Organizations can address this concern by creating reporting structures that protect security independence (such as having the CISO report outside IT) while establishing collaborative processes for security and business leaders to address risks together. This balance helps security leaders maintain necessary independence without creating adversarial relationships with business units.

Career development in integrated governance frameworks concerns security leaders who wonder how business alignment affects their professional growth. Traditional security career paths emphasized technical depth and certifications, while integrated models may require more business acumen and relationship skills. Organizations can address this concern by creating development paths that value both technical expertise and business understanding, providing security leaders with opportunities to develop business skills without abandoning their security focus.

Strategies for influencing without direct authority become important in integrated models where security leaders may have less formal authority over business decisions. Security leaders can maintain influence through several approaches: building credibility through consistent, high-quality risk assessments; developing business fluency to communicate security concepts in business terms; establishing trusted relationships with business leaders; and focusing on business outcomes rather than security compliance. These influence strategies help security leaders remain effective in governance models that distribute decision authority.

Organizations should recognize that security leaders' concerns often reflect legitimate professional commitments rather than simple resistance to change. Security leaders typically value their professional obligations to protect the organization and may worry that integrated governance will compromise these obligations. Acknowledging these commitments while showing how integrated governance can enhance security effectiveness helps address these deeper concerns.

This resistance parallels the objections to security spending discussed in Chapter 5, requiring similar strategies for building stakeholder buy-in and demonstrating business value.

7.10.2 Engaging business leaders in security governance

Business leaders often resist participation in security governance, viewing it as a technical specialty outside their expertise or a compliance function that constrains business operations. Engaging these leaders requires showing the business value of integrated security governance.

Making the business case for integrated governance should focus on outcomes that matter to business leaders: reducing security-related business disruptions, improving customer trust through strong security practices, supporting business initiatives with appropriate security enablement, and making more efficient security investments based on business priorities. This business case should use financial language and business metrics rather than technical security terms, demonstrating how integrated governance supports business objectives.

Techniques for building security ownership among business executives help them see security governance as part of their leadership responsibility rather than a separate technical function. Executive education sessions focused on business implications of security risks can build understanding without requiring technical expertise. Including security metrics in business performance reviews helps establish accountability for security outcomes. Celebrating security successes within business units reinforces the value of security ownership. These techniques help business leaders incorporate security considerations into their management approach.

Balancing business autonomy with security standards represents a key concern for business leaders who worry that security governance will constrain their operational flexibility. Organizations can address this concern through risk-based approaches that scale security requirements based on business risk levels. Providing business leaders with options for meeting security requirements rather than mandating specific controls helps maintain their autonomy while achieving security objectives. Involving business leaders in security standard development ensures that these standards reflect business realities.

Risk appetite frameworks can help align expectations between security and business leaders by establishing agreed boundaries for risk tolerance. These frameworks document which risks the organization will accept, avoid, mitigate, or transfer, providing guidance for both security and business decisions. By participating in risk appetite development, business leaders gain influence over security priorities while accepting accountability for risks within their domains. This shared ownership helps prevent conflicts between security and business objectives.

Organizations should recognize that business leaders' resistance often stems from past experiences with security as a business impediment. Security teams that have focused on control enforcement rather than business enablement (also known as the "department of no") may have created negative associations with security governance. Acknowledging these experiences while demonstrating a fresh approach focused on business partnership helps overcome this historical resistance.

7.10.3 Change management for governance transformation

Implementing integrated security governance represents a significant organizational change that affects roles, responsibilities, and decision processes across the enterprise. Effective change management helps organizations navigate this transformation while minimizing resistance and disruption.

Assessing governance readiness for change helps organizations determine where to start and how quickly to proceed with governance transformation. This assessment typically considers several factors: current governance maturity, executive support for integration, security team capabilities and capacity, business unit receptiveness, and existing change initiatives that might compete for attention. Organizations with low readiness may need to start with small pilot initiatives, while those with high readiness can implement broader changes more quickly.

Stakeholder engagement strategies for governance changes should address the specific concerns and motivations of different stakeholder groups. Executive sponsors need clear business cases and success metrics for governance changes. Security teams need reassurance about role changes and new skill requirements. Business units need to understand how governance changes will affect their operations and decision authority. Tailored communications and engagement activities help each group understand and support the transformation.

Phased implementation approaches help manage resistance by breaking governance changes into manageable steps with visible benefits. Initial phases typically focus on low-resistance, high-value changes that demonstrate the benefits of integration. Middle phases address more significant structural changes once stakeholders have gained confidence in the approach. Later phases refine governance processes based on implementation experience. This phased approach helps organizations maintain business continuity while transforming governance.

Measuring and communicating governance improvements provides evidence of progress and reinforces the value of continued transformation. Metrics might include time required for security decisions, business satisfaction with security governance, security incident impacts, and governance process efficiency. Regular communication of these metrics helps maintain stakeholder support and identify areas requiring adjustment. Success stories highlighting specific benefits of integrated governance provide concrete examples that help stakeholders understand the value of the transformation.

Organizations should apply established change management methodologies to governance transformation, treating it as a significant organizational change rather than a simple process adjustment. These methodologies provide structured approaches for stakeholder analysis, communication planning, resistance management, and benefit realization. Their proven effectiveness helps organizations navigate the complexity of governance transformation.

Chapter 8 addresses the cultural aspects of overcoming this resistance, providing strategies for building support among both security and business leaders.

7.10.4 Building sustainable governance practices

Sustainable security governance requires mechanisms for ongoing adaptation to changing business needs, security threats, and organizational structures. Without these mechanisms, governance models that initially work well may gradually lose effectiveness as conditions change.

Governance review and renewal processes help organizations assess and improve their governance models over time. These processes typically include regular reviews (often annual) of governance structures, charters, and decision processes. Reviews should evaluate whether governance is achieving its intended outcomes, identify gaps or inefficiencies, and recommend specific improvements. Involving both security and business stakeholders in these reviews ensures a balanced assessment of governance effectiveness.

Adapting models as organizations evolve ensures that governance remains appropriate for changing conditions. Organizational changes like mergers, acquisitions, new business lines, or geographic expansion may require governance adjustments. Similarly, evolving security threats, regulatory requirements, or technology environments may require governance updates. Establishing clear triggers for governance review (such as major organizational changes or significant security incidents) helps ensure timely adaptation.

Succession planning for governance roles maintains consistency during leadership transitions. Organizations should identify and develop potential successors for key governance positions, including committee chairs, the CISO, and security directors. This planning should include knowledge transfer mechanisms to preserve institutional memory about governance decisions and rationales. Documented governance processes reduce dependence on specific individuals, ensuring that governance continues to function effectively despite personnel changes.

Connection to security culture development creates a foundation for sustainable governance. While governance structures provide formal mechanisms for security decision-making, culture shapes how individuals and teams approach security in their daily work. Governance and culture should reinforce each other – governance structures should reflect and support desired cultural attributes, while culture should encourage adherence to governance processes. This connection helps ensure that formal governance translates into actual security behaviors throughout the organization.

Organizations should view governance as an ongoing capability rather than a one-time implementation. This perspective encourages investment in governance capabilities that can evolve over time, including skilled governance personnel, effective collaboration mechanisms, and adaptive processes. Organizations that treat governance as a dynamic capability rather than a static structure are better positioned to maintain effective security governance as conditions change.

Downloadable Exercise: Resistance Mapping and Mitigation

7.11 CONCLUSION

Effective security governance balances security expertise with business alignment, creating structures that support both security effectiveness and business objectives. This balance allows organizations to manage security as a true business risk rather than treating it as a technical specialty disconnected from business concerns. Integrating security and business perspectives leads to better-informed decisions about security investments, risk acceptance, and control implementation.

No single governance model works for all organizations. Each organization must design governance structures that match its specific size, industry, risk profile, and culture. Centralized models may work well for organizations with homogeneous operations and strong central authority, while federated approaches may serve diverse, decentralized organizations better. Most organizations benefit from hybrid approaches that combine elements of both models, adapting governance to different business contexts while maintaining enterprise-wide standards.

Decision rights, committee structures, and reporting relationships must work together as an integrated system rather than isolated components. Clear decision authority without appropriate committee structures leaves decisions without proper oversight or stakeholder input. Well-designed committees without clear reporting relationships may lack the necessary information or influence. Effective governance integrates these elements into a cohesive system where authority, oversight, and information flows reinforce each other.

Implementation should follow a maturity-based approach tailored to organizational context. Organizations with limited security governance experience should focus first on establishing clear roles and basic governance processes before implementing more sophisticated approaches. Implementation plans should consider organizational readiness, potential resistance, and change management requirements. Phased approaches help organizations build governance capabilities progressively while demonstrating value at each stage.

Resistance to integrated governance is natural, but can be overcome with thoughtful engagement strategies. Security leaders need reassurance that integration will not compromise their ability to manage security risks effectively. Business leaders need to understand how security governance supports rather than constrains business objectives. Change management approaches that address specific stakeholder concerns and demonstrate concrete benefits help overcome this resistance.

The governance models established in this chapter provide the foundation for the security culture discussed in the next chapter. Without proper governance structures, culture changes will lack sustainability and direction. Governance establishes formal authorities, processes, and expectations that shape cultural norms and behaviors. At the same time, governance without a supportive culture often results in superficial compliance rather than true risk management. The integration of governance and culture creates a powerful foundation for effective security risk management.

With integrated governance in place, organizations can manage security as a true business risk – weighing security investments against potential business impacts, making risk-informed decisions about business initiatives, and ensuring that security enables rather than constrains business objectives. This approach helps organizations succeed in an increasingly complex threat landscape while maintaining business agility and competitiveness.

7.12 ACTION ITEMS FOR READERS

1. Assess your organization's current security decision authority by documenting who actually makes key security decisions today, identifying gaps or conflicts in decision rights, and mapping these against the potential business impact of each decision type.
2. Engage three business leaders outside of IT in structured conversations about their current experience with security governance, their concerns about security participation, and their perspectives on how security decisions affect their operations.

3. Create a RACI matrix for your organization's ten most important security decisions (such as risk acceptance, budget approval, policy exceptions, and incident response), clearly defining who is Responsible, Accountable, Consulted, and Informed for each decision type.
4. Design a governance committee structure proposal that specifies committee membership, meeting frequency, decision authority, and reporting relationships, choosing between centralized, federated, or hybrid approaches based on your organizational context and culture.
5. Conduct a pilot implementation of integrated governance for one specific security domain (such as vendor risk management or access controls), measuring decision speed, stakeholder satisfaction, and business alignment before expanding to other areas.

Chapter 8

Creating a culture of integrated risk management

Chapter in One Sentence: Transforming organizational culture from viewing security as a technical problem to treating it as a shared business responsibility requires reframing risk in business terms, breaking down organizational silos, building broad risk awareness, and aligning incentives with desired risk behaviors.

8.1 EXECUTIVE SUMMARY

This chapter tackles one of the most challenging aspects of integrated risk management: cultural transformation. While technical solutions and governance frameworks are necessary, they cannot succeed without corresponding changes in organizational mindsets, behaviors, and values. The chapter examines how traditional approaches that treat security risks as purely technical concerns managed exclusively by IT departments have proven ineffective in today's complex threat landscape. Organizations that successfully manage security risks recognize them as business risks requiring enterprise-wide integration.

The chapter identifies common cultural barriers, including hierarchical communication patterns, specialized language, and the persistent "security is IT's problem" mindset. It presents an approach to transformation that addresses these barriers through several key strategies. First, by reframing security in business terms rather than technical ones, organizations can make security risks accessible to business stakeholders and integrate them into existing frameworks. Second, building bridges between technical and business teams through shared risk vocabularies and collaborative assessment approaches creates common ground for cross-functional discussion.

The chapter includes practical frameworks for breaking down organizational silos, including cross-functional governance structures and shared risk ownership models that distribute responsibility effectively without creating artificial handoffs. It details approaches for building risk awareness beyond security teams, emphasizing behavior change rather than mere compliance. The chapter also explores incentive systems that align individual and team

DOI: 10.1201/9781003744146-8

goals with risk objectives while avoiding unintended consequences that could undermine security.

The LILAC framework (Leadership, Involvement, Learning, Accountability, Communication) provides a comprehensive model for sustainable cultural change. Throughout the chapter, real-world examples illustrate both successful transformations and common pitfalls. The journey from siloed to integrated risk management requires sustained effort, but organizations that build collaborative risk cultures position themselves for significant advantages: faster response to threats, more effective resource allocation, and the ability to use security as a strategic enabler rather than merely a compliance requirement.

8.2 KEY TAKEAWAYS

- Cultural transformation represents a persistent obstacle to implementing effective integrated risk management, requiring changes in organizational mindsets, behaviors, and values
- Translating technical risks into business impacts creates a common language between security and business functions
- Shared risk ownership models maintain business function responsibility for risks, while security teams provide expertise and support
- Effective risk awareness programs focus on changing behaviors rather than just increasing knowledge
- Incentive systems must be carefully designed to encourage appropriate risk behaviors without creating perverse incentives

8.3 APPLICATION QUESTIONS

1. How does your organization currently distribute responsibility for security risks, and where do you see opportunities to implement more collaborative ownership models?
2. What incentives, both formal and informal, might be driving behaviors that undermine effective risk management in your organization?
3. Which elements of the LILAC framework (Leadership, Involvement, Learning, Accountability, Communication) represent the greatest opportunity for improvement in your organization's risk culture?

8.4 TOOLS REFERENCED IN THIS CHAPTER

All tools available at kaynemcgladrey.com/myth/

- Risk Culture Maturity Assessment
- Risk Translation Framework: From Technical to Business Impact
- Exercise: Stakeholder Mapping for Cultural Change

- Organizational Silo Mapping Exercise
- Role-Based Risk Awareness Program Template
- Exercise: Developing a Risk Awareness Campaign
- Security Incentive Design Framework
- Exercise: Designing Risk Incentives

8.5 INTRODUCTION

Security risks have traditionally been siloed as technical concerns, managed exclusively by IT departments with little input from other business functions. This approach has proven ineffective in today's interconnected threat landscape. According to Hyperproof's 2024 IT Risk and Compliance Benchmark Report (Hyperproof, 2024), "Those who manage risk and compliance in silos are more likely to experience breaches, with 70% of respondents in this category facing security incidents in the last 24 months." The most successful organizations now recognize security risks as business risks requiring enterprise-wide integration. They understand that security incidents threaten revenue, reputation, operations, and strategic objectives – not just technical systems. This recognition demands a fundamental shift in how organizations perceive and manage risk.

Cultural transformation often represents the biggest obstacle to implementing effective organizational changes. Technical solutions and governance frameworks, while necessary, cannot succeed without corresponding changes in organizational mindsets, behaviors, and values. Simply put, a security program is only as strong as the culture supporting it.

This chapter bridges the gap between formal governance structures and the human elements that make them effective. We'll explore practical strategies for changing entrenched mindsets, breaking down organizational silos, and building collaborative risk cultures that engage stakeholders at all levels.

8.6 UNDERSTANDING THE CURRENT STATE OF RISK CULTURE

Before attempting any cultural transformation, organizations must first assess where they stand; a comparison of maturity levels is shown in Figure 8.1. Many leaders assume their risk culture problems stem from a lack of awareness or insufficient training, yet the reality appears more complex. Organizational hierarchies, entrenched communication patterns, and historical divisions between technical and business functions may create barriers that standard awareness programs cannot address. This section examines the structural and cultural factors that shape how organizations currently approach security risks.

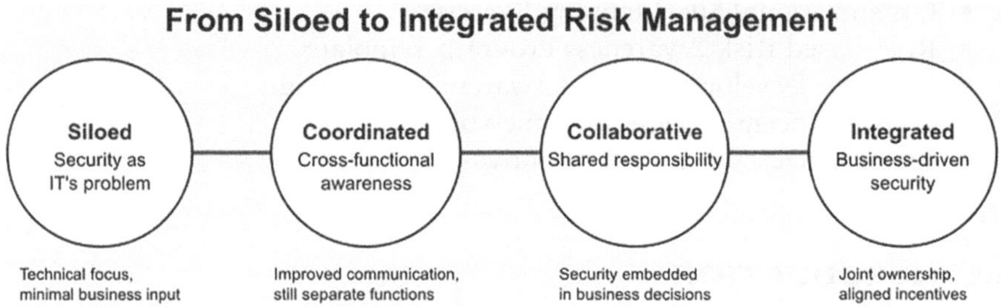

Figure 8.1 From siloed to integrated risk management.

8.6.1 The hierarchical nature of risk management cultures

Organizational hierarchies significantly impact how risks are perceived, communicated, and managed. According to research by Phillip King-Wilson (2022), the hierarchical structure of an organization creates distinct approaches to risk data consumption based on position and role. Those at C-Suite and Board levels focus on formulating corporate objectives and strategies, requiring broader, less granular data. In contrast, those at operational cybersecurity interfaces need highly detailed, focused data for maintaining specific controls.

This natural division creates challenges for integrated risk management. Top-level executives may become overwhelmed with excessive technical detail, undermining timely, unbiased decision-making. Conversely, providing only high-level information to technical teams prevents them from implementing effective controls. As King-Wilson notes, "Too great a volume and the executive levels may be overwhelmed with data to be capable of taking timely and unbiased crucial decisions... Too little, or too coarse... may be omitted, with equal, or greater potential harm posed to an entity."

These hierarchical dynamics often manifest in communication patterns that reinforce silos rather than collaboration. Technical teams communicate upward using overly detailed reports, while leadership communicates downward with vague directives lacking contextual understanding. Neither approach supports integrated risk management.

Organizations with mature risk cultures recognize these hierarchical dynamics and develop systems to provide appropriate information granularity to different levels. They create mechanisms for bidirectional communication that preserve technical accuracy while providing appropriate business context.

8.6.2 Common cultural barriers to integrated risk management

Several cultural barriers typically impede integrated risk management efforts. Primary among these is the "risk management is IT's problem" mindset. This perspective, deeply embedded in many organizations, assumes security risks are primarily technical and should be managed exclusively by technical specialists. These cultural barriers directly impact how organizations measure security; a topic explored in Chapter 6 where we examine why traditional technical metrics fail to resonate with business leaders.

The communication challenges introduced in Chapter 1 become amplified in hierarchical organizations, where specialized terminology can create the appearance of communication while parties maintain fundamentally different interpretations of the same terms. Similarly, the communication barriers and expertise gaps discussed in Chapter 7's governance context can also manifest as cultural barriers.

There is also the challenge of balancing specialized technical expertise with broader business understanding. Technical specialists often struggle to contextualize their work within business objectives, while business leaders may lack the technical knowledge to evaluate security proposals appropriately. This knowledge gap creates mutual frustration that undermines collaboration.

8.6.3 Assessing your organization's risk culture

Before attempting to transform your risk culture, it's essential to understand your starting point. Several frameworks can help assess your organization's current state; a comparison can be seen in Table 8.1.

The risk maturity model described by Paul Hopkin (2019) provides an effective assessment framework. It categorizes organizations along a continuum from "Naïve" (unaware of risk management needs) to "Natural" (with risk awareness fully embedded in organizational thinking). Between these extremes lie "Novice" organizations (aware but just starting implementation) and "Normalized" organizations (with embedded processes requiring ongoing management effort).

The FOIL assessment framework introduced in Chapter 4 provides another lens for cultural evaluation, particularly when examining how embedded risk thinking has become across the organization. For cultural transformation, these maturity levels help identify not just structural gaps but behavioral patterns that require attention.

To apply these frameworks, organizations can conduct internal assessments through interviews, surveys, and documentation reviews. According to the 2025 IT Risk and Compliance Benchmark Report (Hyperproof, 2025), "58% of respondents recognize that IT risk management requires integrated efforts across roles and teams... 38% have automated most of their IT risk management procedures." This statistic highlights that while a majority acknowledge the need for cross-functional collaboration, a significant portion of organizations still face challenges in fully integrating risk management practices, underscoring the cultural barriers that must be addressed.

Table 8.1 Risk culture maturity models comparison

Maturity level	*4Ns model*	*FOIL model*	*Key characteristics*	*Typical behaviors*
Level 1	Naïve Unaware of risk management needs	Fragmented Risk activities focus on compliance	• No formal processes • Reactive approach • Siloed activities	• Crisis-driven decisions • Blame culture • Minimal documentation
Level 2	Novice Aware but just starting implementation	Organized Some coordination emerging	• Basic processes defined • Limited integration • Compliance-focused	• Following checklists • Some risk discussions • Departmental focus
Level 3	Normalized Embedded processes requiring management	Influential Risk influences some decisions	• Systematic approach • Cross-functional teams • Regular reporting	• Proactive planning • Shared ownership • Learning from incidents
Level 4	Natural Risk awareness fully embedded	Leading Risk drives business decisions	• Strategic integration • Continuous improvement • Innovation-enabled	• Risk-informed strategy • Cultural embedding • Competitive advantage

Through careful assessment, organizations can identify specific cultural barriers that limit risk integration and develop targeted strategies to address them. This baseline understanding provides the foundation for meaningful cultural transformation.

Understanding current cultural barriers provides the foundation for transformation, but assessment alone cannot create change. Organizations that recognize their starting point must next address the fundamental assumptions and mental models that shape how different stakeholders view security's role in business operations.

🔗 *Downloadable Resource: Risk Culture Maturity Assessment*

8.7 CHANGING ENTRENCHED THINKING ABOUT SECURITY

Cultural transformation requires more than new policies or procedures – it demands a fundamental shift in how organizations conceptualize security itself. For decades, many companies have treated security as a technical problem requiring technical solutions, managed by technical specialists. This perspective, while understandable, may limit the effectiveness of security programs and perpetuate the very silos that comprehensive risk management seeks to eliminate. This section explores strategies for reframing security as a business capability that enables strategic objectives.

8.7.1 Reframing security as a business imperative

Changing entrenched thinking about security requires reframing security issues in business terms rather than technical ones. This reframing isn't merely semantic – it fundamentally changes how organizations perceive, prioritize, and address security risks.

As established in Chapter 2's business lens framework, translating technical risks into business language forms the foundation for executive engagement. Moving beyond individual vulnerability reports, cultural transformation requires embedding this translation approach into organizational thinking at all levels. Rather than treating business translation as a communication tactic, mature organizations make it a fundamental part of how security risks are conceived, discussed, and managed across all functions.

Engaging non-technical stakeholders in security conversations becomes easier when using this business-oriented framing. Consider creating simple visual aids that connect security controls to business outcomes. These can help business leaders understand security's contribution to business success without requiring technical expertise.

🔗 *Downloadable Resource: Risk Translation Framework: From Technical to Business Impact*

8.7.2 Building bridges between technical and business units

Creating effective bridges between technical and business teams requires intentional effort and structure as illustrated in Figure 8.2. One approach involves

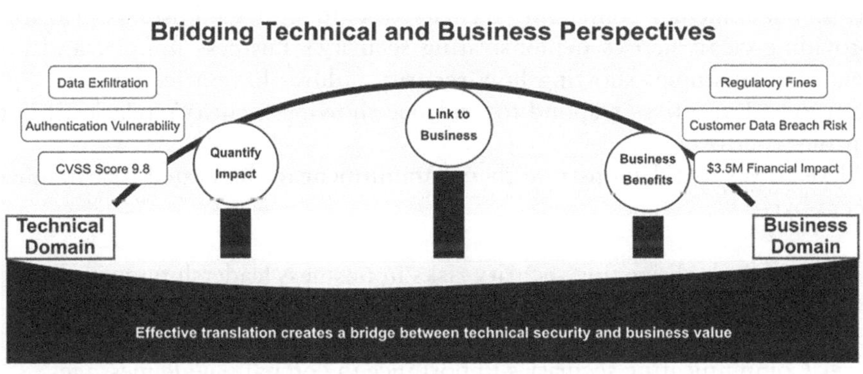

Figure 8.2 Bridging technical and business perspectives.

developing shared risk vocabularies that resonate across departments. When technical and business teams define key terms together, they create a common language for discussing risk that crosses departmental boundaries.

For example, rather than using technical terms like "vulnerability" or business terms like "exposure," teams might jointly define "security risk" as "the potential for harm to business operations, reputation, or compliance status resulting from security weaknesses." This shared definition creates common ground for cross-functional discussion.

Collaborative risk assessment approaches can further strengthen these bridges. Cross-functional risk workshops bring together technical and business stakeholders to identify, assess, and prioritize risks collectively. This collaboration ensures that technical and business perspectives are integrated from the beginning rather than translated after the fact.

Establishing feedback loops between security teams and business units helps maintain these bridges over time. Regular cross-functional meetings, shared metrics, and joint accountability for risk outcomes create an ongoing dialogue that prevents silos from re-forming.

8.7.3 The role of leadership in cultural transformation

Leadership behavior profoundly influences risk culture transformation. The "tone at the top" can significantly affect whether risk management becomes integrated or remains siloed. Leaders who actively model risk-aware behaviors send a powerful message about organizational priorities.

According to the 2024 BDO Board Survey (BDO, 2024), "25% of directors point to cyberthreats and incidents as the most significant risk to their business over the next year," and "37% are changing the treatment of cyber risk from an 'IT responsibility' to a 'company-wide responsibility'." This increased board involvement signals top-down support for cultural change, helping to shift the organizational mindset toward treating security as a business risk and not just a technical concern.

Several techniques can help gain executive buy-in for cultural change initiatives. These include connecting security risks to strategic business priorities, providing clear metrics demonstrating security's business impact, and presenting case studies showing how security failures have affected peer organizations. Executives respond to evidence showing security's relationship to business performance.

Executives can demonstrate their commitment to integrated risk management by:

- Regularly discussing security risks in business leadership meetings
- Including security considerations in strategic planning processes
- Meeting with security leaders to understand current risk landscapes
- Communicating security's importance in company-wide messages
- Allocating resources based on risk impact rather than technical factors

This visible leadership engagement accelerates cultural transformation by signaling that security is truly a business priority.

Reframing security as a business imperative creates the conceptual foundation for change, yet lasting transformation requires structural modifications to how organizations operate. Moving from new ways of thinking to new ways of working means addressing the organizational boundaries that separate functions and limit collaboration.

Downloadable Exercise: Stakeholder Mapping for Cultural Change

8.8 BREAKING DOWN ORGANIZATIONAL SILOS

The fragmented accountability and organizational costs outlined in Chapter 1 manifest most clearly in persistent functional silos. Moving beyond understanding these problems to actively dismantling them requires structural and cultural interventions. These silos, though often created with good intentions, can create dangerous blind spots and missed opportunities for comprehensive risk management.

8.8.1 Case study: SEC v. SolarWinds Corporation

8.8.1.1 Context

SolarWinds Corporation, a Texas-based publicly traded software company, provided network monitoring software to over 300,000 customers worldwide, including 499 Fortune 500 companies and numerous government agencies. Their flagship Orion platform, accounting for 45% of company revenue in 2020, was considered a "crown jewel" asset. As a security software provider, SolarWinds' business model depended on customer trust in its cybersecurity practices and claimed adherence to industry security standards.

8.8.1.2 Challenge

SolarWinds faced a fundamental disconnect between its public security posture and its internal security reality. The company maintained a "Security Statement" on its website that made several key representations about its cybersecurity practices, including following the NIST Cybersecurity Framework, using a secure development lifecycle (SDL), implementing network monitoring, enforcing strong password policies, and maintaining robust access controls. These claims were designed to reassure customers and investors.

However, internally, the company's cybersecurity practices fell significantly short of these claims. Internal assessments, presentations, and employee communications painted a dramatically different picture. According to the SEC investigation, the company routinely granted employees unnecessary administrative rights, contradicting its public claim of providing access on a "need-to-know/least privilege necessary basis." Password practices were equally troubling – in one instance, the password to the company's server used for distributing software updates was discovered to be simply "solarwinds123."

This misalignment created significant risk. Timothy Brown, SolarWinds' Vice President of Security and Architecture, warned in an internal presentation that the "current state of security leaves us in a very vulnerable state for our critical assets" and that "a compromise in these assets would damage [the company's] reputation and [SolarWinds] financially."

8.8.1.3 Approach

Rather than addressing these fundamental security weaknesses, the company maintained its misleading public posture. The Security Statement was used to respond to customer questionnaires about cybersecurity practices, while internally, one engineering manager admitted that the company didn't "do some of the things that are indicated in the [Security Statement SDL Section]."

Instead of implementing proper security controls, the company pursued what appeared to be a "check-the-box" compliance approach. For example, when assessing its compliance with the NIST framework, a 2019 assessment found that SolarWinds had a "program/practice in place" for only 21 of 325 controls (6%), with 198 controls (61%) having "no program/practice in place."

The disconnect between public claims and internal reality extended to incident response. When customers reported suspicious activity involving their Orion software, company personnel downplayed concerns and misrepresented the company's awareness of similar issues. In one notable instance, a SolarWinds employee sent an instant message during a call with a client: "Well I just lied."

8.8.1.4 Outcome

The consequences of this misalignment materialized in December 2020 with the revelation of what became known as the SUNBURST attack. In January 2019, threat actors had accessed SolarWinds' network through a VPN vulnerability that had been identified but not remediated. Between February and June 2020, they inserted malicious code into three Orion software builds, which were then delivered to approximately 18,000 customers worldwide.

The attack compromised numerous federal and state government agencies and more than 1,500 publicly traded companies. On December 14, 2020, when SolarWinds disclosed the attack, its stock price dropped more than 16% in a single day and fell by approximately 35% by month's end.

The damage extended beyond immediate financial impact. In October 2023, the SEC filed charges (Securities and Exchange Commission v. Solarwinds Corp. & Timothy G. Brown, 2024) against SolarWinds and Brown for securities fraud, internal controls failures, and misleading disclosures. A judge dismissed many of these claims in July 2024, but the court allowed claims related to the Security Statement to proceed, finding that the company's representations about access controls and password policies were "well pled as misleading if not outright false." This created substantial, lasting concerns among CISOs throughout 2025. Although the case was dismissed with prejudice in November 2025, CISOs globally remain concerned about the risks of litigation stemming from their actions or statements.

8.8.1.5 Lessons

The SolarWinds case demonstrates several important lessons about alignment between security and compliance:

1. Truthful Representation is Non-Negotiable: As the court noted, "In essence, the [Security] Statement held out SolarWinds as having sophisticated cybersecurity controls in place and as heeding industry best practices. In reality... the company fell way short of even basic requirements of corporate cyber health." Security teams must ensure their public statements align with operational reality.
2. Documentation Without Implementation Creates Liability: Having security policies is insufficient if they aren't enforced. SolarWinds had a password policy requiring complex passwords, yet its Akamai server used "solarwinds123" – a clear violation that created significant risk.
3. Siloed Security and Compliance Functions Lead to Catastrophic Failures: Internal communications at SolarWinds revealed that employees knew about security gaps but continued to make misleading public statements. This disconnect between front-line security knowledge and compliance representation creates an unsustainable risk position.
4. A "Check-the-Box" Approach Provides False Security: SolarWinds' approach to the NIST framework demonstrated that simply claiming compliance without meaningful implementation leaves an organization vulnerable. The company's NIST assessment showed a vast majority of controls were either unimplemented or unverified.

Organizations that deeply embed compliance into their security operations don't merely avoid penalties – they build resilience against attacks. The SolarWinds case shows that misalignment between security reality and compliance claims not only leads to regulatory issues but can result in devastating security breaches that impact customers, shareholders, and the broader ecosystem.

In a related but less-publicized ruling, the Delaware Chancery Court dismissed a derivative lawsuit against the company's directors, finding specifically that cybersecurity risk is a business risk, meaning that boards have discretion under the business judgment rule. The Court stressed that oversight failures leading to corporate trauma do not automatically trigger liability unless they are indicative of bad faith actions.

The SolarWinds case highlights many of the legal and regulatory drivers for integrated governance discussed in Chapter 7, where we examine how these factors are reshaping security oversight requirements.

8.8.2 Creating cross-functional governance structures

Breaking down silos requires formal structures that bring different functions together around shared risk objectives. Cross-functional risk committees represent one effective model. These committees typically include representatives from security, IT, business units, legal, finance, and executive leadership. They create a forum for diverse perspectives on risk identification, assessment, and management.

For these structures to be effective, they must incorporate several key elements:

- Clear charter defining scope, authority, and decision-making processes
- Executive sponsorship providing visible support and resources
- Representation from all key stakeholder groups with decision-making authority
- Regular meeting cadence with structured agendas and follow-up
- Transparent reporting mechanisms sharing insights across the organization

Organizations should measure the effectiveness of these governance structures using metrics that reflect collaboration quality, not just activity levels. Effective metrics include:

- Time to resolve cross-functional risk issues
- Stakeholder satisfaction with risk decision processes
- Percentage of risks identified through cross-functional collaboration
- Business units actively taking part in risk identification
- Reductions in duplicate or conflicting risk management activities

These metrics provide insight into whether governance structures are truly breaking down silos or merely creating additional bureaucracy.

These cross-functional structures require the formal governance models discussed in Chapter 7, which provides detailed guidance on committee structures, reporting relationships, and decision rights.

🔗 *Downloadable Resource: Organizational Silo Mapping*

8.8.3 Implementing shared risk ownership models

The risk ownership models discussed in Chapter 4 require careful implementation to achieve meaningful cultural change. Moving from traditional handoff approaches to true shared ownership means addressing both the structural changes covered previously and the behavioral shifts needed to make these models successful in practice.

Building on the Three Lines of Defense model outlined in Chapter 4, shared ownership implementation requires practical frameworks for distributing risk responsibility effectively. Rather than creating artificial handoffs between functions, these models emphasize collaborative accountability where business and specialist functions work together on risk management outcomes.

Implementing shared ownership often encounters resistance from both business and security teams. Business leaders may resist what they perceive as additional responsibility, while security teams may fear loss of control over risk decisions. Overcoming this resistance requires:

- Clarifying that shared ownership doesn't mean equal expertise requirements
- Providing appropriate tools and training for business teams to fulfill their role
- Ensuring security teams are positioned as enablers rather than enforcers
- Developing shared success metrics that reward collaboration
- Creating escalation paths for managing disagreements
- Organizations that successfully implement shared ownership typically report stronger risk awareness, faster risk response, and more sustainable risk management practices.
- These ownership approaches build on the frameworks introduced in Chapter 4, where we examined different models for distributing risk responsibility across the organization.

8.8.4 Shared risk language and communication practices

Effective collaboration requires common language and communication practices that bridge technical and business domains. This shared language enables meaningful discussion without requiring extensive translation.

Building on the business-centric risk language principles outlined in Chapter 1, organizations must now implement these concepts through deliberate vocabulary development. The shared language framework requires practical application across organizational levels, with particular attention to:

- Risk categories relevant to the organization's operations
- Impact scales connecting technical events to business outcomes
- Likelihood descriptions that all parties interpret consistently

- Risk acceptance criteria and escalation thresholds
- Key risk indicators that drive management attention

Communication procedures should balance transparency with appropriate filtering. Not all stakeholders need all details, but all need an appropriate context for their responsibilities. For instance, executive summaries should provide business context, key findings, required decisions, and expected outcomes – leaving technical details to appendices for those who need them.

Effective risk reporting templates organize information in layers, allowing stakeholders to access the level of detail relevant to their role. A good template includes:

- Executive summary with business context and key decisions required
- Risk overview showing changes from previous reporting periods
- Business impact assessment for identified risks
- Mitigation strategies with responsibilities and timelines
- Technical details for specialized stakeholders

These communication practices create bridges between technical and business perspectives while respecting different information needs.

Structural changes in governance and ownership models create the framework for collaboration, but frameworks alone cannot guarantee participation. Organizations must build the knowledge, skills, and motivation necessary for stakeholders across all functions to contribute meaningfully to risk management.

8.9 BUILDING RISK AWARENESS BEYOND SECURITY TEAMS

Traditional security awareness programs often focus on compliance training and knowledge transfer, yet research suggests that information alone rarely changes behavior. Effective risk awareness requires embedding security thinking into daily business operations, creating opportunities for practical experience, and connecting security concepts to individual roles and responsibilities. This section examines approaches that move beyond checkbox training to build genuine risk intuition across the organization.

8.9.1 Designing effective risk awareness programs

Traditional security awareness programs often focus on compliance rather than engagement, resulting in checkbox exercises that don't change behaviors. More effective programs focus on building actual risk intuition through engagement-driven approaches.

Effective risk awareness programs share several key principles:

1. Focus on behaviors rather than knowledge: Define specific behaviors that demonstrate risk awareness and measure progress against these behaviors rather than quiz scores.
2. Connect to personal experience: Show how security concepts apply both professionally and personally, making the content directly relevant to participants' lives.
3. Use storytelling: Share real examples of security incidents and their impacts using narrative approaches that create emotional connection.
4. Provide contextual learning: Deliver content w it's most relevant – for example, providing phishing guidance when sending sensitive information.
5. Create psychological safety: Encourage reporting of security concerns without fear of punishment, creating a learning environment rather than a blame culture.

Tailoring risk messaging for different organizational roles and functions increases effectiveness. For instance, messaging for finance teams might focus on fraud risks, while development teams might receive content focused on secure coding practices. This customization makes security relevant to daily work rather than an abstract concept.

The effectiveness of awareness programs should be measured through behavioral metrics rather than completion rates. Organizations might track:

- Security incident reporting rates
- Phishing simulation response rates
- Security concern escalations
- Voluntary participation in security initiatives
- Examples of security being considered in business decisions

These metrics help to provide insight into whether awareness is translating into actual behavior change.

Downloadable Resource: Role-Based Risk Awareness Program Template

8.9.2 Embedding risk thinking into business processes

For risk awareness to become sustainable, it must be embedded in existing business processes rather than treated as a separate activity. This integration makes risk consideration a routine part of business operations.

Several techniques can help incorporate risk considerations into everyday workflows:

1. Add security checkpoints to project management methodologies at key decision points
2. Include security impact questions in change management processes

3. Integrate risk assessment into product development lifecycles
4. Add security considerations to procurement and vendor management procedures
5. Include risk perspectives in strategic planning templates and processes

These integrations ensure security is considered naturally within business activities rather than as an afterthought or separate process.

Risk discussions can be integrated into regular business meetings by adding brief security updates to standing agendas, creating "risk moments" for sharing recent learnings, or rotating responsibility for bringing security considerations to meetings. These approaches normalize security discussions without requiring separate meetings.

Successful integration examples include product teams that incorporate threat modeling into design reviews, procurement teams that include security requirements in vendor assessments, and marketing teams that include security features in product messaging. These examples show how security awareness can enhance business processes rather than impede them.

8.9.3 Creating opportunities for practical risk experience

Abstract security training rarely creates true risk intuition. Practical experience provides more powerful learning opportunities that build risk understanding across the organization.

Simulation exercises represent one approach to building practical experience. Tabletop exercises that walk through security incident scenarios help participants understand potential impacts and response requirements. These exercises can be tailored to different business functions – for example, having marketing teams work through a website compromise scenario or finance teams address a business email compromise attempt.

Cross-training approaches help to build a shared understanding between technical and business teams. Security staff might spend time with business units to understand operational constraints, while business staff might observe security operations to appreciate the threat landscape. This exchange of perspectives builds empathy and collaboration.

Post-incident reviews provide powerful learning opportunities when conducted effectively. Rather than focusing on blame, these reviews should identify systemic factors that contributed to incidents and develop improvements that address root causes. Sharing lessons learned across the organization builds collective risk wisdom that improves future decision-making.

Regular practice with security tools and procedures builds comfort and competence. For example, having all employees periodically report suspicious emails using the organization's reporting tool ensures they know how to use these mechanisms when real threats appear.

Risk awareness programs can build knowledge and capability, yet without appropriate incentives, these investments may produce limited behavioral change. Organizations discover that what gets measured and rewarded ultimately determines what behaviors emerge and persist.

8.9.3.1 Exercise: developing a risk awareness campaign

This step-by-step exercise helps design targeted risk awareness initiatives:

1. Define campaign objectives:
   - Identify specific behaviors you want to encourage or discourage
   - Establish measurable outcome goals (e.g., 50% increase in reporting)
   - Define success criteria and evaluation methods
2. Segment your audience:
   - Identify primary audience groups with different needs
   - Map their current awareness levels and specific risk exposures
   - Determine motivators and barriers for each group
3. Develop tailored messaging:
   - Create core messages addressing each group's specific risks
   - Adapt delivery methods to each group's preferences
   - Incorporate real examples relevant to each audience
4. Create a multi-channel communication plan:
   - Select appropriate communication channels for each audience
   - Schedule communications to avoid overload
   - Plan for reinforcement through different formats
5. Establish measurement approach:
   - Define key metrics aligned with behavioral objectives
   - Create baseline measurements before campaign launch
   - Establish regular measurement points to track progress
6. Implement, measure, and refine:
   - Launch campaign with high-visibility kickoff
   - Collect feedback and measure early results
   - Adjust approach based on initial outcomes

This structured approach creates awareness campaigns that drive actual behavior change rather than merely transmitting information.

8.10 INCENTIVIZING COLLABORATIVE RISK MANAGEMENT

Organizational behavior follows organizational incentives, often in ways that surprise well-intentioned leaders. Performance metrics that reward speed without considering security implications, recognition systems that celebrate individual achievement over collaboration, and compensation structures that ignore risk outcomes can undermine the best cultural change initiatives. This section explores how thoughtfully designed incentive systems can support collaborative risk management.

8.10.1 Aligning individual and team incentives with risk goals

Incentive systems often unintentionally discourage good risk management by rewarding speed, cost reduction, or revenue generation without considering risk implications. As Douglas Brooks notes (John R. S. Fraser, 2010), "If these goals do not include proper recognition of risk and reward, then the organization will reap what it sows, and take on inappropriate risk."

Effective performance metrics should encourage appropriate risk behaviors. These might include:

- Security considerations in project planning and execution
- Prompt vulnerability remediation within business applications
- Early identification and escalation of potential security issues
- Cross-functional collaboration on security initiatives
- Business process improvements that enhance security

Organizations must balance individual, team, and organizational risk incentives. Individual metrics might focus on personal security practices, team metrics on collaborative security management, and organizational metrics on overall risk reduction. This balanced approach as shown in Figure 8.3, encourages both personal responsibility and collective action.

Figure 8.3 Incentive alignment pyramid for risk management.

When designing incentives, organizations should carefully consider potential unintended consequences. For example, metrics focusing solely on vulnerability counts might encourage addressing easy, low-impact issues while ignoring complex, high-impact vulnerabilities. Similarly, incident reduction metrics might discourage reporting, creating dangerous blind spots. Effective metrics balance quantitative measures with qualitative assessment to avoid these pitfalls. A comparison is provided in Table 8.2.

Downloadable Resource: Security Incentive Design Framework

8.10.2 Recognition and reward systems for risk collaboration

Beyond formal incentives, recognition systems can powerfully influence risk culture. Several models effectively acknowledge security contributions across functions:

- Security Champion Programs: Recognize individuals who promote security within their business functions through formal designation, additional training, and peer recognition.
- Risk Collaboration Awards: Celebrate teams that successfully integrate security into business initiatives, particularly when they demonstrate innovative approaches.
- Recognition in Performance Reviews: Include security contributions in standard performance evaluation processes, ensuring they receive attention alongside other business objectives.
- Management Acknowledgment: Have senior leaders publicly recognize security-conscious decisions, reinforcing their value to the organization.

Table 8.2 Incentive types effectiveness comparison

Incentive type	*Example*	*Effectiveness*	*Best for*	*Potential risks*
Financial	Bonuses tied to risk metrics	High short-term impact	Clear, measurable goals	Can create perverse incentives
Recognition	Security champion awards	Strong for engagement	Building culture	May seem tokenistic if overused
Career development	Security rotation programs	High long-term value	Skill building	Resource intensive
Autonomy	Risk decision authority	Very effective for seniors	Experienced staff	Requires clear boundaries
Team-based	Shared risk objectives	Builds collaboration	Cross-functional goals	Free-rider problems

Non-monetary incentives often prove highly effective at building risk culture. These might include professional development opportunities, increased autonomy, special project assignments, or formal recognition through organizational communication channels. These rewards signal organizational priorities without creating perverse incentives.

Creating visibility for collaborative risk success stories helps reinforce desired behaviors. Organizations might share these stories through internal newsletters, town hall meetings, or dedicated recognition events. These communications demonstrate that security collaboration is valued and celebrated.

8.10.3 Addressing resistance to change

Resistance to new risk management approaches is natural and should be expected. Common sources of resistance include:

- Perceived Burden: Concern that new approaches will create additional work without commensurate value
- Loss of Authority: Fear that shared responsibility dilutes existing authority structures
- Competence Concerns: Worry about lacking skills needed for new approaches
- Historical Friction: Past negative experiences between security and business teams
- Competing Priorities: Perception that security initiatives compete with business objectives

Identifying resistance factors requires active listening rather than assumption. Techniques include anonymous surveys, facilitated discussions, one-on-one conversations, and observation of behavior patterns. This inquiry helps identify specific concerns rather than generic "resistance."

Addressing resistance effectively requires tailored approaches:

- For perceived burden, demonstrate efficiency improvements from better collaboration
- For authority concerns, clarify decision rights and emphasize expanded influence
- For competence issues, provide appropriate training and support resources
- For historical friction, acknowledge past challenges and reset relationships
- For competing priorities, demonstrate how security enables business objectives

Creating safe spaces for expressing concerns helps surface and address resistance. This might include designated feedback channels, neutral facilitators for difficult conversations, or anonymous suggestion systems. These mechanisms allow concerns to be addressed proactively rather than manifesting as passive resistance.

Well-designed incentives can accelerate cultural transformation, but maintaining momentum requires ongoing measurement and adjustment. Organizations that successfully transform their risk cultures develop systematic approaches to tracking progress, identifying emerging challenges, and sustaining positive changes over time.

8.10.3.1 Exercise: designing risk incentives

This framework helps audit and improve risk incentive structures:

1. Audit current incentives:
    - Identify formal incentives (compensation, promotion criteria, etc.)
    - Map informal incentives (recognition, influence, opportunity access)
    - Assess alignment between stated risk goals and actual incentives
    - Identify conflicting incentives that undermine risk management
2. Design collaborative incentives:
    - Define specific behaviors you want to encourage
    - Create balanced metrics combining leading and lagging indicators
    - Incorporate both individual and collective performance measures
    - Ensure incentives are meaningful to target audiences
3. Implementation planning:
    - Sequence changes to avoid disruption
    - Communicate purpose and mechanics clearly
    - Provide transition support for adjustment periods
    - Establish feedback mechanisms to identify issues
4. Measurement and refinement:
    - Track behavioral changes resulting from new incentives
    - Monitor for unintended consequences
    - Adjust approaches based on observed outcomes
    - Celebrate and communicate early successes

This structured approach helps create incentive systems that genuinely support collaborative risk management rather than merely adding security metrics to existing frameworks.

8.11 MEASURING CULTURAL PROGRESS AND MAINTAINING MOMENTUM

Cultural change initiatives often begin with enthusiasm, but fade without sustained measurement and reinforcement. Unlike technical implementations that produce immediate, visible results, cultural transformation occurs gradually and requires different metrics to track progress. Organizations need approaches that capture both quantitative indicators and qualitative shifts in behavior, communication, and decision-making patterns.

8.11.1 Metrics for risk culture maturity

Measuring cultural change requires both quantitative and qualitative approaches. Key indicators of a maturing risk culture include:

- Risk consideration in business decisions: Percentage of business initiatives that include security risk assessment before approval
- Cross-functional collaboration: Frequency and quality of interaction between security and business teams
- Risk reporting and escalation: Timeliness and accuracy of risk information flow
- Response to security incidents: Speed and effectiveness of cross-functional incident response
- Resource allocation: Alignment between risk priorities and resource decisions

Organizations should balance quantitative metrics (such as incident response times or risk assessment completion rates) with qualitative measures (such as stakeholder interviews or culture surveys). This balanced approach provides a more complete picture of cultural development.

Progress along risk maturity models provides another measurement approach. Using the FOIL model (Fragmented, Organized, Influential, Leading) or the 4Ns model (Naïve, Novice, Normalized, Natural), organizations can assess their advancement along the maturity spectrum. These assessments should be conducted periodically to track progress and identify emerging challenges.

8.11.2 Sustaining cultural change

Creating sustainable cultural change requires embedding new practices into organizational systems and routines. Several approaches help maintain momentum:

- Feedback mechanisms that reinforce positive risk behaviors, including recognition programs, performance reviews, and regular leadership acknowledgment of good risk management practices.
- Integration of risk culture into onboarding processes, ensuring new employees immediately understand the organization's approach to risk management and their role within it.
- Ongoing development programs that build risk management capabilities at all levels, from technical specialists to business leaders to board members.
- Communities of practice that bring together individuals from different functions with shared interest in risk management, creating networks that sustain cultural development.
- Regular reassessment of risk culture, identifying new challenges and opportunities for continued enhancement.

These approaches help prevent cultural regression after initial progress, ensuring that integrated risk management becomes “how we do things” rather than a temporary initiative.

8.11.3 The LILAC framework for risk-aware culture

As shown in Figure 8.4, the LILAC framework, adapted from research by the UK Health and Safety Executive, and cited by Paul Hopkin (Hopkin, 2019) provides a useful summary of essential elements for a risk-aware culture:

- Leadership: Strong leadership within the organization regarding risk strategy and operations is foundational. Leaders demonstrate risk-aware behavior, set clear expectations, and provide necessary resources.
- Involvement: All stakeholders participate in risk management processes, with specialist risk functions serving advisory rather than ownership roles. This broad participation ensures diverse perspectives inform risk decisions.
- Learning: The organization emphasizes training in risk management procedures and learning from events. A learning culture enables organizations to identify and change inappropriate risk behaviors through in-depth analysis and communication.

Figure 8.4 The LILAC framework for risk-aware culture.

- Accountability: The organization maintains appropriate accountability without creating blame culture. Employees feel able to report issues without fear of punishment, while still maintaining clear responsibility for risk management duties.
- Communication: The organization maintains open communication on all risk management issues and lessons learned. Information flows freely up, down, and across the organization with appropriate context and detail for different audiences.

Organizations that excel in these five dimensions as seen in Table 8.3, typically demonstrate mature risk cultures capable of sustaining integrated risk management approaches over time.

Table 8.3 LILAC framework components

Component	*Focus area*	*Key activities*	*Success indicators*	*Common pitfalls*
Leadership	Setting tone and direction	• Visible commitment • Resource allocation • Strategic integration	• Regular risk discussions • Risk-based decisions • Executive sponsorship	• Delegating without involvement • Mixed messages
Involvement	Broad participation	• Cross-functional teams • Stakeholder engagement • Shared ownership	• Active participation • Diverse perspectives • Collaborative solutions	• Token representation • Specialist-only approach
Learning	Continuous improvement	• Training programs • Incident analysis • Knowledge sharing	• Behavior changes • Reduced repeat incidents • Innovation in risk management	• One-time training • Blame-focused reviews
Accountability	Clear responsibilities	• Role definition • Performance metrics • Escalation paths	• Timely decisions • Issue ownership • Psychological safety	• Blame culture • Unclear responsibilities
Communication	Information flow	• Regular updates • Feedback channels • Transparent reporting	• Informed stakeholders • Quick escalation • Shared understanding	• Information hoarding • Technical jargon only

8.12 CONCLUSION

Cultural transformation forms the foundation for truly integrated risk management. Technical controls and governance structures, while necessary, cannot succeed without corresponding cultural elements that support and sustain them. As we've seen throughout this chapter, cultural change requires addressing both structural components (like incentives and governance models) and human factors (like communication practices and leadership behaviors).

The journey from siloed to integrated risk management is neither quick nor simple. It requires sustained effort across multiple dimensions, from leadership commitment to frontline engagement. Organizations should expect this transformation to progress through stages, with setbacks along the way requiring course corrections and renewed commitment.

Organizations that build collaborative risk cultures position themselves for significant advantages. They can respond more quickly to emerging threats, allocate resources more effectively to risk priorities, and make better risk-informed business decisions. Perhaps most importantly, they can use security as a strategic enabler rather than treating it merely as a risk reduction function or compliance requirement.

The frameworks and approaches outlined in this chapter provide a roadmap for this cultural transformation. By understanding current cultural barriers, changing entrenched thinking about security, breaking down organizational silos, building broad risk awareness, incentivizing collaboration, and measuring progress, organizations can develop the cultural foundation necessary for effective integrated risk management.

In Chapter 9, we'll build on this cultural foundation to explore how security can become a strategic business enabler, contributing directly to competitive advantage and business value creation. The cultural transformation described in this chapter creates the necessary conditions for this strategic repositioning of the security function.

8.13 ACTION ITEMS FOR READERS

1. Conduct a risk culture assessment using the LILAC framework (Leadership, Involvement, Learning, Accountability, Communication) to evaluate your organization's current state across these five dimensions and identify specific cultural barriers limiting integrated risk management.
2. Develop a shared risk vocabulary by facilitating workshops with technical and business stakeholders to jointly define key terms like "security risk," "business impact," and "risk tolerance" in language that resonates across all organizational functions.
3. Establish a cross-functional risk committee with representatives from security, IT, business units, legal, and finance, including a clear charter

defining decision-making authority, meeting cadence, and success metrics focused on collaboration quality rather than activity levels.

4. Create risk-aware performance metrics by incorporating security considerations into existing individual and team performance evaluations, ensuring that collaboration on risk management becomes a recognized and rewarded behavior across the organization.
5. Implement embedded risk checkpoints in three existing business processes (such as project management, procurement, or strategic planning) where security impact questions become routine parts of decision-making workflows rather than separate activities.

Chapter 9

From risk reduction to business enablement

Chapter in One Sentence: Security transforms from a cost center to a strategic asset when leaders identify, measure, and communicate how security capabilities enable business objectives, create competitive advantages, and drive growth rather than simply mitigating risks.

9.1 EXECUTIVE SUMMARY

This chapter presents a transformative approach to security, repositioning it from a defensive cost center to a strategic business enabler. The chapter provides frameworks and methodologies for identifying, measuring, and articulating how security creates tangible business value beyond risk mitigation. It begins by examining the evolution of security's business role, noting that 38% of executive leaders now identify privacy and security as important technologies for achieving revenue growth. The chapter introduces the concept of the "upside of risk," where well-designed security enables appropriate risk-taking that delivers business advantages.

The Security Business Enablement Matrix offers a structured approach for mapping security capabilities to business objectives across four dimensions: operational enablement, trust creation, compliance advantage, and innovation support. Through this framework, security leaders can identify untapped business value in existing capabilities and target investments that deliver the greatest impact. The chapter demonstrates how security enables new business models, expands market reach into regulated sectors, and accelerates innovation by providing the foundation for secure experimentation and development.

For competitive differentiation, the Strategic Security Differentiation Framework helps organizations identify unique security capabilities that create business advantages. The chapter details approach for integrating security into brand positioning, targeting security-conscious market segments, and leveraging industry security events to demonstrate comparative advantage. It emphasizes translating technical security features into value statements that resonate with customers and partners.

DOI: 10.1201/9781003744146-9

Finally, the chapter addresses how to measure and communicate security's business contribution using metrics that matter to executives. By quantifying security's impact on revenue generation, customer acquisition and retention, operational efficiency, and innovation velocity, security leaders can build compelling business cases that position security as an investment rather than an expense. Through practical frameworks, templates, and real-world examples, the chapter equips security leaders with tools to transform their positioning from cost center to value creator, ensuring security is recognized as an integral component of business strategy and success.

9.2 KEY TAKEAWAYS

- Security creates business value by enabling operational efficiency, enhancing customer trust, turning compliance requirements into market opportunities, and accelerating innovation
- The Security Business Enablement Matrix helps identify and articulate how security capabilities directly support business objectives across multiple dimensions
- Organizations can leverage security as a competitive differentiator by targeting security-conscious market segments and integrating security into their brand promise
- Business-oriented security metrics that quantify revenue enabled, customer trust enhanced, and efficiency improved communicate security's value more effectively to executives
- Successful transformation requires security leaders to adopt business language, focusing on what security enables rather than what it prevents

9.3 APPLICATION QUESTIONS

1. How could you reframe your existing security capabilities to highlight their business-enabling functions rather than just their protective benefits?
2. Which security-conscious market segments might value your organization's security capabilities as a competitive differentiator?
3. What business metrics could you develop to more effectively communicate the value your security program creates beyond risk reduction?

9.4 TOOLS REFERENCED IN THIS CHAPTER

All tools available at kaynemcgladrey.com/myth/

- Security Business Enablement Matrix
- Security-Enabled Business Opportunity Assessment
- Security Competitive Differentiation Framework

- Security Investment Business Case Template
- Executive Security Value Communication Toolkit

9.5 INTRODUCTION

Security has traditionally been viewed as a cost center focused primarily on risk reduction and defense. Organizations allocate resources to security programs primarily to protect assets, prevent breaches, and ensure compliance with regulatory requirements. This limited perspective has long positioned security departments as necessary expenses rather than strategic contributors to business success.

However, this narrow view ignores the significant business value security can deliver beyond protection. When security is seen only as a defensive function, organizations miss opportunities to leverage security capabilities as catalysts for growth, innovation, and competitive advantage. The true potential of security lies not just in preventing negative outcomes, but in enabling positive business results.

Modern organizations increasingly recognize security as a strategic enabler that can create competitive advantage. Leading companies are transforming their approach to security, positioning it as an integral component of business strategy rather than a separate technical function. This shift represents a fundamental change in how organizations perceive the role and value of security investments.

This chapter explores how to transform security from a necessary expense into a business driver. We will examine practical approaches for identifying, measuring, and articulating the business value that effective security programs can deliver. The focus will shift from simply protecting what exists to enabling what could be.

We'll examine frameworks, metrics, and strategies for positioning security as an enabler of business opportunities. These tools will help security leaders demonstrate how their programs contribute directly to revenue generation, market expansion, operational efficiency, and innovation.

The chapter builds on previous discussions of cultural transformation to provide practical approaches for deriving tangible business value from security investments. By aligning security initiatives with business objectives and measuring their impact in business terms, security leaders can secure their position as strategic partners in organizational success.

9.6 THE EVOLUTION OF SECURITY'S BUSINESS ROLE

The traditional view of security as a necessary expense appears to be shifting across organizations worldwide. Business leaders increasingly recognize that security investments can contribute to revenue generation, operational efficiency, and competitive positioning. This transformation requires security professionals to adopt new perspectives on how their programs create value beyond risk mitigation. Understanding this shift provides the foundation for repositioning security as a strategic business asset that enables growth and innovation.

9.6.1 From cost center to value creator

Historically, security functions have been primarily focused on protection and compliance. Organizations established security programs largely in response to threats, incidents, and regulatory requirements. As discussed in Chapter 1, the historical separation between security and business functions created communication barriers and misaligned priorities. Today's business environment now requires security to deliver measurable business value. As digital transformation accelerates and organizations increasingly depend on technology for core operations, the scope and importance of security have expanded dramatically. Building on the business enablement foundation established in Chapter 5, this transformation represents a fundamental shift from viewing security as an isolated technical function to recognizing its potential for revenue generation, operational efficiency, and competitive positioning as seen in Figure 9.1.

Several key drivers are forcing this evolution. Digital transformation initiatives have embedded technology deeply into core business processes, making security an essential component of operational resilience. Regulatory changes continue to raise the stakes for security failures, with more stringent requirements and higher penalties for non-compliance. Competitive pressures are pushing organizations to move faster and more efficiently while maintaining appropriate controls. Customer expectations regarding data protection and privacy have risen substantially, making security a factor in purchasing decisions and brand reputation.

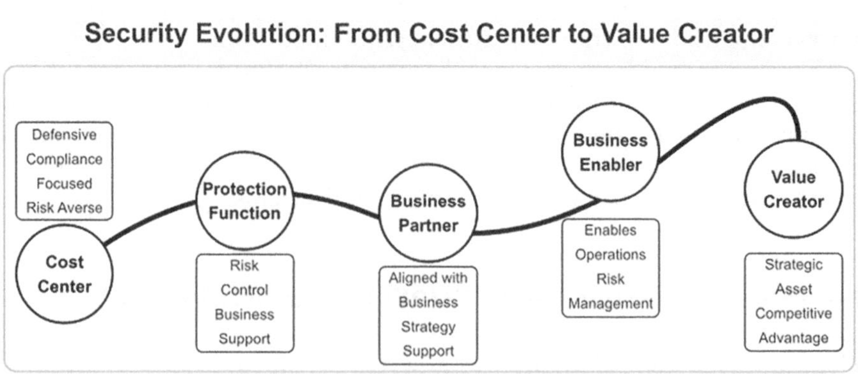

Figure 9.1 From cost center to value creator.

According to Gartner research (Proctor, 2024), 38% of executive leaders involved in their company's growth initiatives identified privacy and security as one of the most important technologies for achieving high enterprise revenue growth in the next three years, demonstrating the business value of security investments. This statistic links security and privacy to business growth, supporting the argument that security is a strategic enabler and not just a cost center.

Leading organizations are repositioning security within their business models. Rather than viewing security as a necessary burden, these companies are integrating security into their value propositions and strategic planning processes. For example, financial institutions now advertise their security capabilities as a competitive advantage when attracting security-conscious customers. Healthcare organizations leverage their robust security and privacy controls to build patient trust and expand partnerships with other providers. Technology companies embed security features into their products as value-added differentiators rather than compliance checkboxes.

This transition from cost center to value creator doesn't happen automatically. It requires security leaders to reframe their approach, speak the language of business, and clearly articulate how security investments contribute to business outcomes. Organizations that successfully make this transition gain both enhanced security and strategic business advantages.

9.6.2 Understanding the upside of security risk

The concept of the "upside of risk" in terms of security represents a significant shift in perspective. Traditionally, risk management in security has focused almost exclusively on preventing negative outcomes. However, as described in Fundamentals of Risk Management (Hopkin, 2019), there are multiple ways to interpret the upside of risk, from "fewer disruptions to normal operations" to "achieving a positive outcome in difficult circumstances."

Effective security management creates opportunity spaces for organizations. When security controls are properly designed and implemented, they provide a foundation of trust and resilience that enables organizations to pursue new initiatives with confidence. Rather than simply preventing bad things from happening, security can create the conditions necessary for good things to happen. This perspective transforms security from a purely defensive function to an enabler of strategic business opportunities.

There is an important distinction between viewing security as limiting risk versus enabling controlled risk-taking. The traditional approach to security often emphasizes restrictions, limitations, and barriers. This can create friction with business objectives and lead to security being viewed as an obstacle. A more mature approach recognizes that all business activities involve some degree of risk, and the goal of security is not to eliminate risk entirely but to enable appropriate risk-taking within defined parameters.

As described in Fundamentals of Risk Management (Hopkin, 2019), "In simple terms, the upside of risk is achieved when the benefits obtained from taking the risk are greater than any benefit that would have resulted from not taking it." This perspective applies directly to security, where well-designed controls can help organizations assess, understand, and manage risks associated with new business ventures.

Risk appetite relates directly to business enablement. Organizations with a clear understanding of their risk appetite can make informed decisions about which opportunities to pursue and how to manage the associated risks. Security functions that understand the organization's risk appetite can design controls that align with business objectives, enabling rather than impeding strategic initiatives. This approach allows organizations to take calculated risks in pursuit of business goals while maintaining appropriate security guardrails.

As security leaders shift their mindset from risk elimination to risk management, they position their programs as strategic enablers rather than compliance checkboxes. This perspective allows security to be integrated into business planning processes, ensuring that security considerations enhance rather than hinder strategic decision-making.

9.6.3 Case study: Dittman v. UPMC, Supreme Court of Pennsylvania

9.6.3.1 *Context*

The University of Pittsburgh Medical Center (UPMC), one of Pennsylvania's largest healthcare providers, collected and stored sensitive personal and financial information from its 62,000 employees as a condition of their employment. This information included names, birth dates, social security numbers, addresses, tax forms, and bank account information, which was stored on the organization's internet-accessible computer systems.

9.6.3.2 *Challenge*

In 2014, UPMC experienced a significant data breach when cybercriminals accessed their systems and stole the personal and financial information of all 62,000 current and former employees. The stolen data was subsequently used to file fraudulent tax returns, causing actual financial damages to the affected employees. The breach revealed several critical security vulnerabilities, including alleged failures to:

- Properly encrypt data
- Establish adequate firewalls to handle server intrusion
- Implement adequate authentication protocols to protect confidential information

The fundamental challenge stemmed from UPMC's apparent misalignment between their security practices and their legal compliance obligations. The organization seemed to operate under the assumption that they had no legal duty to implement reasonable security measures to protect employee data from breaches, focusing instead only on their notification requirements after a breach occurred.

9.6.3.3 Approach

Rather than taking responsibility for the breach, UPMC took a defensive legal approach. When employees filed a class-action lawsuit claiming negligence, UPMC argued two main defenses:

1. They had no legal duty to protect employee data against cybercriminals
2. The economic loss doctrine barred claims for purely financial damages

UPMC maintained they weren't in the business of providing data security and couldn't be held liable for third-party criminal conduct. They also argued that being held accountable for data breaches would create "hundreds of thousands of lawsuits" that could overwhelm the judicial system and potentially put entities out of business.

9.6.3.4 Outcome

After years of litigation, the Supreme Court of Pennsylvania ruled against UPMC in November 2018 (Barbara A. Dittman, Gary R. Douglas, Alice Pastirik, Joann Decolati, Tina Sorrentino, Kristen Cushman And Shannon Molyneaux, Individually And On Behalf Of All Others Similarly Situated v. UPMC D/B/A The University Of Pittsburgh Medical Center, And UPMC Mc, 2018), making this a landmark legal decision. The court determined that:

1. Employers have a legal duty to exercise reasonable care to safeguard employees' sensitive personal information when stored on an internet-accessible computer system
2. The economic loss doctrine does not bar negligence claims seeking purely financial damages when based on the breach of a legal duty that exists independently from any contractual obligations

Following the litigation, UPMC eventually reached a settlement of $2.65 million to resolve the class action lawsuit.

9.6.3.5 Lessons

The Dittman v. UPMC case highlights several important lessons about the risks of non-compliance and misalignment between security and compliance teams:

1. Proactive Security vs. Reactive Compliance: UPMC focused narrowly on breach notification requirements while neglecting their broader duty

to implement reasonable security measures. Organizations must move beyond checkbox compliance to proactive security.

2. Evolving Legal Landscape: The court recognized that traditional legal principles apply to modern technological contexts. Companies must anticipate how established legal duties extend to emerging technologies and data protection.
3. Financial Consequences: Beyond the $2.65 million settlement, UPMC faced years of litigation costs and reputational damage. The financial impact of non-compliance often far exceeds the investment needed for proper security measures.
4. Organizational Alignment: The case demonstrates how silos between legal, compliance, and security teams can create significant blind spots. When these functions operate separately rather than in coordination, organizations face increased liability and risk exposure.

For security and executive leaders, this case underscores why embedding compliance into security operations isn't just about avoiding penalties - it's about building resilience, reducing risk, and improving security outcomes. Organizations that treat compliance as separate from security operations create dangerous gaps that adversaries can exploit, leading to both security breaches and legal consequences.

Forward-thinking organizations leverage such obligations to strengthen stakeholder relationships. Rather than viewing the ruling as an additional compliance burden, these organizations see it as an opportunity to demonstrate their commitment to protecting sensitive information. By exceeding minimum security requirements, they build confidence among employees, customers, and partners, leading to stronger relationships and potential business advantages.

Recognizing security's potential for business enablement represents an important first step, but organizations need practical approaches to identify and develop these opportunities. The frameworks and methodologies that follow provide structured approaches for mapping security capabilities to specific business objectives and measuring their impact.

9.7 FRAMEWORK FOR IDENTIFYING SECURITY'S BUSINESS ENABLING FUNCTIONS

Identifying specific ways security creates business value requires structured approaches and practical frameworks. Organizations often struggle to connect their security capabilities to measurable business outcomes, missing opportunities to show their programs' contributions. The frameworks presented in this section provide methodologies for mapping security investments to business objectives across multiple dimensions. These tools help security leaders articulate their value in terms that resonate with business stakeholders and executive leadership.

9.7.1 The Security Business Enablement Matrix

To effectively position security as a business enabler, organizations need a structured approach for identifying and articulating the business value of security investments. The Security Business Enablement Matrix provides a comprehensive framework for mapping security capabilities to business objectives, helping security leaders identify and communicate how their programs contribute to organizational success. This enablement matrix provides a structured approach to the investment alignment discussed in Chapter 5, helping security leaders identify and articulate how security investments support business goals.

As shown in Figure 9.2, the matrix consists of four key quadrants, each representing a different aspect of security's business enabling functions:

1. Operational Enablement: How security ensures business continuity, supports business functions, and enables operational efficiency
2. Trust Creation: How security builds confidence among customers, partners, and other stakeholders
3. Compliance Advantage: How security helps meet regulatory requirements while creating business advantages
4. Innovation Support: How security enables controlled risk-taking and supports new initiatives

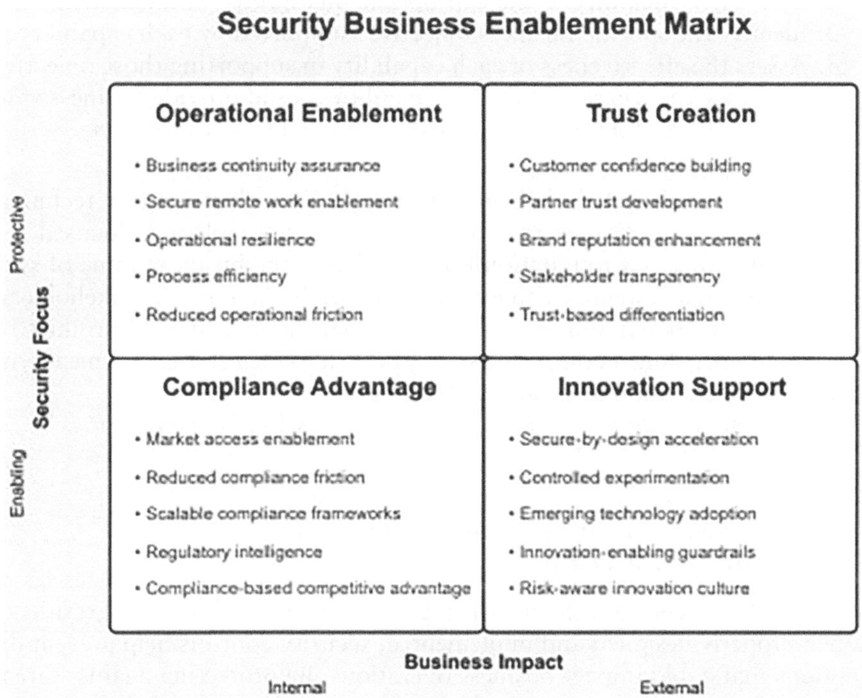

Figure 9.2 Security Business Enablement Matrix.

Each quadrant contains specific security capabilities that contribute to business objectives in that area. For example, within Operational Enablement, capabilities might include identity and access management, secure remote access, and business continuity controls. Within Trust Creation, capabilities might include data protection, transparent security practices, and privacy controls.

Organizations can use this framework to identify untapped business value in existing security capabilities. By mapping current security investments against the four quadrants, security leaders can identify areas where they are already creating business value but may not be measuring or communicating it effectively. This process often reveals that existing security capabilities provide business benefits beyond their primary security functions.

The framework also helps identify gaps where additional security investments could create significant business value. By understanding how security capabilities map to business enablement functions, organizations can make more strategic decisions about security investments, prioritizing those that deliver the greatest business impact.

The process for mapping current security investments against business enablement opportunities involves several steps:

1. Inventory existing security capabilities and investments
2. Map each capability to the appropriate quadrant(s) in the matrix
3. Identify the specific business objectives supported by each capability
4. Assess the effectiveness of each capability in supporting those objectives
5. Identify gaps where additional capabilities could provide business value
6. Prioritize capabilities based on their potential business impact

This structured approach helps security leaders shift from a technical, protection-focused mindset to a business-oriented, enablement-focused perspective. It provides a foundation for articulating the business value of security in terms that resonate with executive leadership and other stakeholders.

This framework expands on the business enablement concept introduced in Chapter 5, providing a comprehensive approach to identifying and measuring security's contribution to business objectives.

Downloadable Resource: Security Business Enablement Matrix

9.7.2 Operational enablement: supporting business functions

Security plays a central role in ensuring operational continuity and resilience. When properly designed and implemented, security controls help prevent disruptions that could impact business operations. By protecting against threats that could compromise systems, data, or processes, security helps organizations to maintain consistent operations even in challenging environments.

The ability to enable secure remote work and distributed business operations has become particularly valuable in recent years. As organizations adopt more flexible work models, security provides the foundation necessary for employees to access systems and data securely from any location. This capability supports business objectives related to talent acquisition, employee satisfaction, and operational resilience. For example, services like Secure Access Service Edge (SASE) and multi-factor authentication (MFA) support distributed workforces securely, facilitating remote work policies while maintaining data protection standards.

Security also supports business agility through secure-by-design architectures. When security is integrated into systems and processes from the beginning, organizations can move more quickly and confidently. Rather than adding security as an afterthought that might slow down operations, secure-by-design approaches ensure that security enables rather than inhibits business agility. This approach allows organizations to adapt quickly to changing business conditions while maintaining appropriate security controls.

An often-overlooked aspect of operational enablement is how security can reduce friction in business processes while maintaining appropriate controls. Well-designed security controls balance protection with usability, ensuring that security measures don't create unnecessary obstacles for legitimate business activities. This balance is essential for security to be viewed as an enabler rather than a hindrance to business operations.

Security helps ensure systems remain operational, which is a part of maintaining business continuity. This is vital for revenue generation and customer satisfaction, as uninterrupted operations mean consistent service delivery and customer engagement. This direct connection between security and operational continuity illustrates how security enables core business functions rather than simply protecting them.

By focusing on operational enablement, security leaders can show how their programs directly contribute to the organization's ability to operate efficiently and effectively. This perspective shifts the conversation from what security prevents to what security enables, highlighting its role as a business driver rather than just a protective function.

9.7.3 Trust creation: building security into your brand promise

Trust represents one of the most valuable currencies in modern business, and security plays an increasingly central role in creating and maintaining that trust. When organizations effectively communicate their security practices and demonstrate genuine commitment to protecting stakeholder data, they build confidence that translates directly into measurable business value. This trust becomes a powerful differentiator that influences customer decisions, partner relationships, and brand perception.

9.7.3.1 From security feature to brand asset

Security has evolved from a behind-the-scenes technical function to a front-and-center brand differentiator. Organizations that recognize this shift can transform their security capabilities into powerful trust-building assets. Strong security measures directly increase customer trust, leading to increased loyalty and retention - impacts that can be quantified through metrics like Net Promoter Score (NPS) and Customer Lifetime Value (CLV).

The key lies in integrating security elements into brand positioning and messaging in ways that resonate with stakeholders. This integration involves identifying the security capabilities that support the brand promise and incorporating them into brand messaging, marketing materials, and customer communications. When done effectively, this positions security as an integral part of the brand rather than a separate technical function.

9.7.3.2 Building multi-stakeholder confidence

Security creates value by building confidence across multiple stakeholder groups, each with distinct concerns and priorities:

9.7.3.3 Customer trust enhancement

- Transparent communication about data protection practices
- Demonstrable commitment through certifications and audits
- Proactive security updates that reinforce reliability
- Clear, accessible privacy policies and security documentation

9.7.3.4 Partner confidence for business growth

Organizations with strong security programs find it significantly easier to establish partnerships, particularly in industries involving data sharing. Partners require assurance that shared data will be protected appropriately, and organizations with demonstrated security excellence can provide that assurance. This creates opportunities for expanded business relationships that might not be available to organizations with weaker security postures.

9.7.3.5 Investor and board confidence

Security excellence increasingly influences investment decisions and board confidence. Organizations that can demonstrate mature security practices often enjoy:

- Higher valuations because of reduced risk profiles
- Easier access to capital and partnerships
- Stronger board support for strategic initiatives
- Enhanced credibility during due diligence processes

9.7.3.6 Communicating security value in customer language

The most sophisticated security capabilities create little business value if stakeholders cannot understand their benefits. Effective communication requires translating technical security features into value statements that resonate with different audiences:

9.7.3.6.1 Instead of technical features, emphasize business benefits

- Rather than "256-bit AES encryption," communicate "Your data is protected with bank-level security"
- Replace "Multi-factor authentication" with "Extra protection ensures only you can access your account"
- Transform "SOC 2 Type II certification" into "Independent verification of our commitment to protecting your data"

9.7.3.6.2 Tailor messages to stakeholder priorities

- For customers: Focus on privacy, control, and peace of mind
- For partners: Emphasize reliability, compliance, and risk reduction
- For investors: Highlight risk management, competitive advantage, and market access

9.7.3.7 Avoiding trust-destroying pitfalls

While security can build trust, poorly managed security communications can destroy it. Organizations must navigate several critical pitfalls:

9.7.3.7.1 Overpromising on security

Making absolute security claims creates legal exposure and erodes trust when incidents occur. Instead of claiming "unbreakable security," communicate continuous improvement and commitment to protection.

9.7.3.7.2 Security Theater vs. Substance

Stakeholders increasingly distinguish between genuine security practices and superficial security theater. Trust comes from demonstrable capabilities, not marketing claims.

9.7.3.7.3 Reactive vs. Proactive Communication

Organizations that only discuss security after incidents lose credibility. Proactive communication about security investments and improvements builds confidence before it's tested.

9.7.3.7.4 Measuring trust impact

To demonstrate security's contribution to trust creation, organizations should track specific metrics:

- Customer Trust Indicators: NPS scores, customer satisfaction ratings specific to security/privacy, retention rates among security-conscious segments
- Partner Confidence Metrics: Partnership conversion rates, time to establish data-sharing agreements, partner satisfaction scores
- Brand Trust Measurements: Brand perception surveys including security components, competitive positioning on trust factors, media sentiment analysis
- Business Impact Metrics: Revenue from trust-sensitive segments, price premiums achieved through security differentiation, CLV improvements

By focusing on trust creation through security, organizations transform a technical capability into a business asset that drives customer acquisition, retention, and partner relationships. This positions security as a creator of business value rather than just a preventer of business losses.

9.7.4 Market expansion through security: turning compliance and capabilities into growth

Security capabilities and compliance achievements often serve as keys that unlock new markets, customer segments, and partnership opportunities. Forward-thinking organizations recognize that security requirements - whether regulatory, industry-specific, or customer-driven - represent gateways to growth rather than barriers to entry. By building robust security and compliance capabilities, organizations can access markets and opportunities that remain closed to less-prepared competitors.

9.7.4.1 The security-enabled market opportunity

Every industry and geographic region presents unique security requirements that organizations must meet to compete effectively. These requirements, often viewed as burdensome obstacles, actually create protected market opportunities for organizations with the right capabilities:

9.7.4.2 Geographic expansion through compliance

Different regions impose varying security and privacy regulations that serve as de facto market entry requirements:

- GDPR compliance opens access to European markets and privacy-conscious customers globally
- HIPAA capabilities enable entry into U.S. healthcare sectors worth trillions in annual revenue

- Regional data residency requirements create opportunities for locally-compliant providers
- Emerging privacy regulations in Asia-Pacific and Latin America favor prepared organizations

9.7.4.3 Industry-specific security as market access

Many high-value industries maintain security requirements that filter out unprepared competitors:

- Financial services requiring SOC 2, PCI DzSS, and specialized financial compliance
- Healthcare sectors demanding HIPAA, HITRUST, and medical device security standards
- Government contracts requiring FedRAMP, FISMA, or security clearances
- Defense and aerospace markets with CMMC and ITAR requirements

9.7.4.4 Creating scalable compliance frameworks for growth

The key to leveraging compliance for market expansion lies in building scalable frameworks rather than point solutions. Organizations that create flexible, comprehensive compliance architectures can:

9.7.4.4.1 Accelerate market entry

- Pre-built compliance capabilities reduce time to enter new markets from years to months
- Modular frameworks allow rapid adaptation to regional variations
- Documented processes speed up certification and audit processes
- Established relationships with auditors and assessors streamline validations

9.7.4.4.2 Reduce incremental costs

- Shared controls across multiple compliance frameworks minimize redundant investments
- Automated compliance monitoring reduces ongoing operational costs
- Centralized governance structures prevent duplication of effort
- Economies of scale make each additional compliance requirement less expensive

9.7.4.5 Generate business intelligence

Compliance processes often require deep visibility into operations, creating valuable data collection opportunities:

- Risk assessments reveal operational improvement opportunities
- Compliance metrics highlight efficiency gains and process maturity

- Audit findings identify areas for competitive differentiation
- Regular assessments provide benchmarking against industry standards

9.7.4.5.1 Security certifications as competitive qualifiers

In many markets, security certifications function as essential qualifying credentials. Organizations with comprehensive certification portfolios gain significant advantages:

9.7.4.5.2 Premium market access

- Fortune 500 enterprises often require specific certifications from all vendors
- Government contracts explicitly require security attestations
- Regulated industries mandate certified security practices
- International businesses demand region-specific compliance proof

9.7.4.5.3 Shortened sales cycles

- Pre-existing certifications eliminate months of security assessments
- Documented compliance reduces due diligence requirements
- Third-party validations build immediate credibility
- Standardized security practices simplify contract negotiations

Partnership Enablement Security certifications facilitate strategic partnerships by:

- Demonstrating readiness for data sharing arrangements
- Satisfying partner risk management requirements
- Enabling inclusion in partner ecosystems and marketplaces
- Supporting joint go-to-market initiatives requiring security standards

9.7.4.5.4 Building trust in emerging and high-risk markets

Security capabilities become particularly valuable when entering markets where trust is scarce or risk perceptions are heightened.

9.7.4.5.5 Post-breach market opportunities

When competitors experience security incidents, prepared organizations can capitalize by:

- Highlighting superior security practices without directly referencing incidents
- Accelerating sales conversations with security-conscious buyers

- Capturing market share from damaged competitors
- Establishing long-term relationships with risk-aware customers

9.7.4.5.6 Emerging market differentiation

In rapidly growing markets where security standards are still developing:

- Early security investments establish market leadership positions
- Strong security practices attract sophisticated early adopters
- Proactive compliance positions organizations for future requirements
- Security excellence helps build critical government and enterprise relationships

9.7.4.6 Measuring market expansion impact

To quantify security's contribution to market expansion, track these key metrics:

9.7.4.6.1 Market access metrics

- Number of new markets entered because of security/compliance capabilities
- Revenue from previously inaccessible market segments
- Geographic expansion enabled by security certifications
- Industry verticals opened through specialized compliance

9.7.4.6.2 Growth acceleration indicators

- Time-to-market reduction for new geographic or industry expansion
- Sales cycle compression because of pre-existing compliance
- Win rate improvement in competitive deals where security is a factor
- Partner acquisition rate improvement from security capabilities

9.7.4.6.3 Financial returns

- Revenue per compliance dollar invested
- Market share gains in security-sensitive segments
- Price premiums achieved in high-security markets
- Cost avoidance from efficient compliance frameworks

By viewing security and compliance as market enablers rather than operational burdens, organizations can transform regulatory requirements into competitive advantages. This perspective shift turns the cost of compliance into investments in market access, creating sustainable growth opportunities that justify security spending through revenue generation rather than just risk reduction.

Understanding how to identify security's business enabling functions creates the foundation for actively pursuing new opportunities. The next step involves examining specific ways organizations can leverage their security capabilities to drive business growth, innovation, and competitive advantage.

9.8 SECURITY AS A DRIVER OF BUSINESS OPPORTUNITIES

Security capabilities can serve as catalysts for new business opportunities and revenue streams when properly positioned and implemented. Organizations that view security as an enabler rather than a constraint often discover pathways to innovation, market expansion, and operational improvement. This section examines how security investments can unlock business potential by supporting new models, accelerating innovation, and creating competitive advantages in the marketplace.

9.8.1 Enabling new business models

Enhanced security capabilities can unlock additional revenue streams for organizations across various industries. For example, financial institutions with robust security controls can offer premium services that involve higher-value transactions or more sensitive data, creating new revenue opportunities. Healthcare organizations with strong security and privacy capabilities can expand into telehealth and remote monitoring services that might otherwise present unacceptable risks. Technology companies can develop new service offerings based on their security expertise, turning internal capabilities into marketable services.

Expanding on the digital transformation enablement discussed in Chapter 5, this support extends beyond simply securing new technologies to actively accelerating transformation initiatives through proactive risk management. Rather than slowing down digital transformation, well-designed security programs accelerate it by addressing security requirements proactively and efficiently.

The ability to enable secure customer experiences creates competitive differentiation. Organizations that can provide convenient, frictionless customer experiences while maintaining appropriate security controls gain a significant advantage over competitors that sacrifice either security or convenience. This balance is particularly valuable in industries where both security and customer experience are important competitive factors, such as financial services, healthcare, and e-commerce.

Security provides the foundation for innovative business models like subscription services, platform businesses, and data-driven services. These models often involve continuous access to customer data and systems, requiring strong security controls to maintain customer trust and meet regulatory requirements. With strong security capabilities, organizations can pursue these models confidently, knowing they can protect customer data and maintain appropriate controls.

By viewing security as an enabler of new business models rather than just a protector of existing ones, organizations can identify opportunities to create value through security investments. This perspective transforms security from a defensive function to a strategic business driver.

Downloadable Resource: Security-Enabled Business Opportunity Assessment

9.8.2 Accelerating innovation

Secure-by-design approaches support faster product development by addressing security requirements from the beginning of the development process. Rather than adding security as an afterthought that might require significant rework, secure-by-design methodologies integrate security into the development lifecycle from the start. This integration reduces delays and rework, allowing new products and features to reach the market more quickly.

Security enables rapid experimentation while maintaining appropriate risk controls. Organizations with mature security programs can implement controls that protect core systems and data while allowing controlled experimentation in less sensitive areas. This approach enables innovation while managing risk appropriately, creating a balance that supports both security and agility.

Providing confidence to explore emerging technologies represents another important way security accelerates innovation. Technologies like artificial intelligence, blockchain, and the Internet of Things offer significant business potential but also introduce new security challenges. Organizations with strong security capabilities can explore these technologies more confidently, knowing they can identify and address security risks appropriately. This confidence helps them to adopt new technologies more quickly than competitors with less mature security programs.

Creating security guardrails that encourage rather than restrict innovation involves designing controls that provide necessary protection without impeding legitimate business activities. This approach requires a deep understanding of both security requirements and business objectives, allowing security leaders to implement controls that address risks without creating unnecessary obstacles. When done effectively, this creates an environment where innovation can flourish within appropriate boundaries.

By viewing security as an accelerator of innovation rather than a barrier to it, organizations can identify opportunities to leverage their security investments for competitive advantage. This perspective positions security as a strategic enabler of innovation rather than just a protective function that preserves the status quo.

Creating business opportunities through security provides valuable organizational benefits, but maximizing these advantages requires strategic positioning in competitive markets. Organizations can amplify their security investments' impact by positioning their capabilities as differentiators that influence customer decisions and market perception.

9.9 POSITIONING SECURITY AS A COMPETITIVE DIFFERENTIATOR

Security capabilities can become powerful differentiators when strategically positioned in competitive markets. Organizations with strong security programs often find opportunities to distinguish themselves from competitors, particularly in industries where trust and protection are valued by customers. This section provides frameworks for identifying unique security capabilities and positioning them as competitive advantages that influence customer decisions and market positioning.

9.9.1 Strategic Security Differentiation Framework

To effectively position security as a competitive differentiator, organizations need a structured methodology for identifying unique security capabilities that create competitive advantage. The Strategic Security Differentiation Framework (seen in Figure 9.3) provides this methodology, helping security

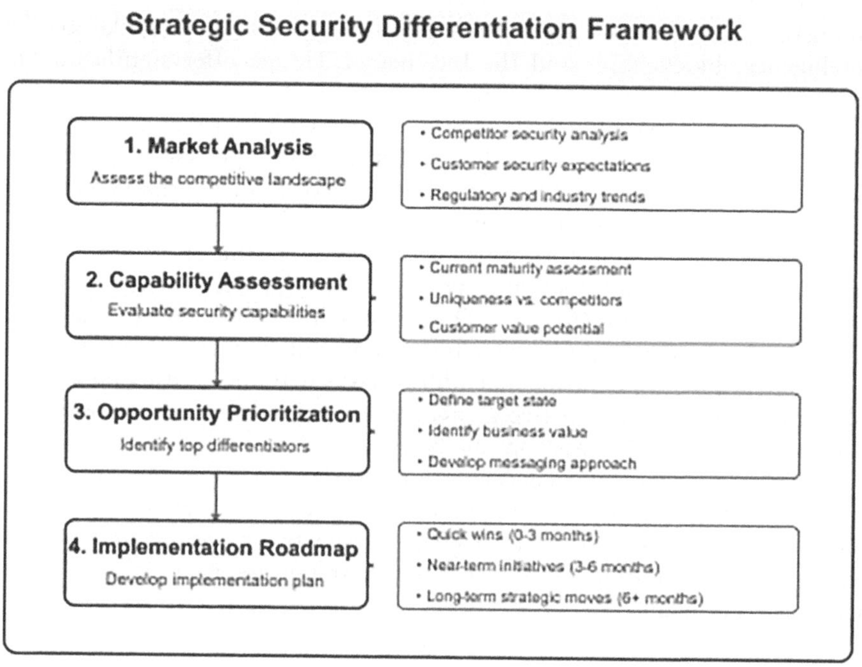

Figure 9.3 Strategic Security Differentiation Framework.

leaders identify, develop, and communicate security capabilities that distinguish their organizations from competitors.

The framework begins with assessing competitor security postures to identify differentiation opportunities. This assessment involves analyzing the security capabilities, messaging, and reputations of key competitors to identify areas where the organization has or could develop superior capabilities. This competitive intelligence provides valuable insights into potential differentiation opportunities and helps security leaders focus their efforts on areas with the greatest potential impact.

Creating messaging and positioning that highlights security advantages requires translating technical security capabilities into business language that resonates with customers and partners. This translation involves identifying the business benefits that security capabilities deliver and articulating those benefits in terms that matter to the target audience. For example, rather than emphasizing technical details of encryption, the messaging might focus on how data protection builds customer trust and supports regulatory compliance.

Developing a security differentiation roadmap aligned with business strategy ensures that security investments support broader business objectives. This roadmap identifies the security capabilities that will create the greatest competitive advantage and outlines the steps necessary to develop or enhance those capabilities. By aligning this roadmap with business strategy, security leaders ensure that security investments contribute directly to strategic business goals.

By applying the Strategic Security Differentiation Framework, organizations can identify and develop security capabilities that create meaningful competitive advantages. This approach positions security as a strategic business asset rather than just a necessary overhead cost.

Downloadable Resource: Security Competitive Differentiation Framework

9.9.2 Targeting security-conscious market segments

Identifying customer segments that prioritize security in purchasing decisions represents an important opportunity for security differentiation. Some customer segments, such as financial institutions, healthcare organizations, government agencies, and security-conscious consumers, place particularly high value on security capabilities. Organizations that can meet the security requirements of these segments often gain access to premium pricing, longer-term contracts, and greater customer loyalty.

Tailoring security messaging for different buyer personas and journeys involves understanding the specific security concerns and priorities of each persona and addressing those concerns at each stage of the buying process. For example, technical buyers might focus on specific security controls and certifications, while business buyers might prioritize risk reduction and compliance capabilities. Effective messaging addresses the concerns that matter most to each persona.

Creating sales enablement materials that effectively communicate security value helps sales teams articulate the business benefits of security capabilities. These materials translate technical security features into business value statements, provide competitive comparison information, and offer responses to common security-related questions and objections. When properly equipped, sales teams can leverage security as a selling point rather than treating it as a technical hurdle to be overcome.

Training customer-facing teams to articulate security as a business benefit ensures that security messaging remains consistent across all customer touchpoints. This training helps customer-facing employees understand the organization's security capabilities, translate those capabilities into customer-relevant terms, and address security-related questions and concerns effectively. This consistent messaging reinforces the organization's security differentiation and builds customer confidence.

By focusing on security-conscious market segments, organizations can identify opportunities to create business value through security investments. This targeted approach positions security as a creator of competitive advantage rather than just a general protective function.

9.9.3 Turning security incidents into opportunities

Industry security incidents provide opportunities to show a comparative advantage. When competitors or other industry participants experience security incidents, organizations with strong security programs can highlight their superior capabilities without directly capitalizing on others' misfortunes. This comparative advantage can be particularly valuable when security concerns are heightened following publicized incidents.

Developing a proactive communication strategy for industry security events ensures that the organization responds appropriately when incidents occur. This strategy should include guidelines for internal and external communications, roles and responsibilities for key stakeholders, and pre-approved messaging for common scenarios. With this strategy in place, the organization can respond quickly and appropriately to industry events, positioning itself as a security leader.

Building executive communication skills around security differentiation helps leaders articulate the organization's security advantages effectively. These skills include understanding the organization's security capabilities, translating those capabilities into business terms, and addressing security-related questions and concerns confidently. When executives can communicate security value effectively, they enhance the organization's security credibility and differentiation.

Creating thought leadership that positions the organization as a security leader involves developing and sharing insights on security trends, challenges, and best practices. This thought leadership can take many forms, including articles, white papers, webinars, conference presentations, and media interviews. By establishing itself as a source of security expertise, the organization enhances its reputation and creates competitive advantages in security-conscious markets.

By turning security incidents into opportunities, organizations can transform industry challenges into competitive advantages. This approach positions security as a strategic business asset rather than just a reactive defensive function.

Positioning security as a competitive differentiator creates significant business value, but this value must be measured and communicated effectively to maintain executive support and strategic alignment. Developing appropriate metrics and communication approaches helps organizations demonstrate security's business contribution and secure continued investment in strategic security initiatives.

9.10 MEASURING AND COMMUNICATING SECURITY'S BUSINESS VALUE

Demonstrating security's business contribution requires metrics that connect security activities to business outcomes executives understand and value. Traditional security measurements often fail to communicate business impact effectively, limiting security leaders' ability to secure resources and strategic support. This section presents approaches for quantifying security's business contribution and developing executive communications that position security as a strategic business enabler.

9.10.1 Metrics that matter to business leaders

Developing business-oriented security metrics that resonate with executives represents an important step in positioning security as a business enabler. These metrics should focus on business outcomes rather than technical outputs, connecting security activities to business objectives such as revenue growth, cost reduction, customer satisfaction, and operational efficiency. By using metrics that matter to business leaders (such as are shown in Figure 9.4), security leaders can communicate their value in terms that executives understand and appreciate.

Moving beyond technical measures to business impact indicators involves identifying the specific ways security contributes to business success and developing metrics that capture those contributions. For example, rather than reporting the number of vulnerabilities patched, security leaders might report the reduction in downtime or the improvement in system availability resulting from vulnerability management activities. This business-focused approach makes security metrics more relevant and valuable to non-technical stakeholders.

Creating a balanced scorecard approach for security business contribution provides a comprehensive view of security's impact on the organization. This scorecard might include metrics related to risk reduction, operational enablement, compliance advantage, and competitive differentiation. By presenting a balanced view of security's business contribution, the scorecard helps security leaders demonstrate the full range of value their programs provide.

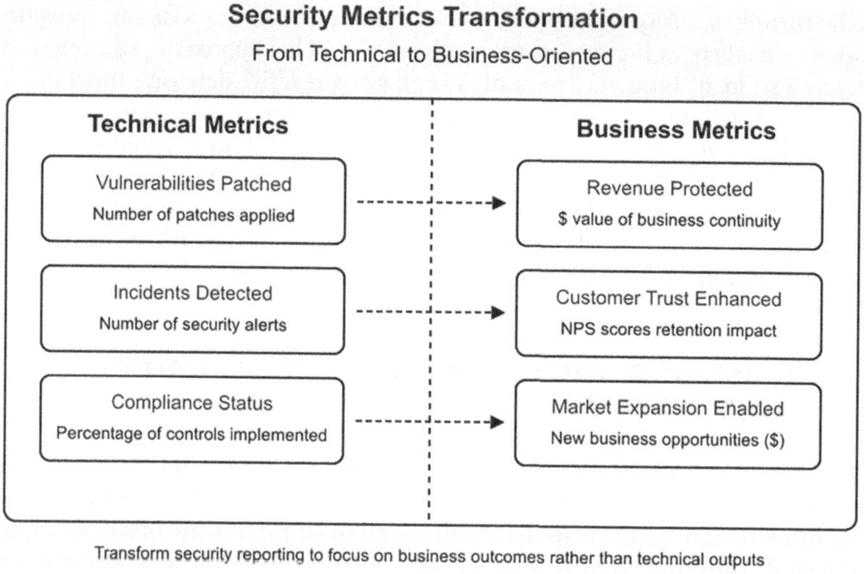

Figure 9.4 Security metrics transformation.

9.10.2 Quantifying security's business contribution

Methods for calculating security's contribution to revenue generation help show the business value of security investments. These methods might include analyzing the revenue from security-conscious customer segments, quantifying the value of contracts where security capabilities were a deciding factor, or measuring the revenue enabled by security-dependent products and services. By connecting security capabilities directly to revenue generation, security leaders can demonstrate their contribution to the organization's financial success. These quantification approaches build on the translation techniques discussed in Chapter 6, converting technical security activities into measurable business contributions.

Techniques for quantifying customer acquisition and retention benefits provide another perspective on security's business value. These techniques might include analyzing the impact of security messaging on conversion rates, measuring the influence of security incidents on customer churn, or assessing the value of security certifications in customer acquisition. This customer-focused approach highlights security's contribution to one of the most important business metrics: CLV.

Approaches for measuring operational efficiency improvements connect security activities to cost reduction and productivity enhancement. These approaches might include analyzing the reduction in incident response costs, quantifying the efficiency gains from automated security processes, or measuring the productivity improvements resulting from streamlined security controls. By demonstrating how security contributes to operational efficiency, security leaders can position their programs as business enablers rather than business constraints.

Frameworks for evaluating security's impact on innovation velocity help quantify one of the most valuable but difficult-to-measure aspects of security's business contribution. These frameworks might include analyzing the time-to-market impact of secure-by-design approaches, measuring the innovation enabled by secure development environments, or assessing the competitive advantages created by security-enabled technologies. This innovation-focused approach highlights security's role in driving business growth and competitive advantage.

By quantifying security's business contribution across multiple dimensions, security leaders can show the full range of value their programs provide. This comprehensive approach positions security as a multifaceted business enabler rather than just a one-dimensional protective function.

Downloadable Resource: Security Investment Business Case Template

9.10.3 Developing executive communications

Building on the translation principles outlined in Chapter 1, effective board and C-suite presentations require specific executive-focused approaches that highlight the business value of security investments and address executive concerns about risk, compliance, and competitive positioning. By developing presentations that address executive priorities, security leaders can more effectively communicate their value to senior leadership.

As described in the translation principles in Chapter 2, business cases that highlight security as investment, not expense, require demonstrating the return on security investments rather than just their cost. These business cases should identify the specific business outcomes enabled by security investments, quantify the value of those outcomes, and compare that value to the investment required. This investment-focused approach positions security as a creator of business value rather than just a consumer of business resources.

Developing visual dashboards that connect security activities to business outcomes helps make security's business contribution more visible and understandable. These dashboards should present key metrics in a clear, concise format that highlights trends, patterns, and relationships. By visualizing security's business impact, these dashboards make it easier for executives to understand and appreciate the value that security provides.

Building on the stakeholder-specific proposal techniques from Chapter 5, executive communications for security's business value require similar audience tailoring but with emphasis on realized outcomes rather than investment justification.

By developing effective executive communications, security leaders can ensure that their business value is understood and appreciated at the highest levels of the organization. This executive-level understanding is essential for positioning security as a strategic business enabler rather than just a tactical protective function.

Downloadable Resource: Executive Security Value Communication Toolkit

9.11 CONCLUSION

Security's transformation from cost center to business enabler represents a fundamental shift in organizational thinking. This transformation requires security leaders to move beyond traditional risk reduction mindsets and embrace a broader perspective that recognizes security's potential to create business value. By positioning security as an enabler of trust, operational efficiency, compliance advantage, and innovation, security leaders can show their contribution to organizational success in terms that resonate with business executives.

- The frameworks and approaches outlined provide practical paths to identify, measure, and communicate security's business value.
- The Security Business Enablement Matrix helps identify how security capabilities support business objectives across multiple dimensions.
- The Strategic Security Differentiation Framework provides a methodology for positioning security as a competitive differentiator.

Business-oriented metrics and executive communication approaches help security leaders articulate their value in terms that matter to business leaders.

Organizations that successfully position security as an enabler gain significant competitive advantages. They can enter new markets more confidently, build stronger customer relationships, operate more efficiently, and innovate more quickly than competitors that view security primarily as a defensive function. These advantages translate directly into business success metrics such as revenue growth, customer satisfaction, operational efficiency, and market share.

This transformation requires not just new metrics and frameworks, but cultural change throughout the organization. Security must be integrated into business planning processes, executive discussions, and strategic decision-making. Security leaders must adopt business-oriented mindsets and language, and business leaders must recognize security's potential to create business value. This cultural change is essential for realizing the full business potential of security investments.

Security leaders who can articulate business value become strategic partners in organizational success. By demonstrating how their programs enable business objectives rather than just protecting assets, these leaders earn seats at the strategic planning table. This partnership ensures that security considerations are integrated into business decisions from the beginning, creating better outcomes for both security and the business.

9.12 ACTION ITEMS FOR READERS

1. Conduct a comprehensive inventory of your organization's current security capabilities and map each capability against the four quadrants of the Security Business Enablement Matrix (Operational Enablement, Trust Creation, Compliance Advantage, and Innovation Support) to identify existing business value that may not be measured or communicated effectively.
2. Identify three specific competitor organizations and analyze their public security messaging, certifications, and market positioning to uncover differentiation opportunities where your security capabilities could create competitive advantage in target market segments.
3. Collaborate with sales, marketing, and business development teams to create a list of lost opportunities or delayed deals where security requirements were a factor, then develop specific security capabilities or messaging that could have addressed those situations.
4. Develop a balanced scorecard of business-oriented security metrics that connects your security activities to measurable business outcomes such as revenue generation, customer acquisition, operational efficiency, or market access, moving beyond traditional technical security measurements.
5. Create an executive presentation template that positions a specific security investment as a business enabler rather than a cost center, including quantified business benefits, competitive advantages, and return on investment calculations that resonate with C-suite priorities.

Chapter 10

Putting it all together

Integrated risk management in action

Chapter in One Sentence: Transforming security from a technical function to a business enabler requires assessing your organization's current integration maturity, implementing a tailored roadmap, addressing common challenges, and measuring progress through business-aligned metrics.

10.1 EXECUTIVE SUMMARY

This chapter provides a practical framework for integrating security risk management into business operations, transforming it from a siloed technical function into a strategic business enabler. This integration is both necessary and achievable regardless of an organization's current maturity level. The chapter begins by illustrating the disconnect between security teams and business leadership through a realistic scenario of a CISO's rejected budget proposal, highlighting how only 2% of organizations are optimizing cyber resilience across all areas.

The chapter outlines characteristics of successful integration, including board-level engagement, alignment between security and business goals, risk-based decision-making, cross-functional collaboration, and a common risk language. These traits manifest in organizational structures with appropriate reporting relationships, cross-functional risk committees, and clear roles across business units.

Through case studies like Capital One, the chapter identifies common success patterns including executive sponsorship, cultural change strategies, and appropriate resource allocation. The implementation roadmap section provides tailored guidance based on an organization's maturity level – Traditional (siloed), Initial, Advanced, or Optimal – with specific steps for each stage of the journey.

The chapter addresses common transformation challenges, including organizational resistance, resource constraints, and technical limitations of legacy systems, providing practical strategies for each. Integration progress should be measured using process metrics (such as percentage of projects with security reviews), outcome metrics (such as reduction in incidents), and perception metrics (such as business satisfaction with security collaboration).

DOI: 10.1201/9781003744146-10

For sustainable integration, the chapter emphasizes the importance of institutionalizing practices, succession planning, and continuous improvement frameworks to maintain momentum through leadership changes and changing business needs. The path to integration may be challenging, but the business value is compelling: better protection, more efficient resource use, faster decision-making, and enhanced ability to pursue business opportunities with appropriate risk management.

10.2 KEY TAKEAWAYS

- Successful security integration requires executive sponsorship, cross-functional collaboration, and a common risk language that connects security concerns to business impacts.
- Organizations should assess their current maturity level and follow an implementation roadmap specific to their starting point, focusing first on high-value, low-difficulty initiatives.
- Integration efforts must address organizational resistance, resource constraints, and technical challenges through targeted strategies that demonstrate business value.
- Measuring integration progress requires a balanced approach using process, outcome, and perception metrics that show both the mechanics and business results of integration.
- Sustainable integration depends on institutionalizing practices through policies, procedures, and governance frameworks that can withstand leadership changes.

10.3 APPLICATION QUESTIONS

1. What is your organization's current security-business integration maturity level, and which specific characteristics from the assessment tool indicate this level?
2. Which integration initiatives would deliver the highest business value with the lowest implementation difficulty for your organization?
3. How might you adapt your communication about security risks to better resonate with other leaders in your organization?

10.4 TOOLS REFERENCED IN THIS CHAPTER

All tools available at kaynemcgladrey.com/myth/

- Exercise: Benchmark Your Organization
- Security-Business Integration Maturity Assessment

- Exercise: Identify Your Organization's Transformation Opportunities
- Exercise: Build Your Custom Implementation Plan
- Exercise: Develop Your Challenge Mitigation Strategy
- Security Integration Challenge Resolution Toolkit
- Integration Progress Dashboard
- Exercise: Design Your Progress Measurement System

10.5 INTRODUCTION

The CISO sat at the conference room table, staring at his rejected budget proposal. For the third consecutive quarter, the executive team had declined his request for additional security investments. Despite the detailed technical justifications and compliance requirements he had meticulously documented, the CFO's feedback was painfully clear: "We don't see how these security investments tie to our business goals. What's the return on investment here?" This scenario plays out daily across organizations worldwide, demonstrating the fundamental disconnect between security teams and business leadership.

This chapter provides actionable guidance for integrating security risk management into business operations, breaking down the silos that create this disconnect. Building on the PwC research (PwC, 2024) discussed in Chapter 1, their 2024 findings also reveal that only 2% of organizations are optimizing cyber resilience across all areas, demonstrating significant opportunity for the integration approaches we'll explore in this chapter. This statistic may seem discouraging, but it also reveals a significant opportunity for advancement.

The transformation from siloed security functions to integrated risk management is both necessary and achievable, regardless of your organization's current maturity level. Organizations that successfully integrate security risk management into business operations not only protect themselves more effectively but also gain competitive advantages through enhanced decision-making, improved operational efficiency, and greater business agility.

In the following sections, we will explore what successful integration looks like in practice, examining the characteristics of effectively integrated risk management and the organizational structures that support it. You'll receive a practical implementation roadmap tailored to your organization's current maturity level, along with strategies for overcoming common challenges in the transformation journey. Finally, we'll provide assessment tools to measure your progress and methods for sustaining momentum.

Building on the previous chapter's discussion of security as a business enabler, this chapter provides the practical framework for putting those principles into action. By the chapter's conclusion, you'll have the tools needed to begin – or accelerate – your organization's journey toward truly integrated security risk management.

10.6 WHAT SUCCESSFUL INTEGRATION LOOKS LIKE IN PRACTICE

Understanding what successful integration looks like provides a clear target for your organization's transformation efforts. Organizations that effectively integrate security risk management into business operations share distinct characteristics that can be identified, measured, and replicated. These traits (illustrated in Figure 10.1) manifest in specific organizational structures, governance approaches, and measurable business outcomes that separate high-performing organizations from their peers.

10.6.1 Characteristics of effectively integrated risk management

Organizations that successfully integrate risk management demonstrate several distinctive characteristics that separate them from their peers. First and foremost is board and executive-level engagement and ownership. In these organizations, security isn't delegated to technical teams but is actively overseen at the highest levels. Executive leadership regularly reviews security risks alongside other business risks, making informed decisions based on a holistic view of the organization's risk landscape.

Alignment between security objectives and business goals represents another critical characteristic. Integrated organizations don't treat security as

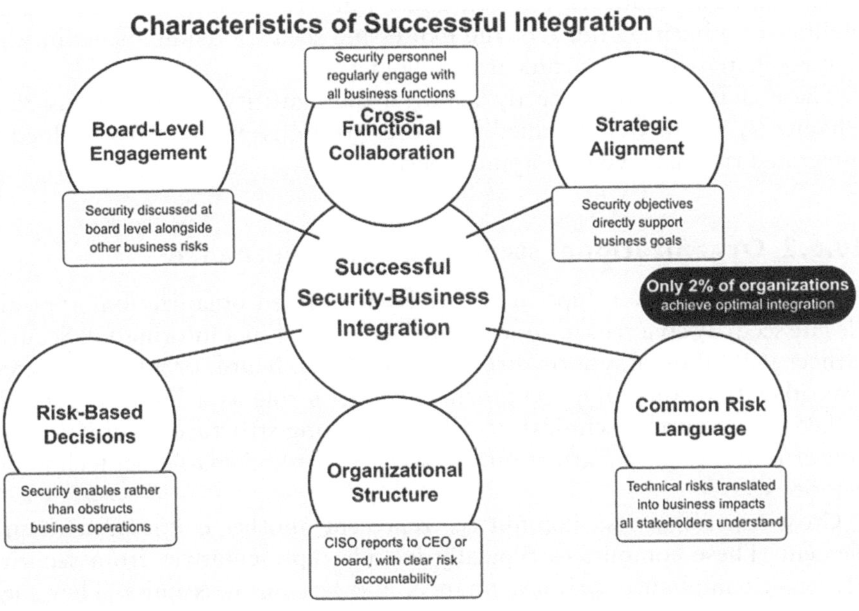

Figure 10.1 Characteristics of successful integration.

a separate function with its own agenda but as an enabler of business strategy. Security teams understand business objectives and tailor their approach to support these goals rather than obstruct them. They focus on what matters most to the business, prioritizing the protection of critical assets and processes that drive revenue and competitive advantage.

Risk-based decisions enable rather than obstruct business operations in integrated organizations. Security teams work with business units to find acceptable ways to manage risk while allowing business innovation to proceed. They offer options rather than mandates, clearly articulating the risk implications of different approaches and allowing business leaders to make informed choices.

Cross-functional collaboration and communication serve as the foundation for effective integration. Security professionals in these organizations regularly engage with colleagues from legal, compliance, privacy, IT, operations, and business units. They participate in strategy sessions, project planning, and operational reviews, bringing a security perspective to discussions from the beginning rather than as an afterthought.

The trend toward centralized GRC programs discussed in Chapter 7 reflects this growing recognition of integration's value, with year-over-year increases demonstrating accelerating adoption. This trend indicates a growing recognition of the need for integration and maturity in managing risk across the enterprise.

Perhaps the most telling characteristic is the development of a common risk language across departments. Integrated organizations speak about risk in consistent terms that everyone can understand, translating technical vulnerabilities into business impacts and expressing security requirements in ways that resonate with non-technical stakeholders.

These characteristics directly relate to the maturity models discussed in Chapter 4, where we examined how organizations progress from siloed to integrated risk management approaches.

10.6.2 Organizational structure and governance

The reporting relationships in effectively integrated organizations typically elevate security concerns to appropriate levels. The Chief Information Security Officer (CISO) often reports directly to the CEO, board, or a C-suite executive other than the CIO, recognizing security's role as a business function rather than a purely technical one. This reporting structure ensures security concerns receive proper attention and aren't subordinated to other technology priorities.

Cross-functional risk committees represent another common structural element. These committees typically include representatives from security, IT, legal, compliance, privacy, finance, and key business units. They meet regularly to review risks, set priorities, and make decisions that balance security requirements with business needs. The diversity of perspectives ensures more robust risk management and better alignment with overall business objectives.

Clear roles and responsibilities across business units are essential for effective integration. Business unit leaders understand their accountability for risk within their areas, while security teams recognize their role as advisors and enablers rather than enforcers. This shared responsibility model distributes the burden of security across the organization rather than concentrating it within a single department.

Decision-making processes incorporate security perspectives through structured approaches like security review boards for major initiatives and security checkpoints in project management methodologies. These processes ensure security considerations are addressed at appropriate points without causing undue delays or obstacles.

Engagement models between security and business teams are formalized in mature organizations. They may include security liaisons assigned to specific business units, regular touchpoints between security leaders and business executives, and formal processes for security consultation on new initiatives. These structured engagement models prevent security from becoming a bottleneck while ensuring risks are properly addressed.

10.6.3 Measuring success: the business impact of integration

The business impact of integration can be measured through several key performance indicators. Reduction in security incidents and their severity is perhaps the most direct indicator, showing that integrated risk management is effectively protecting the organization. Time-to-market metrics also reveal integration success, as streamlined security processes reduce delays in launching new products and services.

Cost avoidance represents a significant benefit, though it's challenging to quantify. This includes preventing security breaches, avoiding compliance penalties, and reducing rework that would be necessary if security were considered late in development cycles. Beyond cost avoidance, business enhancement metrics demonstrate how security enables business growth, innovation, and competitive advantage.

The 2025 IT Risk and Compliance Benchmark Report (Hyperproof, 2025) provides compelling evidence for the value of integration: "60% of respondents who manage risk ad-hoc or when a negative event happens experienced a data breach in 2024. Respondents who use integrated and automated GRC tools are less likely to experience a data breach at only 41%." This 19-percentage-point difference translates to significant financial benefit when considering the average cost of a data breach.

Integrated security risk management may also contribute to improved customer trust, as measured by customer satisfaction scores, retention rates, and willingness to share sensitive information. For some organizations, security has become a competitive differentiator, allowing them to win business from security-conscious customers and enter markets with strict security requirements.

Employee productivity metrics can also show improvements from integrated security approaches that streamline workflows rather than adding friction. And the speed of risk assessment and decision-making often increases as organizations mature in their integration, allowing them to respond more quickly to changing business needs.

While understanding the characteristics of successful integration provides important guidance, examining how real organizations have achieved these outcomes offers practical insights into implementation approaches and common pitfalls to avoid.

10.6.3.1 Exercise: benchmark your organization

Take a few minutes to assess your organization's current level of integration using the following questions. Rate each item on a scale of 1 (not present) to 5 (fully mature):

Governance Structure:

- Does security leadership have direct access to the board and executive team?
- Are business leaders held accountable for security risks in their areas?
- Do cross-functional teams regularly discuss security risks?
- Is security represented in strategic planning processes?

Reporting Relationships:

- Does the CISO report to a position that ensures security has appropriate visibility?
- Are security metrics and status updates included in executive reporting?
- Do business unit leaders report on security risks alongside other business risks?
- Is there clear escalation for security issues that need executive attention?

Risk Frameworks:

- Does your organization use a consistent approach to assess and manage security risks?
- Is the same terminology used to discuss risks across departments?
- Are security risks evaluated using the same criteria as other business risks?
- Do risk assessments consider both technical and business factors?

Scoring Guide:

- 48-60: Advanced integration
- 36-47: Developing integration

- 24-35: Basic integration
- 12-23: Early stages of integration
- Below 12: Siloed approach to security

Use this assessment to identify your organization's strengths and areas for improvement. The results will help you target your integration efforts more effectively as you work through the remainder of this chapter.

Downloadable Resource: Security-Business Integration Maturity Assessment

10.7 HOW REAL ORGANIZATIONS HAVE TRANSFORMED THEIR APPROACH TO SECURITY RISK

Real-world examples offer valuable insights into how organizations achieve integration between security and business functions. Examining both successes and setbacks reveals practical lessons about implementation approaches, resource allocation, and change management strategies. These case studies demonstrate that transformation is possible across different industries and organizational contexts, while highlighting common patterns that contribute to success.

10.7.1 Case study: Capital One's integration journey

Capital One's case study (from Chapter 2) contains valuable lessons about the journey toward integrated security risk management. Before the breach, the company had made substantial progress in integrating security into its business operations, particularly as it migrated to the cloud. The company had established cross-functional teams, implemented a cloud governance framework, and invested in advanced security technologies.

However, the 2019 breach revealed a critical gap between their governance framework and actual implementation. Despite having policies and procedures in place, the misconfiguration that led to the breach went undetected. This underscores the importance of ensuring that integration extends beyond policies and frameworks to day-to-day operations and technical implementations.

Following the breach, Capital One significantly enhanced its integration approach. The company strengthened the connection between security governance and technical implementation, improved their security testing methodologies, and further integrated security considerations into their cloud deployment processes. They also enhanced board-level oversight of cybersecurity risk, creating more direct reporting lines between security leadership and the board.

The company's commitment to learning from the breach and improving their integrated approach to security risk was evident in their subsequent launch of DataBolt at the RSA Conference 2025. This new security product demonstrated how Capital One had turned their hard-won security lessons into both improved internal practices and a product offering for other organizations facing similar challenges. Their journey shows how even setbacks can become opportunities for deeper integration when the organizational commitment is present.

10.7.2 Common success patterns across organizations

Despite differences in industry, size, and starting point, organizations that successfully transform their approach to security risk tend to share several common patterns. Executive sponsorship and commitment consistently appear as critical success factors. Transformation efforts that lack visible support from the CEO, board, or other senior executives typically stall when they encounter resistance. Successful organizations secure this sponsorship early and maintain it through regular engagement and demonstrable progress.

The approach to transformation – incremental versus comprehensive – appears to be less important than consistent progress. Some organizations succeed with a gradual approach that focuses on specific integration points and builds momentum through small wins. Others thrive with comprehensive transformation programs that redesign security governance and processes across the enterprise. The key is in selecting an approach that fits the organization's culture and change tolerance.

Cultural change strategies that have proven effective in successful transformations include emphasizing security as an enabler rather than an obstacle, recognizing and rewarding collaborative behavior, and actively involving business leaders in security decisions. Many organizations find that embedding security professionals within business teams accelerates cultural change by building relationships and mutual understanding.

Timeline expectations for meaningful integration vary widely depending on the organization's size, complexity, and starting point. However, most successful transformations show significant progress within 12–18 months, with early wins often visible within the first six months. Setting realistic expectations about the timeline helps maintain executive support and momentum through the inevitable challenges.

Resource allocation patterns in successful transformations typically include investing in people as much as technology. Organizations often find that dedicated integration roles – people who bridge the gap between security and business units – accelerate progress significantly. Technology investments tend to focus on tools that improve visibility and streamline processes rather than simply adding more security controls.

Learning from other organizations' experiences helps inform your approach, but successful transformation requires a systematic implementation plan that addresses your organization's specific starting point and target outcomes.

10.7.2.1 *Exercise: identify your organization's transformation opportunities*

Use this worksheet to identify the highest-value integration points in your organization:

1. Quick Win Opportunities:
   - List 3-5 areas where security and business objectives currently conflict
   - For each area, identify potential solutions that would benefit both security and business goals
   - Rate each opportunity based on (a) value to the business, (b) security impact, and (c) ease of implementation
2. Relationship Building:
   - Identify key business leaders whose support is essential for integration
   - For each leader, note their primary business objectives and concerns
   - Outline an approach to engage each leader that addresses their priorities while advancing security integration
3. Business Case Elements:
   - What specific business metrics could improve through better security integration?
   - What costs (direct and indirect) result from the current siloed approach?
   - How does your proposed integration align with strategic business initiatives?
   - What competing priorities might conflict with your integration efforts?
4. Transformation Approach:
   - Based on your organization's culture and change readiness, would an incremental or comprehensive approach be more likely to succeed?
   - What level of executive sponsorship is needed, and from whom?
   - What resources (people, funding, tools) would be required for your preferred approach?
   - What timeline seems realistic given your organization's specific circumstances?

Use the results of this exercise to develop a preliminary transformation strategy tailored to your organization's unique context and opportunities.

10.8 IMPLEMENTATION ROADMAP FOR YOUR ORGANIZATION

Implementing integrated risk management requires a structured approach that accounts for your organization's current capabilities and maturity level. Organizations at different stages of integration face distinct challenges and opportunities, requiring tailored strategies that build on existing strengths while addressing specific gaps. This roadmap approach allows you to focus resources on the most impactful initiatives for your situation.

10.8.1 Assessing your starting point

Before you can chart a course for security integration, you need to assess your current position accurately. Chapter 4 introduced the concept of maturity progression in security risk management. Here, we'll use a complementary assessment framework, shown in Figure 10.2, that focuses specifically on implementation readiness rather than general ERM integration maturity. The GRC maturity model that I wrote for Hyperproof provides a useful framework, segmenting organizations into four levels: Traditional, Initial, Advanced, and Optimal.

Organizations at the Traditional level operate with ad-hoc risk management processes, relying heavily on individual knowledge rather than established procedures. Security functions are isolated from business operations, with a limited awareness of security concerns among business leaders. Communication about risk is inconsistent and often technical, making it difficult for non-security personnel to understand security implications. Risk decisions are typically reactive, responding to incidents rather than proactively managing potential issues.

At the Initial level, organizations have established basic risk management processes and begun to formalize security governance. There is growing awareness of security concerns among business leaders, though security is still viewed primarily as a technical function. Some communication channels exist between security and business teams, but integration remains limited. Risk assessments occur, but they may not consistently influence business decisions.

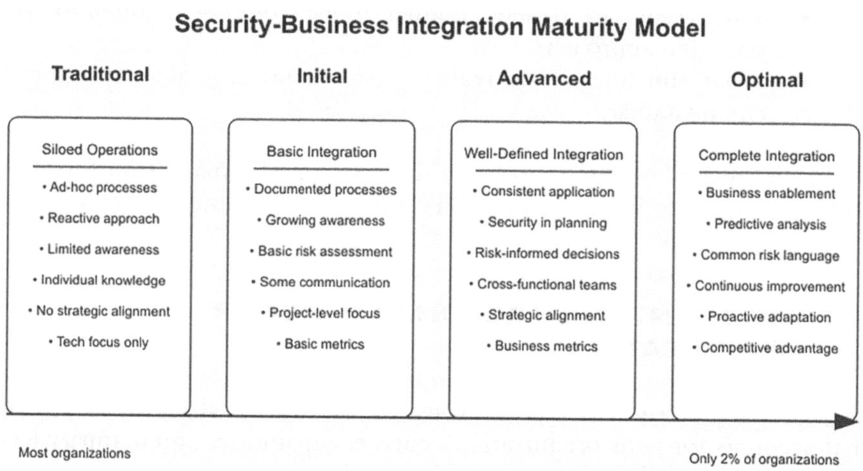

Figure 10.2 Security-business integration maturity model.

Advanced organizations demonstrate well-defined risk management processes that are consistently applied across the enterprise. Security considerations are regularly included in business planning, with established channels for communication between security and business teams. Risk assessments directly inform business decisions, and security metrics align with business objectives. Cross-functional teams address security risks, with clear roles and responsibilities.

At the Optimal level, risk management is fully integrated into business processes and strategic planning. Security and business objectives are aligned, with security viewed as a business enabler rather than a separate function. A common risk language exists across the organization, and risk-based decisions balance security requirements with business needs. Continuous improvement processes refine the integration approach based on changing conditions and lessons learned.

To determine your organization's current state, consider the following characteristics:

- How consistently are security risks identified and assessed?
- To what extent do business leaders understand and take responsibility for security risks?
- How are security concerns incorporated into business decisions?
- What communication channels exist between security and business teams?
- How aligned are security metrics with business objectives?

Be realistic in your assessment, recognizing that most organizations have strengths in some areas and weaknesses in others. Your goal is to identify your overall maturity level to select the most appropriate next steps in your integration journey.

10.8.2 Roadmap for traditional organizations (Siloed operations)

Organizations operating at the Traditional level face the most challenging journey, but they also can design their integration approach without having to overcome entrenched practices. The roadmap for these organizations focuses on establishing foundational elements and demonstrating early value.

First steps toward integration from a siloed starting point should include establishing basic governance structures. Create a cross-functional security committee with representatives from business units, IT, legal, and other relevant departments. This committee provides a forum for discussing security risks and their business implications, helping to break down silos and build relationships.

Quick wins are essential for demonstrating the value of integration and building momentum. Look for opportunities to solve business problems through security improvements, such as streamlining access management processes that currently frustrate employees or implementing security controls that also improve operational efficiency. Document and communicate these wins to build support for further integration efforts.

Essential governance changes include clarifying security roles and responsibilities across the organization. Develop a RACI (Responsible, Accountable, Consulted, Informed) matrix for key security activities, ensuring business units understand their role in managing security risks. Establish regular reporting on security risks to executive leadership, using business language rather than technical jargon.

Foundational processes to establish include a basic risk assessment methodology that considers both security and business factors. Develop a simple but consistent approach to evaluating security risks based on potential business impact, and use this approach to prioritize security efforts. Create standard operating procedures for including security considerations in project planning and system implementations.

For organizations at the Traditional level, a realistic timeline for achieving basic integration is typically 12–18 months, with noticeable improvements possible within the first six months. Resource expectations should include dedicated time from security leaders and business representatives, plus modest investments in process development and communication efforts. The focus at this stage should be on building relationships and establishing fundamental practices rather than implementing complex technical solutions.

10.8.3 Roadmap for initial integration organizations

Organizations at the Initial level have established some integration between security and business functions but still have significant opportunities for improvement. Their roadmap focuses on strengthening existing integration points while expanding integration across the organization.

Strengthening existing integration points involves evaluating what's working well and what's not in current integration efforts. Identify successful collaboration models between security and specific business units, and document the practices that make these relationships effective. Work to replicate these successful patterns in other parts of the organization.

Formalizing risk processes across departments is a key priority for organizations at this level. Develop a consistent risk assessment methodology that all departments use, ensuring security risks are evaluated alongside other business risks. Establish clear escalation procedures for significant risks, and implement a regular cadence of risk reviews with business leadership.

Enhancing communication channels between security and business teams can accelerate integration progress. Consider embedding security liaisons within major business units to facilitate ongoing communication and collaboration. Work to create security dashboards that present information in business terms, helping executives understand security status and trends without requiring technical expertise.

Developing common risk metrics that tie security performance to business outcomes helps build a shared understanding of security's value. Work with business leaders to identify metrics that matter to them, then show how security activities contribute to these metrics. For example, connect improvements in vulnerability management to reductions in system downtime or link enhanced access controls to improved operational efficiency.

Education and awareness strategies should focus on building security knowledge among business leaders while helping security teams understand business priorities. Cross-training sessions where business and security personnel share their perspectives can be particularly effective. Executive education should emphasize the business value of security rather than technical details or compliance requirements.

Organizations at the Initial level can typically advance to the Advanced level within 12–24 months, depending on the breadth and complexity of their operations. Resource requirements increase at this stage, often requiring dedicated integration roles and investments in tools that support risk assessment and monitoring across the enterprise.

10.8.4 Roadmap for advanced and optimal organizations

Organizations that have reached the Advanced or Optimal levels of integration face different challenges than those at earlier stages. Rather than building basic integration capabilities, they focus on refinement, efficiency, and innovation in their integrated risk management practices.

Refinement strategies include conducting detailed gap analyses to identify remaining areas where security and business functions aren't fully aligned. Even advanced organizations typically discover opportunities to deepen integration in specific business units or processes. Regular maturity assessments help track progress and identify gaps before they become problematic.

Automation and efficiency improvements become increasingly important at higher maturity levels. Advanced organizations often find that manual processes for risk assessment and monitoring don't scale effectively as integration expands. Investments in GRC platforms, automated risk analysis tools, and integrated dashboards can significantly enhance efficiency while providing more consistent results.

Continuous improvement frameworks ensure that integration practices improve as the organization and its environment change. Establish processes for regularly reviewing and updating risk assessment methodologies, governance structures, and communication approaches. Incorporate lessons learned from incidents and near-misses into these improvement efforts.

Innovation in integrated risk management may involve exploring advanced analytics to identify patterns and trends in risk data, developing predictive risk models that anticipate emerging threats, or creating novel approaches to measuring security's business value. Advanced organizations often lead their industries in developing new methods for integrated risk management.

According to the 2024 Global Digital Trust Insights from PwC (PwC, 2024), only "5% of IT and tech respondents say they're 'very satisfied' with the technology capabilities of their cyber solutions," indicating widespread dissatisfaction even among advanced organizations. This suggests that technology enhancement remains a priority even at higher maturity levels, with opportunities to implement more integrated and effective solutions.

Organizations at the Advanced level typically require 18–36 months to reach Optimal integration, with ongoing refinement continuing indefinitely. Resource requirements at this stage focus on specialized skills in areas like risk analytics, process optimization, and change management, along with strategic technology investments.

Having a clear implementation roadmap provides direction for your transformation efforts, but expecting and preparing for common obstacles can mean the difference between successful integration and stalled initiatives.

Downloadable Exercise: Build Your Custom Implementation Plan

10.9 OVERCOMING COMMON CHALLENGES IN THE TRANSFORMATION JOURNEY

Transformation efforts consistently encounter predictable obstacles that can derail progress if not addressed proactively. Understanding these common challenges allows you to develop targeted strategies before resistance emerges or resource constraints become limiting factors. Organizations that successfully navigate these obstacles share specific approaches to managing change, allocating resources, and addressing technical limitations. These challenges and their potential solutions are shown in Figure 10.3.

10.9.1 Organizational resistance and cultural barriers

The journey toward integrated security risk management inevitably encounters resistance, often stemming from deeply ingrained organizational cultures and individual concerns. Understanding the types of resistance you may face allows you to develop effective strategies for addressing them.

The resistance patterns we explored in Chapter 4's discussion of risk ownership changes manifest more broadly during integration initiatives. While Chapter 4 focused on ownership-specific resistance, integration efforts face additional challenges across the organization. Overcoming this resistance involves demonstrating how integrated security can enable business agility and innovation while managing risks appropriately.

Strategies for addressing skepticism and fear include creating safe spaces for open dialogue about concerns, acknowledging past failures in security-business relationships, and showcasing early successes where integration

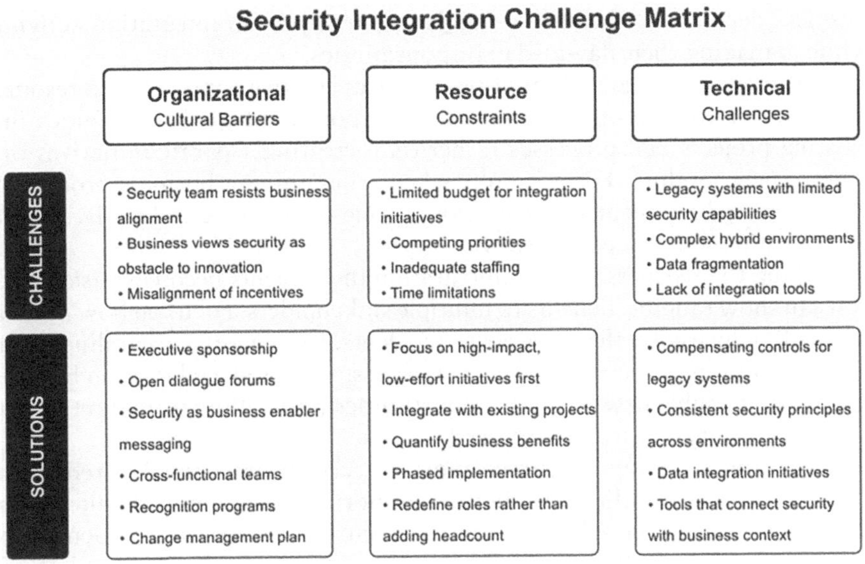

Figure 10.3 Security Integration Challenge Matrix.

has delivered business benefits. Involving skeptics in planning and decision-making can transform them from opponents to advocates as they see their input shaping the integration approach.

Building a culture that values security as business enablement requires consistent messaging from leadership about security's role in supporting business objectives. Recognition programs that highlight collaborative problem-solving between security and business teams reinforce this cultural shift. Celebrating examples where security considerations have improved business outcomes – rather than just prevented negative events – helps change perceptions about security's value.

Change management approaches that work for security integration typically emphasize the "what's in it for me" factor for different stakeholders. Frame integration benefits in terms that resonate with each audience: operational efficiency for business units, risk reduction for executives, improved system reliability for IT, and enhanced job satisfaction for security professionals who spend less time fighting resistance and more time adding value.

10.9.2 Resource constraints and competing priorities

Limited resources present significant challenges for organizations undertaking security integration initiatives. Budget constraints often force difficult choices between investing in integration efforts and addressing immediate security needs or business priorities. Time limitations affect both security and business personnel, who may struggle to participate in integration activities while managing their day-to-day responsibilities.

Working within budget limitations requires creative approaches to resource allocation. Look for opportunities to incorporate integration activities into existing projects and processes rather than creating separate initiatives that require new funding. For example, when redesigning a business process for efficiency, include security integration as one of the design objectives rather than treating it as a separate effort.

Making the business case for integration investments becomes easier when you can show tangible benefits to multiple stakeholders. Focus on how integration will reduce costs (fewer security incidents, less rework, streamlined compliance), improve efficiency (faster risk assessments, reduced friction between teams), and enable new business opportunities (faster time-to-market, ability to serve security-sensitive customers).

Leveraging existing resources more effectively may involve redefining roles and responsibilities to better support integration without adding headcount. Consider whether current security resources are focused on the right activities. Resources devoted to manual security tasks that add little value might be redirected to integration efforts with greater business impact.

Prioritization frameworks help organizations make difficult decisions when resources are limited. A simple but effective approach is to evaluate potential integration initiatives based on business value, security impact, and resource requirements. This allows you to identify "low-hanging fruit" – initiatives that deliver significant value for relatively modest investment – and "high-value targets" that may require more resources but deliver transformative benefits.

Demonstrating early ROI is essential for securing additional resources as your integration journey progresses. Document and communicate the tangible benefits of initial integration efforts, whether they're efficiency improvements, risk reductions, or enhanced business capabilities. Quantify these benefits whenever possible, and connect them directly to the integration activities that produced them.

10.9.3 Technical challenges and legacy systems

Legacy technologies present particular challenges for security integration. These systems often lack modern security capabilities, may not support current security standards, and could be difficult to modify without risking stability. Integration efforts must address these limitations while still providing appropriate risk management.

Integrating security into legacy technologies often requires compromise and creativity. Rather than attempting to retrofit modern security controls that the legacy system can't support, focus on implementing compensating controls in the surrounding environment. For example, if a legacy application can't support modern authentication methods, implement strong access controls and monitoring at the network level to reduce the risk.

Cloud and hybrid environment integration strategies need to address the complexity of managing security across multiple technology platforms with different capabilities and operational models. Successful approaches typically include developing consistent security principles that apply across all environments, implementing tools that provide unified visibility, and establishing governance processes that work for all platforms.

Data integration to support risk-based decisions is often hampered by fragmented security information spread across multiple tools and systems. Organizations may need to invest in security information management platforms or data integration projects to create the unified view of risk that effective integration requires. Start by identifying the most critical data needed for risk-based decisions, then work incrementally to bring that data together.

Tool selection to support integrated risk management should prioritize solutions that connect security with the business context. Look for tools that can map security risks to business processes, assets, and objectives, and that provide reporting capabilities suitable for both technical and business audiences. Evaluate whether existing GRC platforms can be enhanced to support integration needs before investing in new technologies.

When developing technology roadmaps, consider how each planned change will affect the integration between security and business functions. Adding new security capabilities without addressing how they'll integrate with business processes may create additional friction rather than increasing protection. Similarly, business technology initiatives should include security integration considerations from the start, rather than addressing them as an afterthought.

Successfully addressing transformation challenges moves you closer to your integration goals, but measuring progress and building sustainable practices protects your investment and maintains momentum over time.

🔗 *Downloadable Exercise: Develop Your Challenge Mitigation Strategy*

🔗 *Downloadable Resource: Security Integration Challenge Resolution Toolkit*

10.10 MEASURING PROGRESS AND SUSTAINING MOMENTUM

Measuring progress and maintaining momentum requires systematic approaches to assessment and continuous improvement. Effective measurement combines quantitative metrics with qualitative indicators to provide a comprehensive view of integration success. Building sustainable practices protects your investment in integration by creating systems that can withstand leadership changes and adapt to changing business conditions.

10.10.1 Assessment tools for measuring integration progress

Measuring progress is essential for maintaining momentum in your integration journey. Building on the performance measurement framework established in Chapter 4, organizations need specific indicators to track integration progress. These indicators fall into three categories that extend the risk management metrics we discussed earlier: process metrics that track integration mechanisms, outcome metrics that measure integration results, and perception metrics that gauge stakeholder acceptance. The key difference here is focusing specifically on integration progress rather than general risk management effectiveness. These metrics demonstrate the business value of integration.

Perception metrics gauge how stakeholders view the integration effort, measured through surveys of business and security personnel, executive feedback sessions, and analysis of support tickets or complaints related to security processes. Improvements in these metrics indicate that the cultural aspects of integration are progressing.

Qualitative measurement approaches complement quantitative metrics by providing context and depth. Case studies of successful collaboration between security and business teams, documented examples of security enabling business innovation, and stories about improved decision-making all help illustrate integration success in ways that numbers alone cannot.

Regular assessment cadence recommendations vary based on the pace and scope of your integration efforts. Monthly tracking of process metrics helps identify issues early, while quarterly reviews of outcome and perception metrics provide time for changes to show measurable results. Annual comprehensive assessments offer opportunities for more thorough evaluation and strategic adjustments.

These measurement approaches leverage the business-relevant metrics frameworks from Chapter 6, focusing specifically on metrics that show integration progress and success.

🔗 *Downloadable Resource: Integration Progress Dashboard*

10.10.2 Sustaining integration through leadership changes

Leadership changes present significant risks to integration efforts, particularly when key sponsors or champions leave the organization. Institutionalizing integrated risk management helps maintain momentum regardless of personnel changes.

Institutionalization strategies include embedding integration requirements in formal policies, procedures, and job descriptions. When integrated risk management is part of how the organization formally operates rather than a special initiative, it's more likely to survive leadership transitions. Similarly, including security integration in strategic planning documents and corporate governance frameworks reinforces its importance to the organization's operations.

Succession planning for security leadership should focus on identifying and developing individuals who understand both security and business perspectives. Look for security professionals who demonstrate business acumen and relationship-building skills, and provide them with opportunities to broaden their experience through cross-functional projects and executive exposure.

Documentation and process formalization create an institutional memory that preserves knowledge through leadership transitions. Comprehensive documentation of integration approaches, decision-making frameworks, and risk assessment methodologies ensures that new leaders have clear guidance on existing practices. Process automation further cements these practices by building them into the organization's workflows.

Building broad organizational support for integration reduces dependence on individual champions. The more people who understand and value integrated risk management, the more resilient it becomes to leadership changes. Developing a network of advocates across different departments and levels of the organization creates a support system that can maintain momentum during transitions.

Chapter 8 addresses the cultural elements necessary for sustainable integration, complementing these structural approaches with strategies for building lasting risk awareness.

10.10.3 Continuous improvement

Integration is not a one-time achievement but an ongoing journey that requires continuous refinement and adaptation. Feedback loops for integration refinement ensure that processes evolve based on practical experience and changing conditions.

Structured feedback mechanisms might include regular after-action reviews following major projects or incidents, periodic surveys of business and security personnel, and focused discussion sessions to evaluate specific aspects of the integration approach. The key is ensuring that feedback is systematically collected, analyzed, and acted upon.

Learning from near-misses and incidents provides valuable opportunities to strengthen integration. When security events occur, analyze not just the technical aspects but also how effectively security and business teams collaborated in response. Identify gaps in communication, decision-making, or risk assessment that contributed to the event, and implement improvements to address these gaps.

Adaptation to changing business and threat landscapes requires regular reassessment of integration approaches. Business strategies, priorities, and operations evolve over time, as do security threats and regulatory requirements. Integration practices that worked well in the past may need adjustment to remain effective as these conditions change.

Innovation in integrated risk practices keeps the approach fresh and responsive to new challenges. Encourage experimentation with new methods for risk assessment, communication, and collaboration. Create forums where security and business teams can propose and evaluate innovative approaches to shared challenges.

Downloadable Exercise: Design Your Progress Measurement System

10.11 CONCLUSION

Integration of security risk management into business operations is a journey, not a destination. Organizations continually refine and adapt their approach as business strategies evolve, security threats change, and new technologies emerge. The path to integration may be challenging, but the business value is compelling: better protection against threats, more efficient use of resources, faster decision-making, and enhanced ability to pursue business opportunities with appropriate risk management.

Throughout this chapter, we've explored what successful integration looks like in practice, how real organizations have transformed their approach to security risk, and practical roadmaps for implementation regardless of your starting point. We've addressed common challenges in the transformation journey and provided tools for measuring progress and sustaining momentum.

The key message is that transformation is possible for any organization, regardless of size, industry, or current maturity level. The most important first step is an honest assessment of your current state, followed by selecting the most appropriate next steps from the roadmaps provided. Begin with the self-assessment exercises in this chapter, and use the results to guide your integration journey.

Your organization has the potential to transform how it manages security risk. By putting the principles and practices from this chapter into action, you can begin that transformation today.

10.12 ACTION ITEMS FOR READERS

1. Assess your organization's current integration maturity level using the Traditional-Initial-Advanced-Optimal framework outlined in Section 3.1, evaluating how consistently security risks are identified, the extent of business leader engagement, and the alignment between security metrics and business objectives.
2. Establish a cross-functional security committee with representatives from business units, IT, legal, compliance, and other relevant departments to create a forum for discussing security risks and their business implications while breaking down organizational silos.

3. Develop a common risk language by working with business leaders to translate technical security vulnerabilities into business impact terms and creating standardized risk communication templates that resonate with non-technical stakeholders.
4. Create quick wins that demonstrate integration value by identifying specific business problems that can be solved through security improvements, such as streamlining access management processes or implementing security controls that also enhance operational efficiency.
5. Implement measurement systems to track integration progress using the process, outcome, and perception metrics framework from Section 5.1, establishing monthly tracking of integration mechanisms and quarterly reviews of stakeholder satisfaction with security-business collaboration.

References

Association of Corporate Counsel (2024). *2024 ACC Chief Legal Officers Survey.* Retrieved May 16, 2025, from https://www.acc.com/resource-library/2024-acc-chief-legal-officers-survey

Barbara A. Dittman, Gary R. Douglas, Alice Pastirik, Joann Decolati, Tina Sorrentino, Kristen Cushman and Shannon Molyneaux, Individually and on Behalf of All Others Similarly Situated v. UPMC D/B/A The University of Pittsburgh Medical Center, and UPMC Mc, J-20-2018 (Pennsylvania Supreme Court 2018).

BDO. (2024). *2024 BDO BOARD SURVEY.* Retrieved May 18, 2025, from https://insights.bdo.com/2024-BDO-Board-Survey.html

Chandrani Chatterjee, N. A. (2024). *Data Breach Notification Laws and Cost of Debt.* Retrieved May 16, 2025, from https://papers.ssrn.com/sol3/papers.cfm?abstract_id=4812852

Coalition. (2024). *The State of Active Insurance: 2024 Cyber Claims Report.* Retrieved May 17, 2025, from https://www.coalitioninc.com/blog/2024-cyber-claims-report

COSO. (2017). *COSO Enterprise Risk Management – Integrating with Strategy and Performance.*

CVE-2025-47657. (2025, May 16). Retrieved from CVE: https://www.cve.org/CVERecord?id=CVE-2025-47657

Deloitte. (2025). *Audit Committee Practices Report.* Retrieved May 16, 2025, from https://www2.deloitte.com/content/dam/Deloitte/us/Documents/audit/us-audit-committee-practices-report-2025.pdf

Federal Trade Commission v. Equifax, Inc., 1:19-mi-99999-UNA (United States District Court for the Northern District of Georgia, Atlanta Division 2019).

Firemen's Ret. Sys. of St. Louis v. Sorenson, 2019-0965-LWW (Chancery Court of Delaware 2021).

Hopkin, P. (2019). *Fundamentals of Risk Management: Understanding, Evaluating and Implementing Effective Risk Management.*

Hyperproof. (2024). *IT Risk and Compliance Benchmark Report.*

Hyperproof. (2025). *Spring IT Risk and Compliance Benchmark Report.* Retrieved May 16, 2025, from https://hyperproof.io/it-compliance-benchmarks/

IANS Research and Artico Search. (2024). *2024 Security Budget Benchmark Report.* Retrieved from https://www.iansresearch.com/resources/ians-security-budget-benchmark-report-2

IBM. (2023). *Cost of a Data Breach Report.* Retrieved from https://www.ibm.com/reports/data-breach

In Re Anthem, Inc. Data Breach Litigation, 5:15-md-02617-LHK (U.S. District Court for the Northern District of California 2018).

In Re: Capital One Customer Data Security Breach Litigation, 1:19-md-02915-AJT-JFA (U.S. District Court for the Eastern District of Virginia 2022).

In Re: Marriott International, Inc., Customer Data Security Breach Litigation, 8:19-md-02879 (U.S. District Court, District of Maryland 2019).
In re: Target Corporation Customer Data Security Breach Litigation, 0:14-md-02522-PAM (U.S. District Court District of Minnesota 2014).
In re: Target Corporation Customer Data Security Breach Litigation, 0:14-md-02522-PAM (U.S. District Court for Minnesota 2015).
ISO. (2018). *ISO 31000:2018.*
John R. S. Fraser, B. S. (2010). *Enterprise Risk Management.*
King-Wilson, P. (2022). *Volume V Cybersecurity Risk Management.* (K. J. Witty, Ed.)
LabMD, Inc. v. Federal Trade Commission, 14-12144 1:14-cv-00810-WSD (U.S. Circuit Court of Appeals for the Eleventh Circuit 2019).
Mandiant. (2025). *M-Trends.* Retrieved May 16, 2025, from https://cloud.google.com/security/resources/m-trends
Myers, L. (2018, December 18). *Target targeted: Five years on from a breach that shook the cybersecurity industry.* Retrieved from We Live Security: https://www.welivesecurity.com/2018/12/18/target-targeted-five-years-breach-shook-cybersecurity/
Office of the Comptroller of the Currency (OCC). Capital One, N.A., and Capital One Bank (USA), N.A., AA-EC-20-51 (August 6, 2020).
Proctor, P. (2024). Support Enterprise Growth Through Cybersecurity Value Investments. Gartner.
PwC. (2024). *Global Digital Trust Insights.* Retrieved May 16, 2025, from https://www.pwc.com/gr/en/publications/specific-to-all-industries-index/global-digital-trust-insights.html
Sean Steinberg, A. S. (2021). *Target Cyber Attack: A Columbia University Case Study.* Columbia University School of International and Public Affairs. Retrieved May 16, 2025, from https://www.sipa.columbia.edu/sites/default/files/2022-11/Target%20Final.pdf
Securities and Exchange Commission v. Solarwinds Corp. & Timothy G. Brown, 1:23-cv-09518-PAE (United States District Court Southern District of New York 2024).
World Economic Forum. (2025). *Global Cybersecurity Outlook.* Retrieved May 16, 2025, from https://www.weforum.org/publications/global-cybersecurity-outlook-2025/

Index

For Product Safety Concerns and Information please contact our
EU representative GPSR@taylorandfrancis.com Taylor & Francis
Verlag GmbH, Kaufingerstraße 24, 80331 München, Germany